# Discovering
# Annuals

*Graham Rice*

# Discovering Annuals

FRANCES LINCOLN

*Author's note to readers in the Southern Hemisphere*

*This is the point, right at the very beginning, where I must make a request. Annuals are easy to grow all over the world, but it's impossible to write a book to suit gardeners in two hemispheres without reducing the text to generalities. So please be tolerant if you find that your favourite varieties are not mentioned, or techniques especially appropriate to where you live are not discussed. Fortunately, the appeal of annuals is universal and I'm sure that you'll find the book both interesting and entertaining. For additional specialized information the* Discovering Annuals *website (http://discoveringannuals.com) has a page for readers in Australia and New Zealand.*
GRAHAM RICE

Frances Lincoln Limited
4 Torriano Mews
Torriano Avenue
London NW5 2RZ

Graham Rice: Discovering Annuals
Copyright © Frances Lincoln Limited 1999
Text copyright © Graham Rice 1999

First Frances Lincoln edition: 1999

British Library Cataloguing in Publication data.
A catalogue record for this book is available from the British Library.

ISBN 0 7112 1293 7
Set in Hiroshige
Printed in Hong Kong by Kwong Fat

9 8 7 6 5 4 3 2 1

HALF TITLE PAGE *Three pink annuals from a colour-themed seed mixture:* Iberis *'Red Flash',* Collomia grandiflora *'Neon' and* Silene *'Rose Angel'*

TITLE PAGE *'Gallery Yellow' perennial lupins surge through the yellow foliage and white daisies of* Tanacetum parthenium *'Aureum, while the purple foliage of* Plantago major *'Rubrifolia' creates contrast.*

FAR RIGHT *The wild form of the pot marigold,* Calendula officinalis, *with its unusually reddish eye, peeps through* Alchemilla mollis *while a small-flowered blue viola fills in behind.*

# Contents

# What are Annuals?

It's an unusual book, you have to admit, which feels the need to devote a specific page to ensuring that readers understand what the book they've just opened is actually about. But 'annual' is one of those words which seems to create a haze of uncertainty amongst gardeners, so it seems wise to set things straight – although, as you will soon see, 'straight' is hardly the word for it.

Ask any botanist and they will probably tell you that an annual is a plant the seed of which germinates, and that develops, flowers, produces its own seed and then dies all in one year; they may say it all takes place over a 'course of seasons'.

So most annuals germinate in the spring, flower in late spring and summer, and die in the late summer or autumn; alyssum, clarkia and zinnia are familiar examples. A few, however, can also behave as winter annuals, germinating in the late summer and autumn, then remaining partially dormant over the winter before starting into growth again in spring and completing their cycle in summer. Annual chrysanthemums from the Mediterranean fall into this group.

Now the situation becomes rather less clear. For many of the plants which we grow in gardens as annuals, plants like petunias and salvias, are not truly annuals at all. Usually these are shrubs or perennials from warm climates which, once they germinate in spring, develop so quickly that they flower well in their first summer. In many areas, they're not sufficiently tough to survive the autumn frosts so are quickly wiped out.

Both these groups – true annuals and those plants which can be grown as annuals – are included in this book, along with a third smaller group of short-lived plants, the biennials. Like annuals, biennials usually pass through their entire life cycle in one 'course of seasons' but their growth is always spread across two years. So their seed germinates in summer, established plants overwinter, then flower in spring.

Now, at the risk of adding further confusion, it must be admitted that many of the plants we grow as biennials are, in their natural habitats, perennials or shrubs! However, when sown in summer, plants like wallflowers and double daisies have the capacity to flower so prolifically in their first spring that we naturally take advantage.

Finally (yes, finally) a few biennials, like some foxgloves and sweet Williams, have been so transformed by plant breeders that when sown in late winter or early spring they flower in their first summer – as annuals! This only applies to certain varieties, and frankly, turning some of our relatively few spring flowering bedding plants into summer flowers (of which we already have so many) hardly seems progress.

All these various groups are discussed in this book. All are raised from seed and, at the time of writing, all are available from the mail order seed companies listed at the back of the book.

LEFT *The bold black Tuscan kale, 'Nero di Toscana', is surrounded by flowers which pick up its blue colouring. Yellow-throated* Nolana paradoxa *creeps underneath,* Salvia farinacea *'Strata'peeps through the spaces and* Nemesia *'KLM' snuggles into* Senecio cineraria *'Silver Dust'.*

RIGHT *This happy conjunction of bluish flowers, all from a direct sowing in the open ground of a blue-themed mixture , features three different phacelias together with echiums, annual flax and cornflowers.*

LEFT *Some of the best colour-themed plantings are the result of thoughtful planning. Here,* Nicotiana sylvestris *is set in the middle ground to open in front of white hydrangeas and amongst the Shasta daises (*Leucanthemum × superbum*) while white petunias fill the foreground under the silver leaves of* Convolvulus cneorum.

# Catching the Wave

There's an old song by the Beach Boys called 'Catch a Wave'. The point of the song is that when you're out in the surf, waiting for a wave to come, you must choose the right wave and exactly the right moment to grab the best chance of riding the wave all the way in. 'Seize the day', 'Strike while the iron is hot' . . . there are other metaphors for the same thing. The point is this: annuals have been in a flat calm for years, but now their moment has come.

Hardy and half-hardy annuals, and biennials too, have spent a long period out of fashion. Tainted by association with gaudy bedding schemes in seaside parks, all were dismissed and many despised. But a change of spirit is taking place, a change which mirrors our times, a change ignited by enthusiasm for carefully planned colour schemes in the garden and by enthusiasm for container plants like Surfinia petunias. And that's the key to it all: change.

We've reached a time when change is a feature of our lives as never before. Change is more rapid, the changes themselves are more dramatic and we've responded in two ways. We look to preserve elements of stability in our lives and at the same time we learn not to battle against change, but to thrive on it.

It's possible to see the results of these reactions, these two complimentary elements of our adaptability, in our gardens. Gardeners have become more interested in permanence. For example, there's a special fascination with large and long-lived trees and the statistics associated with them; we are planting more trees and we plant fast-growing trees which quickly give an illusion of longevity. Even our enthusiasm for topiary and low box hedges is rooted in some inclination to replicate the old and established.

Gardeners are also making more connections with the past: investigating the origins of plants, searching out old cultivars, and wherever possible reviving and re-introducing lost plants. Indeed the reappearance of Victorian annuals has been a significant factor in encouraging enthusiastic gardeners to look beyond the dreaded African marigolds to older annuals which are more akin to the perennials that have so gripped the attention of gardeners in recent decades.

While looking for stability, permanence and connections with the past, we're also responding to change by revelling in it. And of the full range of garden plants, annuals best represent this change – for annuals demand change.

True annuals, and other plants grown as annuals, last only a single season. Once planted, trees, shrubs, perennials and most climbers reappear in the same place every year, changing only by growing steadily larger, while annuals die at the end of the season. So it takes a great effort of will to make one year's planting at all similar to that of the previous year. This opportunity to make each year's planting of annuals different makes growing annuals so exciting. Of course, there's no insistent imperative for each year's annual borders to be entirely different; it's just that when the plants must be raised afresh there's an annual opportunity to grow something new. The most successful elements of one year's planting can be repeated or adapted, those which worked less well can be abandoned and a new scheme can integrate the best of both.

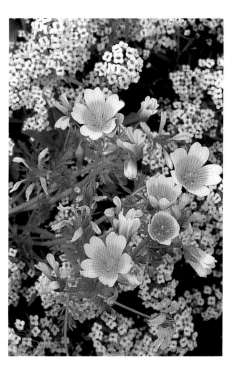

LEFT *White alyssum,* Lobularia maritima, *makes a creeping backdrop for the floppy stems of the poached egg flower,* Limnanthes douglasii.

LEFT *Flowers in the marigold colours make a bright yet satisfying association. In the front,* 'Seven Star Red' *triploid marigolds, which flower incessantly and age harmoniously, are backed by an unusual bronze-leaved foliage plant, a relative of the gunnera no less,* Haloragis erecta 'Wellington Bronze'. *To its left* Bulbine annua *makes vertical marks and to its right the large daisies of* Rudbeckia 'Toto' *are overhung by the greyish foliage and pale flowers of* Chrysanthemum 'Primrose Gem'. *At the back* Calendula 'Indian Prince' *with its chestnut-backed petals, picks up a similar shade in the* 'Mahogany Midget' *coreopsis.*

But if there was nothing more to annuals than the fact that they die every autumn, no one would grow them. Of course there's more, and first among many valuable qualities is colour.

## *Using colour*

It's colour – too much of it used with too little grace and a stunning lack of artistry – which has discouraged so many gardeners from growing annuals over the years. None of us enjoys the wrong plants grown in the wrong place in the wrong way. But the *right* plants grown in the *right* way . . .

The truth is that, especially amongst the mainstream annuals, there's a vast range of colours and shades. The fact that one catalogue lists well over a hundred different cultivars of pansy is a cause not for complaint but for celebration, for however close in colour and habit some of them may be they are all actually different. And whatever colour scheme you have in mind, whatever your preferences and dislikes, it's possible to choose exactly the shade you require. Far from lacking subtlety, as is normally supposed, annuals are chock-full of it.

Consider marigolds. Although many are far too ugly to be tolerated in any garden, or in this book, within a very narrow spectrum of colour from mahogany to palest lemon there's such a wealth of flower form and flower size, plant size and habit, as well as the many tiny differences in colour, that it's possible to pick precisely the shade you need in the height you need in an attractive form. And if the plan doesn't work out *exactly* right, you can try a variation the following year. If you're planning a special display it's even possible to experiment with a number of similar cultivars one year and to choose precisely the right one for the year after. You can't do that with rhododendrons.

The use of single colours rather than mixtures is absolutely crucial. Mixtures are unpredictable in their colour and colour balance, and however they turn out the colours usually clash. It's impossible to plan precision planting schemes if you introduce the inherent unpredictability of a mixture. Would you go into a shop and buy six mixed socks, chosen at random by somebody else? Of course not. You choose the brand and colour of socks you need and you buy them to match your favourite jumper. Likewise annuals. Buying annuals in individual colours gives you the control of planting you expect with perennials and bulbs, and allows you to create personal schemes which reflect your own taste and preferences. The problem is that the availability of these colours changes from year to year so gardeners are kept locked into the cycle of change whether we like it or not!

Most African marigolds may be ugly but there are individual cultivars of annuals which are as beautiful and as entrancing as any plants usually considered more choice. The delicacy of patterning in *Pelargonium* 'Sensation Picotee' is simply captivating – if I were to grow just one summer annual, this would be the one (when it finally becomes widely available). Or it might be *Ipomoea* 'Heavenly Blue', the very sight of which makes me shiver with delight. The purity of the white of *Antirrhinum* 'Sonnet White' is unrivalled; the delicate flecking on the flowers of *Agrostemma* 'Ocean Spray' is delightful; the tender variation in shade between pale lavender-pink and white in *Petunia* 'Pearly Wave', especially when grown as ground cover, is deliciously cool and relaxing.

It's true that many of these plants are not available in garden centres, where the emphasis, in the limited range offered both as plants and as seed, is often on mixtures, but mail order sources offer a much wider range of single colours. Of course, for some gardeners the challenge of hunting down exactly the right cultivar is part of the fun; some gardeners enjoy the chase. Fortunately, there are so many seed companies around the country, and indeed around the world, that there's always the chance of turning up a new colour or even a new species. (You'll find information on ordering seeds on the *Discovering Annuals* website; see page 186.)

## *Annuals for foliage*

Flower colour need not be the sole focus of attention; annuals have many other fine qualities, especially foliage. The bold, rounded leaves of nasturtiums are attractive in themselves; variegated forms like 'Alaska', 'Tutti Frutti', 'Jewel of Africa' and 'Out of Africa' add cream-and-white speckling. The variegated *Antirrhinum* 'Powys Pride' has foliage streaked in cream; silver foliage appears in senecios, tanacetums and even in eschscholzias; ornamental beetroots, many fibrous-rooted begonias, the tuberous begonias 'Midnight Beauties' and 'Non Stop Ornament', and the taller *Hibiscus acetosella* 'Red Shield' all feature dark foliage in the bronze or purple range. The foliage of new *Solenostemon* (*Coleus*) 'Palisandra' is almost black.

Edible plants, not normally considered ornamental, are amongst the most valuable of all foliage annuals. Red cabbage, whose leaves are, often, more of a bluish shade, and purple Brussels sprouts are very useful; the kale 'Redbor' is invaluable; the many coloured-stemmed chards like the startling 'Bright

Lights' mixture and separate colours of scarlet and white are good even when they run up to flower; red lettuce such as 'Red Salad Bowl', 'New Red Fire', 'Malibu' and 'Red Sails' hold their shape well before bolting and also make amusing dark spires as they stretch. Curly parsley is an old favourite.

Some annuals also boast good seed heads. Nigellas, opium poppies, columbines, hollyhocks, teasels, honesty, nicandra, verbascum – these all bring an extra dimension both to the autumn garden and to dried arrangements for the house.

Annuals are also prolific bloomers. It's true that some sacrifice elegance for a punch between the eyes, but most annuals do produce a great many flowers. This is a characteristic which breeders have encouraged in their creations for centuries and in most cases it's combined with a long flowering season. Many annuals are in flower when you plant them in late spring and continue to flower until they die naturally or the frost kills them in the autumn. Even those sown direct in the garden may well flower six or eight weeks after sowing and continue for months.

## Elegance – or the lack of it

This book is nothing if not realistic. Annuals inspire some strong feelings in many gardeners – hatred, disdain, snobbishness, disregard and, I have to say, plain ignorance – and I've tackled

LEFT *The crisp seed heads of* Carthamus tinctorius *make a bold autumnal statement while the contrastingly dainty heads of* Gypsophila elegans *and the final fling from the blue cornflowers fill the background. What started out as a colourful floral sowing in the open ground is transformed into a more restful late season planting.*

RIGHT *In the rough and tumble of this pink, purple and white planting,* Salvia viridis *'Claryssa Pink', with its long-lasting pink bracts, will slowly overwhelm the 'Oriental Night' alyssum, white candytuft, Sutera 'Krysna Hills' and probably the empty spaces as well. Judicious use of the secateurs (and arranging in the house) will solve the problem. The Claryssa Series is a little less lank and a little more prolific than older types of salvia.*

them head on. Some annuals are ugly. My solution: don't grow them – grow the many which are beautiful, stylish and elegant instead.

The very fact that some annuals are simply too crudely garish offends many people – and quite right too. And the fact that many are mostly seen in thoughtless mixtures does them no favours. My solution: don't grow them – choose the separate colours you enjoy.

There's no point trying to hide the fact that some annuals are almost impressively inelegant. The squat, dumpy habit (those words will surely appear elsewhere in this book) of some – most of them relatively modern – cultivars disqualifies them from serious consideration. So don't grow them – grow the many more elegant cultivars instead.

And annuals are so easy to grow. Oddly enough, this lessens their appeal to some gardeners – those who enjoy a challenge. Perhaps the fact that most gardeners can grow annuals well throws more emphasis on how badly their plants are often placed in the garden – a more artistic and less practical skill in which many gardeners are less assured. But here again the very fact that with annuals you can fling your mistakes on the compost heap at the end of the season allows you to learn quickly.

There's little mystique or history about many of the more familiar annuals, which perhaps explains why, for some gardeners, they excite no interest. It also explains, perhaps, the disproportionate enthusiasm, mine included, for the Victorian cultivars which are being reintroduced, along with those of the 1920s and 1930s, and which feature throughout in this book.

## *Intimate (not bedding) schemes*

The factor that turns people's stomachs at the very mention of annuals and bedding plants is the singularly unimaginative way in which they're so often used, especially in our public spaces. The very phrase 'bedding schemes' offends many people and this is all to do with the crude and offensive ways in which the plants are chosen and organized.

Filling a roundabout with orange African marigolds, as I've seen more than once, certainly ensures that they're noticed. But

capturing our brief attention by way of offending even the very broadest definition of taste and discrimination is clearly counterproductive. Surely it's better to have roadside displays that are attractive and intriguing, rather than blindingly garish. So, how should annuals be grown and in particular how should they be grown in gardens?

Replications of formal bedding schemes are unsuited to today's gardens. Large blocks of bold colours sit uneasily in small spaces, where they visually overpower everything else in the garden, often by virtue of their scale. And classic park combinations, in which a bed of scarlet geraniums is edged with

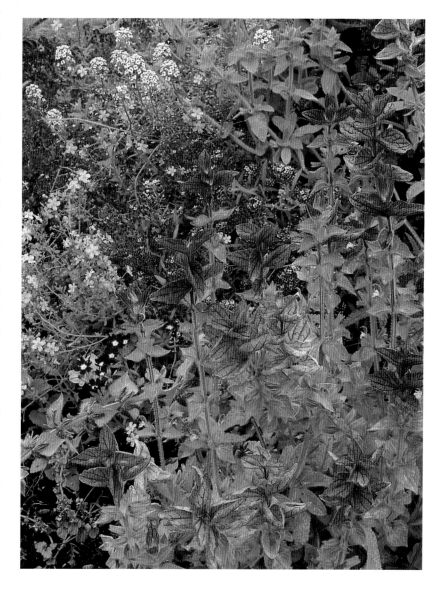

white alyssum and blue lobelia, jar horribly with the more subtle mixed borders which are a feature of so many modern gardens. The sheer brilliance of colour used in blocks dominates so totally that the more delicate and careful colourings of perennials, shrubs and climbers retreat into oblivion.

So the answer is to banish anything resembling old-fashioned bedding schemes, to reduce the scale of the plantings from those great bedrolls of scarlet, and to avoid choosing garish colour combinations and planting them in large blocks.

Instead, plantings should be on a much more intimate scale. Cultivars with a slightly taller, more open and more elegant habit should have priority over the dwarfer types which concentrate more colour into a small space at the expense of grace and distinction. Each cultivar should be planted in smaller numbers; in some cases one is enough; in many cases three or perhaps five is ideal. If more are planted, they should never be set in a concentrated block but should be interplanted with two or three other cultivars which extend beyond the boundary of the main block and into neighbouring groups.

Plantings should be organized in such a way, and maintained in such a way that, as they mature, the plants grow into one another and mingle intimately, creating an ever-changing tapestry of colour associations, intricate conjunctions of form in both flowers and foliage and a display which changes its emphasis as the season develops. There's more excitement in one square metre of intimate planting than in a whole garden full of old-fashioned bedding.

There's also far more opportunity for gardeners to express their own individuality in plantings of this style. Once you start using small groups of a large number of different cultivars there's space to try far more ideas.

The success of this style of planting depends on choosing the right cultivars. As I said earlier, avoid mixtures unless they are formula mixtures in pre-determined colours which can be guaranteed to fit in with the planned scheme. And even in cases where the choice seems clear – a pansy in lemon yellow, for example – you need to select carefully from the range of flower sizes and habits of growth available.

## Colour themes

One of the most striking and satisfying ways of planning intimate plantings is by colour. In my experiments with colour-themed plants the most successful have been in the marigold colours: mahogany, rust, orange, deep yellow, gold and primrose. Plants which fit here include French and triploid marigolds, 'tagetes', calendulas, rudbeckias, bidens, chrysanthemums, zinnias, antirrhinums, eschscholzias, pansies, coreopsis, gazanias and more. Foliage colour comes from dark-leaved dahlias, haloragis, coprosma, nasturtiums, red lettuce and ornamental beetroot.

Rose-pink, silver and white work well, red and white too; blue-flowered plants come in less variety so blue and white plantings need to be on a smaller scale. But almost any combination of colours will work – even red, white and blue – if the plants are chosen carefully and allowed to grow into one another rather than kept resolutely separate.

Bicoloured flowers, of which there are many amongst the annuals, are a great boon. An individual flower featuring two different colours can connect visually with neighbours which relate to each of the two shades, providing links and transitions into more mixed plantings.

A few seed companies offer colour-themed mixtures. The best provide over 100 different cultivars in each colour and are packeted in three height ranges to give the gardener better control. These are full of happy surprises, with rare species jostling with both familiar and unknown cultivars of better-known species in a constantly refreshing sequence of colour.

## Mixed plantings

Choosing annuals carefully also allows them to meld more effectively with plants of other types. A fat block of 'Blaze of Fire' salvias would look ridiculous in a mixed border; a smaller group of the taller, and far more relaxed, *Salvia coccinea* 'Lady in Red' has the elegance of habit and the balance of colour and habit to fit perfectly. Never exclude annuals from mixed plantings on the assumption that they won't fit aesthetically; choose cultivars that do. These may be tall, such as 'Lady in Red', 'Mother of Pearl' poppies, *Eryngium giganteum* or sunflowers; or they may be

RIGHT *New Guinea impatiens from seed are still developing, but the Java Series marks a significant improvement on Spectra and Firelake. In cool areas, they're best grown in a container on a sheltered patio as here. Their companions are* Heuchera *'Palace Purple' and the sinuous stems and grey foliage of* Helichrysum petiolare *in front. Only overwintered specimens of the helichrysum usually flower and although routinely raised from cuttings it can also be raised from seed.* Antirrhinum *'Black Prince' has been cut back after its first flowering and is again in bud. In warm area and in rich soil New Guinea impatiens will also thrive in beds and borders.*

OVERLEAF *What a spectacle! This interplanting of tall annuals makes a captivating display with the sparse but stiffly upright* Verbena bonariensis *surging through* Cosmos *'Imperial Pink' and 'Helen Campbell' and 'Purple Queen' cleomes. All can be brought on in pots then carefully set out in the border to ensure the right degree of intermingling before planting. The cleomes often germinate best in fluctuating temperatures so may need individual sowing treatment.*

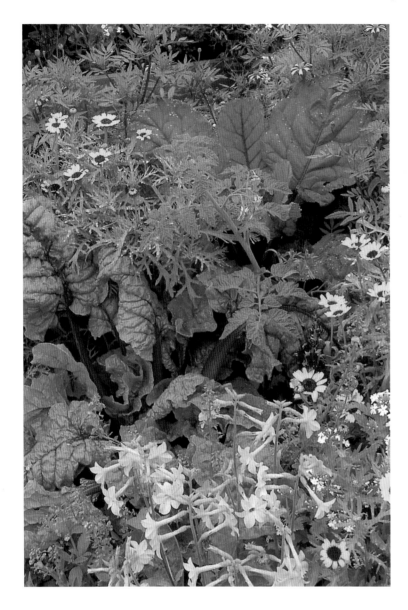

ABOVE *Two vegetables provide the structure here, the purple Brussels sprout 'Falstaff' with its coloured veins is fronted by the ruby chard 'Vulcan'. Chrysanthemum segetum 'Prado' expands from either side,* Antirrhinum *'Night and Day' sneaks through, while in front* Nicotiana *'Lime Green' is almost too vigorous for neighbouring* Alonsoa *'Amber Queen'.*

FAR RIGHT *Annual meadows can be undeniably colourful and here calendulas in their trademark yellows and oranges are interrupted by Shirley poppies in occasional reds and pinks, and cornflowers and echiums in deep blue. Next year, when they all self-sow the colour balance could be entirely different.*

dwarf and spreading like *Bidens* 'Golden Eye', nasturtiums, some of the newer pansies and *Pelargonium* 'Breakaway Red'.

## *Companions for annuals*

There are, it has to be said, some especially valuable companions for flowering annuals which I frequently (forgive any over-enthusiasm) recommend in the book. These are plants whose colour and habit allow them to intermingle with their neighbours, drawing them together visually so they dance together rather than simply plod. The various forms of *Helichrysum petiolare* are especially useful, their arching trails insinuating themselves through their neighbours and their openness of habit allowing nearby plants to return the compliment. The silver foliage of the familiar species is invaluable, as is the limy yellow of 'Limelight'. The yellow-centred silver leaves of 'Variegatum', and its less vigorous form 'Roundabout', are also useful; the neater silver form 'Goring Silver' is usually the best choice for containers. *Plecostachys serpyllifolia*, often listed as a helichrysum, develops especially long sinuous branches.

Two other immensely useful plants, the dark-leaved ornamental beetroots, 'Bull's Blood' and 'MacGregor's Favourite', combine relatively compact yet loose growth in an invaluable colour. The enormous range of colours and colour combinations amongst vegetatively propagated coleus also create contrasts, harmonies and links with a wide range of other plants.

This way of growing annuals in intimate harmonies and contrasts is not the only way. Annuals fit well into Mediterranean-style plantings; indeed, with a gravel mulch amongst cistus, euphorbias, brooms and other Mediterranean shrubs, they can be all too free with their seedlings. Choose wild species, or cultivars close in style to them, and they fit perfectly. Enthusiastic dead-heading and the rigorous removal of wayward seedlings is crucial.

Annuals have been used in wildflower gardens for some time, if only as temporary colour while perennial wildflowers become established. The vogue for meadow-style plantings of perennials has also taken hold, and now there's an interest in growing annuals in meadows in a similar style. Given the space, the results can be impressive. But allowing plants to self-sow freely over a number of years can make each year's display startlingly unpredictable; this approach also demands a continual and sophisticated regime of dead-heading, thinning seedlings and the addition of new plants. Some cultivars self-sow more easily than others so must be dead-headed more thoroughly to prevent their taking over. Some shed a great deal of seed yet new seedlings rarely appear, so may need augmentation from plants raised under protection. Such wild gardens are an enjoyable way to grow annuals if you not only have the space and time to devote to them but also if there are other areas of the garden which can provide a more dependably satisfying display.

However, the point of this book is to show that, in small gardens in particular, annuals need to be chosen carefully. With thoughtful precision to bring colours and forms together, imaginative planting combinations can be created which are neither garish nor unpredictably chaotic but which allow the expression of the gardener's own character and taste. And, frankly, if you enjoy growing annuals in ways about which I do not enthuse in these pages – take no notice of me . . . plant your annuals in your own way. In so doing, we'll all continue to rediscover and re-invent the continuously changing pleasure of annuals.

# *Ageratum* Ageratum

Blue is a rare and therefore precious colour amongst annuals and we fall gratefully upon those few we have. So ageratums are invaluable – provided always that you choose carefully. But there are two problems.

Ageratum blue reproduces badly in photographs – the camera cannot lie but the film certainly can. Where there should be blue there is mauve, and where there should be mauve there is also mauve. So in both books and catalogues, we find pictures that are either an unnaturally lurid blue thanks to computer manipulation . . . or mauve. It makes choosing difficult.

What's more, there are few varieties, other than those here, worth growing because the plant breeder has ignored the gardener. What use are plants which reach little more than 15cm/6in across and 10cm/4in high in a whole season? Four varieties break this sad rule.

'Blue Horizon' is a valuable, cultured, slightly airy plant reaching about 75cm/2½ft, its flowers naturally tinted purple. With a salpiglossis like 'Kew Blue', *Salvia farinacea* 'Victoria' and 'Redbor' kale it makes a pretty grouping. And there's a white version, 'Highness'. Whites can be disappointing, since as the florets age to brown they detract from the pure white of the fresher flowers. With 'Highness' this is a less of

a problem than with tiny edging sorts. Both these are triploid varieties, sterile hybrids which flower especially prolifically in their fruitless struggle to produce seed. The latest in this type is 'Red Sea'. Its buds actually are red but the open flowers are more of a purplish-red shade.

Coming down in scale as far as we'll go, 'Blue Mink' is an old favourite which sometimes varies a little in height but, at 23–30cm/9–12in and with its slightly open habit, is the best blue for frontal plantings. Better still, yet at about the same height, is 'Bavaria', also known as 'Southern Cross'; with its white pads and slim blue filaments this is a truly wonderful variety. We need the plant breeders to work on a tall version.

Like petunias and geraniums, the best ageratums were once raised from cuttings; a revival is perhaps overdue. This would allow bicoloured types in the style of 'Bavaria' to be created in other combinations in a genus which seed breeders find intractable.

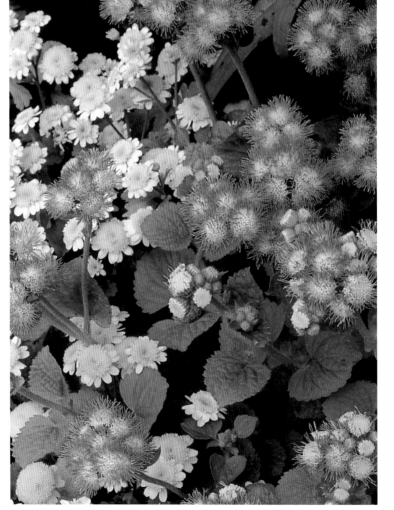

LEFT *'Bavaria' is the best of all the ageratums. Its unique combination of blue and white surges through Tanacetum parthenium 'White Gem' in a low-level combination which will last for months as long as both plants are regularly deadheaded. Sneaky snips low down on both plants will leave the plants rejuvenated yet not looking butchered.*

# *Alcea* **Hollyhock**

The humble hollyhock is enjoying an exciting revival. The widespread destructiveness of rust disease had led to a dramatic decline in their popularity; now, with the introduction of effective fungicides, gardeners happy to use non-organic methods can again grow good hollyhocks.

The plant breeders have responded. Consistency in the seed-raised doubles such as the Chater's Doubles Series is much improved and 'Powder Puffs', in five pure colours, is an excellent refinement. New shades with winsome names like 'Peaches 'n' Dreams' have been introduced, and the mixtures of single-flowered types, usually known simply as 'Single Mixed', have improved their flower forms and the range of colours.

Plant breeders were also tempted – they just can't resist – into creating dwarf hollyhocks to be grown as annuals rather than biennials. The resulting 'Majorette' is an ugly creation that demeans the good name of this classic cottage garden plant.

Rather than try these monstrosities, there's a much neglected group of hybrids which deserve better attention. *Alcea ficifolia* has leaves shaped like those of a fig, as the name suggests, and the wild form usually features flowers in a pretty primrose shade. This species has two advantages: it's a more consistent perennial than the much more widespread and better developed *A. rosea;* and it is also more resistant to rust – an advantage which so far seems sadly unexploited.

When eastern Europe was isolated from developments in the West, a number of interesting forms were grown there, including some with ruffled flowers; these have not yet appeared in catalogues for home gardeners. However, from Holland comes a mixture which includes pinks, reds, yellows and white. This is listed, in the few catalogues which carry it, simply as *A. ficifolia* 'Mixed'. I suspect we'll see more of this group in the future.

There are two ways to grow good hollyhocks. Allow them to self-sow in good soil and a sunny site, and they develop extensive root systems, their crowns bursting with buds. This works best if you grow just one colour; self-sown mixtures are too unpredictable. Hollyhocks can also be raised in pots from a late spring sowing. Prick them out into 9cm/3½in pots and as these fill with roots plant them where they're to flower. If, as is likely, there's no room in your borders in summer, move them on so they finish in 20cm/8in pots; then either plant them in autumn or overwinter them in a cold frame for planting in early spring. And keep rust at bay through regular preventative spraying.

*Alcea rosea* 'Chater's Double Rose'

OVERLEAF *At Hadspen House in Somerset, Nori and Sandra Pope have created the finest colour-themed planting in Britain. Here, black hollyhocks,* Alcea rosea *'Nigra', mingle with self-sown seedlings of the dark-leaved orache,* Atriplex hortensis *var.* rubra. *This valuable foliage plant self-seeds all too generously, so most seedlings must be removed; the trick is to leave those which will associate most successfully with neighbouring perennials. The reddish-magenta of the perennial* Knautia macedonica *in front and the scattering of* Cosmos *'Dazzler' pick up the colour in the paler edges of the hollyhock flowers, while the pink spikes of* Veronica *'Pink Damask' mingling with* Linaria *'Canon Went' behind add fresh sparks.*

# Amaranthus *Amaranthus*

Nowhere else in this book will you find two such contrasting groups of plants under the same heading. United only in their botanical similarities, this likeness is totally overshadowed by their startling, if more superficial, differences and in the scorn in which both groups are commonly held. But this is my plea: don't be too hard on them.

In cooler areas those with tasselled flowers are the more widely grown. They cover a range of species including *Amaranthus caudatus* (Love-lies-bleeding) *A. hypochondriachus* (Prince's feather), *A. cruentus* and *A. paniculatus*. The crowded tassels trail downwards in the first type, hence the common name, and stand up more cheekily in the rest.

A mature plant of the dusty red *A. caudatus*, or its pale green-flowered variant var. *viridis*, is a spectacular creature. At its best it is perhaps 1.2m/4ft high and as much across, but only rich soil and no shortage of water produces a specimen of this majestic stature. The waterfall of tassels tumbles to the soil or, better, on to a stone pathway from a narrow border, and plants are best with a wall behind to which the stout stems can be secured; heavy rain can beat them down and, while tying in an annual as if it were a climber may seem unusual, believe me it's necessary.

Displayed as specimen plants in a large container, with three perhaps planted together, and supported discreetly on stout canes, the effect is both surprising and impressive, adding an unsuspected grandeur to this sometimes despised plant.

The tall, dark-leaved and dark-flowered 'Hopi Red Dye', and the uncomfortably similar 'Foxtail', makes a bold and rather imposing, long-season border feature. For many gardeners the shorter and more stiffly upstanding 'Pygmy Torch', crimson in both leaf and flower, and the yellowish green 'Green Thumb' will be more convenient, although the lack of vigour of the dwarf types can lead to their flowering for a relatively short season. Recently a number of new forms have appeared; the 1.2m/4ft *A. cruentus* 'Golden Giant' is especially useful. Its biscuit-brown, arching tassels hang forward over lower, frontal neighbours like striped, speckled or mahogany-centred yellow *Coreopsis* 'Tiger Stripes', originally introduced from Arkansas in 1823, and always slightly variable. In rich soil some support may be needed to prevent the plant from toppling over as rain collects in its densely packed flower heads.

But beware those varieties which are advertised as mixtures; check the catalogue text carefully. Should you think to plant a large container with a combination of colours, once the range extends beyond green and red

Amaranthus tricolor *'Splendens'*

Amaranthus cruentus *'Golden Giant'*

RIGHT *Adding a sultry light to this red planting, already sparked by the blues of Salvia farinacea 'Strata', 'Hopi Red Dye' is an elegant but rarely grown hybrid amaranthus whose flowering side shoots give it an unusually long season. Dianthus 'Red Feather' flutters daintily around. In the background is the strain of lime green nicotiana from Unwin's Seeds, alongside the tall Salvia splendens 'Rambo'.*

ABOVE *The forerunner of the startlingly colourful 'Poinsettia Mixed' and 'Joseph's Coat' amaranthus is this A.* tricolor, *which is softer in colour, more vigorous and easier to grow. Here the dark markings are picked up by 'Black Night' coleus, while defiantly sparking through the centre is one of the two most elegant of the celosias for annual plantings, 'Flamingo Purple' (the other is the silvery pink 'Flamingo Feather'). The purple tint to its foliage reinforces the sympathetic colouring.*

plants, with their trailing habit, the additional colours will be supplied by plants more upright in growth – creating an unpredictable and perhaps unbalanced display.

All the varieties in this group have one unfortunate characteristic in common, a tendency to shed truly vast quantities of seed – almost all of which seems to germinate. Gravel paths disappear under a carpet of lush green, the slender seed leaves soon giving way to fatter foliage and more vigorous roots; pulling them up brings soil into the gravel mulch . . . soil from which, and into which, weed seeds, not to mention more amaranthus, will germinate. You will have to combine thoughtful and, where necessary, prompt dead-heading with timely weed control.

In warmer climates the foliage plant *A. tricolor* is the more commonly grown species. Most of its varieties, even the long established 'Splendens', are positively garish by comparison with the wild form. They can be raised successfully in cool areas if treated as half-hardy annuals, moving them into 12.5cm/5in pots, keeping them growing well then planting out into a pot or into rich soil in a sunny and sheltered place. But in a cool and dingy summer they languish and remain colourfully foolish runts.

However, if you start plants well, they grow on strongly and you plant them outside from pots, in warmer areas the 90cm/3ft mass of foliage of 'Joseph's Coat', the most widespread variety, develops a luxuriant yet preposterous blend of scarlet, yellow and green – all on the one plant. 'Poinsettia Mixed' looks to be even more outrageous, with three different colour forms in the mixture. For colour-themed planting, select individual plants in appropriate colours from the mixture as they develop.

The success of these colourful foliage forms depends entirely on the plants being big, bold, lush and luxuriant. In cool areas, they often fail, combining wimpish stature with lurid colouring; such sickly specimens prompt ridicule or, at best, a pitying look from visitors. At their most exuberant they create a real spectacle and provide sharper colourings, to be used sparingly, in tropical summer plantings with bananas, ricinus, solanums, the unique black leaves of 'Palisandra' coleus and other plants that revel in similar conditions.

# *Antirrhinum* Snapdragon

Antirrhinums are a sad case: so much potential yet the cause of so much disappointment. We should, perhaps, take the Buddhist approach; Buddhists teach (this is a rather curt, nay brutal, paraphrase but you'll get the idea) that suffering is the result of unfulfilled desire and to avoid suffering we should cease desiring. Taking the tortuous ride from there to horticulture . . . if we didn't expect so much of the humble snapdragon we would not be quite so disappointed.

For antirrhinums are almost unique amongst annuals. Plants of real character which also provide a very colourful display, they're in a class of their own compared with African marigolds, impatiens and dumpy little ageratums. They come in three different flower forms and a wide and intriguing range of colours and bicolours; they make good cut flowers; and, when planted in herbaceous and mixed borders, they actually look as if they belong there. They're tough, they can be raised at lower temperatures than most half-hardy annuals, they can be planted out without damage before the last spring frosts are over . . . not bad, eh?

The problem is rust. This is a dramatic and devastating disease which can wipe out a whole planting in a fortnight, often when the plants are at their peak, and for which, unfortunately, there is no cure. Recent research has shown that resistance is controlled by nine separate genes and even if breeders could create a full range of resistant colours (they managed two then gave up) it would be a short time before the rust mutated into a form which could overcome the resistance. Fortunately, modern fungicides will do a good job if used regularly as a preventative spray and if you choose an appropriate brand (not all fungicides are effective against rust). Rust is much easier to prevent than to cure, so don't wait until you see the first pale spots on the tops of the leaves with the corresponding dark rusty marks underneath before spraying.

Recent developments have revealed an interesting transatlantic distinction in attitudes. Until recently, most American introductions have been very dwarf with a tightly rounded, almost flat habit and are very early flowering but lack the long flowering season which most gardeners appreciate. In Europe there has been more interest in reviving old, usually taller varieties – some going back to the nineteenth century – and those with an unusually long flowering season. Gardeners have downplayed those which start to flower exceptionally early then fizzle out in midsummer.

The Chimes Series and the open-throated Bells Series may be colourful, but so what? 'Can be sold in flower in April from a late January sowing' it says in a trade catalogue. The natural following sentence 'and will be dead by midsummer' is, not unexpectedly, omitted. The French-bred Kim Series flowers for far longer but starts later – so is largely ignored by suppliers of garden centres in spite of RHS Awards of Garden Merit for seven out of the nine colours. Frankly, even the best of these dwarf varieties is difficult to use in the garden. The exception is 'Lampion', developed for hanging baskets, yet rather sparse when used in this way; it's prolific, even elegant, on the flat.

Antirrhinum *'Bells Yellow'*

Antirrhinum *'Brighton Rock'*
*(single colour)*

Move up a size, to about 38–45cm/15–18in, and a world of possibilities opens. The Sonnet Series provides a splendid range including the purest of the whites, and it's in this height range that most of the Victorian revivals appear.

The striped antirrhinums were a speciality of the nineteenth century – the Victorians liked almost anything in stripes. Now listed as 'Brighton Rock', 'Bizarre' or 'Candyman', almost all are mixtures which include a small percentage of unstriped plants, a genetic quirk which cannot be eliminated; 'Torbay Rock' is a red-and-yellow available separately, with 50% pure reds – forget it, the blend of stripes and solid red is very uncomfortable. No other separate colours are available. The mixtures are, it has to be said, rather spangly creations. The only way to ensure harmonious plantings is to grow the plants in pots, then select individual plants for specific plantings from their first flowers.

'Black Prince', with its blood-red foliage and slightly brighter red flowers is another old sort which has not been replicated in modern series. With dark-leaved beetroot 'Bull's Blood' or 'MacGregor's Favourite', and *Dianthus* 'Telstar Crimson' or the even darker, white picoteed 'Black and White Minstrels' (also known as 'Chianti'), plus the sprawling trails of silver-leaved *Helichrysum petiolare* peeping out where they will, you have a very classy grouping. 'Night and Day', a white-tubed form of 'Black Prince' recently rediscovered in Holland, replicates another Victorian style and would pick up the silver foliage and white picotee of the dianthus. This colour combination has now appeared as the open-throated 'La Bella Red and White'.

The other popular shade, apart from white, has long been rose-pink and, amongst the huge range of separate colours in three or four different heights listed in turn-of-the-century catalogues, rose-pink seems to feature strongly. Pale pinks from the

RIGHT *Orange, yellow and rusty colours make a hot and attractive association, here focusing on* Antirrhinum *'Sonnet Bronze' and* Chrysanthemum *'Primrose Gem'. The slender spikes of* Bulbine annua *peep through behind, with a stray flower of* Salpiglossis *'Chocolate Pot', while the sparky little* Linaria *'Fantasia Yellow', which flowers in as little as six weeks from seed, snuggles in at the front.*

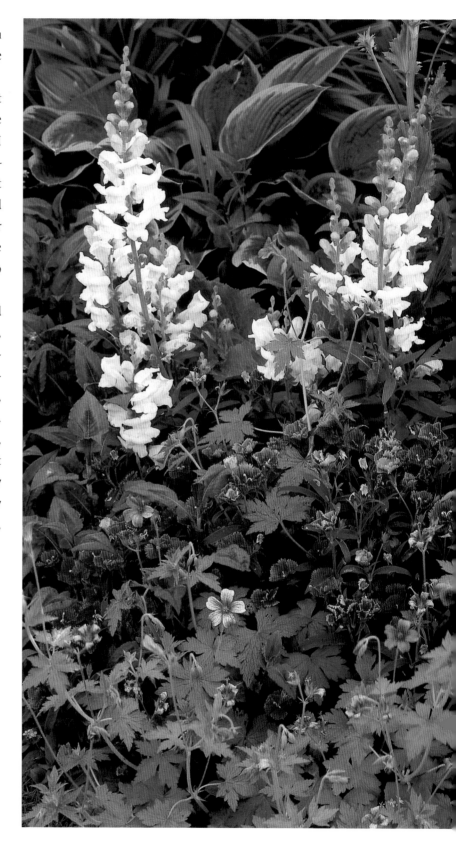

modern Sonnet and Liberty series are noticeably chunky in habit, a result of their otherwise welcome tendency to produce far more than a single solitary spike at first flowering.

If you need taller varieties then single colours become almost impossible to find. 'Forerunner', 'Rocket' and 'Madame Butterfly' all make 90cm/3ft but come only in mixtures (as I write, one catalogue lists 'Rocket' in a few separate colours – please, hunt them out) and are too vigorous to raise to first flower successfully in pots – so their colours cannot be sorted before planting. Occasionally, seed companies list cut-flower types intended for glasshouse use; these are available in a fine range of shades, especially pastels, but are rarely listed. They do surprisingly well outside.

For many years I was at a loss to know why anyone would want to grow the open-throated types like 'Madame Butterfly', the dwarf Bells Series and the recent La Bella Series, a companion for Liberty, because one of the main attractions of antirrhinums is the form of their flowers. When that is transformed, sometimes into rather a muddled shape, they lose their appeal. But it's not that simple. With the flower form changed so much, bees are less able to pollinate the flowers successfully. The result is that the individual flowers stay open for longer so the display lasts longer. In 'Madame Butterfly' the flowers are also partially double, with a few extra segments in the throat; I don't like them, but I can see the point.

LEFT *Tall pink antirrhinums are not easy to find in catalogues as separate colours but, clearly, it's worth hunting them out. Here 'Yosemite Pink', bred as a glasshouse cut flower but superb outside, stands just above drifts of* Consolida *'White Cloud' and* Nemesia denticulata, *with the pretty dwarf sweet pea 'Cupid' in the foreground. If you pinch this tall and relatively unbranched antirrhinum at planting time, rather than letting it run straight up, it will send out a whole colony of slightly shorter stems.*

RIGHT *Individual half-hardy annuals can often be slipped into a perennial border very effectively. Here, a single plant of* Antirrhinum *'Liberty White' is set in front of hostas alongside autumn sedums, while dark pink dianthus mingle with paler hardy geraniums.*

LEFT *'Black Prince' is one of two Victorian antirrhinums never to have quite disappeared from catalogues (the other is 'Rembrandt', an orange and gold bicolour). Here 'Black Prince' snuggles up in front of the modern 'Rocket Yellow', developed as an outdoor cut flower but superb in borders. Blue echium sprawls in from the side with the silvery Artemisia 'Powis Castle', and the seed heads of the opium poppy stand out boldly against the dark flowers.*

# *Aquilegia* Columbine

Still sparking a fond nostalgia amongst all but the most determinedly progressive gardeners, the granny's bonnets, or columbines, of traditional cottage gardens have been joined in recent years by a great variety of flower forms and colour combinations; with the rediscovery of those with coloured foliage there's now an almost bewildering choice. There are even cultivars to be grown as pot plants. What's more, their innocent promiscuity ensures the garden is swiftly peopled with the unpredictable offspring of the few with which you started.

Most columbines are naturally perennial plants but, because they develop so quickly, growing them as biennials is easy. Invaluable midsummer plants, they provide delightful leaf patterning followed by a long succession of flowers. Raised in pots from an early sowing, forms with yellow or yellow-speckled foliage have proved a fine foil for summer flowers.

The first yellow-leaved aquilegia was seen at the RHS trials of 1914; it was called 'Vervaeneana', a name still encountered, but the difficulty in developing a true stock soon led to its rarity. Now breeders have developed two dependable forms: 'Woodside Variegated Mixed' has mainly mottled foliage with flowers in a wide range of colours; from this came 'Mellow Yellow', with unmottled, soft yellow foliage which flowers only in palest blue and white.

Aquilegia viridiflora

In the rich conditions of a container, 'Mellow Yellow' develops a glowing mound of deep yellow foliage in its first summer – but no flowers. It is superb with the yellow daisies of the neat *Bidens* 'Goldie', the chocolate-coloured (and chocolate-scented) flowers of *Cosmos atrosanguineus*, cuphea or the old dwarf striped French marigolds. At the end of the season, the plant can be set out in the garden to flower the following year.

Columbines, of course, are best known for their flowers. Most carry nectar-producing spurs projecting from the back of the flower – sometimes short and stout, sometimes elegantly curved, and maybe in a contrasting colour. Cultivars with names like 'McKana Giants', 'Long Spurred Hybrids' and 'Mrs Scott-Elliot's Strain' all have bright, even multicoloured flowers with long spurs. Choose these for the classic cottage combinations of the June English garden with bearded irises, Oriental poppies, white sweet rocket and lupins.

Aquilegia *McKana Group*

But the spurless doubles are today's choice. 'Nora Barlow', named for the geneticist granddaughter of Charles Darwin who discovered it in her garden around fifty years ago (although a similar form had been known since the sixteenth century), was urgently sought after for many years yet rarely found. With its dense head of slim petals in pink, white and pale apple

Aquilegia vulgaris *Vervaeneana Group*

green, its urgent licentiousness led to all manner of variations turning up under the name.

More controlled selection has produced a stable series of colours and combinations, sometimes known as 'Nora Barlow's Relatives'! Sow inside in spring, grow outside in a nursery bed, then transplant in autumn with plenty of soil on the roots for the most spectacular specimens. The gorgeous blue and white 'Adelaide Addison', with its rippled skirt, and the deep purple and white 'William Guiness' ,can be treated in the same way.

The newer 30cm/1ft-high Music Series, the Cameo Series and the rather taller Songbird Series have their niche as the first columbines which can be grown in window-boxes and small tubs without looking silly. Most of these have also been developed to flower in summer from a spring sowing – an interesting, if dubious, achievement. Columbines should be over when summer annuals are at their best.

The dusky *A. viridiflora* is different from all these, being more demure; it's sometimes seen masquerading under such pretentious cultivar names as 'Chocolate Soldier'. A delicate species, it appreciates a choice place and repays close inspection.

# *Begonia* **Begonia**

The first reaction of most gardeners to begonias is to say that they're difficult to raise from seed. Happily, the seed companies have recognized the problem and developed a number of ways to help gardeners solve, or perhaps skirt round, the undoubted pitfalls.

It does take a certain crazed optimism to raise begonias from seed in the *traditional* way. Just open the packet and you can see why: is there anything in there at all? Begonia seed is so minute that 5,000 can weigh the same as just one sunflower seed. It is, weight for weight, more valuable than gold.

Such tiny seed can be difficult even to get out of the packet. Sowing it evenly is often a matter of chance, and damping off and drought are constant threats. Fortunately, some companies now supply begonia seed in phials from which it's easier to sow evenly; some supply pelleted seed which is much more manageable than natural seed; and more varieties are now available as seedlings and young plants.

Begonias fall into two unexpectedly different groups: the fibrous-rooted begonias, called *Begonia semperflorens*, and the more flamboyant tuberous-rooted begonias, *B.* x *tuberhybrida*. Fibrous-rooted begonias have small single flowers (seed-raised doubles are coming) in reds, pinks and white with fleshy bronze or bright green leaves. Scarlet, white and picoteed flowers especially suit bronze leaves; white and rose suit bright green leaves. In recent years

plant breeders have made them all increasingly tight and inhibited in habit.

And so many are so very similar; most are too small to be grown in open borders. The Stara Series is much less compact but the leaves are large and coarse; better, but less often seen, are the noticeably taller and more open Thousand Wonders Series, and the All Round Series, which is more vigorous and spreading in growth. Both come in fewer leaf/flower colour combinations than smaller types.

In containers where the conditions are richer, generous feeding and constant watering will make even the smaller fibrous-rooted begonias more acceptable; with good living they grow larger and more open in habit. The Victory Series comes in a total of eight colours, both green- and bronze-leaved; the slightly larger-flowered, bronze-leaved Vision Series, in five.

The picotee types are outstanding, especially when combined with bronze foliage. 'Coco Ducolor' was the old favourite and, if you can find it, develops a more open habit than the modern 'Malaga Bicolour' – although when I grew a single plant of the latter in a terracotta pot and fed and watered it well, it did look very fine. These bicolours are delightful, but rarely listed. Unfortunately, the hideous 'Paint Splash', with white-blotched leaves, is much more common.

Tuberous begonias are bolder – positively spectacular compared with fibrous-rooted

Begonia semperflorens 'Victory White'

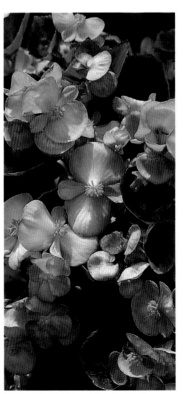

Begonia semperflorens 'Victory Pink'

RIGHT *Picotee fibrous begonias are the most attractive of them all; even filling a container without companions they look good. Here, it's 'Coco Ducolor', but any of the admittedly hard-to-find dark-leaved picotees will fit. Silver Senecio cineraria 'Silver Dust' and a dainty blue viola have been added to create a richer blend; the pink and white Nicotiana 'Havana Appleblossom' would be a more suitable taller neighbour than the lime green.*

Begonia x tuberhybrida *'Happy End'*

ABOVE *Bronze-leaved scarlet begonias make a good specimen display for small spaces. Here, they're enhanced by their dark container and the backing of grassy foliage, which provides contrast in both colour and form.*

sorts. Their flowers are huge, almost always fully double, and yet they have so many orange and yellow shades in addition to the reds, pinks and white seen in fibrous sorts, that they make an altogether more uncomfortable mixture. Look for single colours. Most types have green leaves, but search out those with bronze foliage and orange, apricot or scarlet flowers in particular.

'Nonstop' is the big name in Britain, but not necessarily the best. Most cultivars are too neat and bushy; with one exception, it's the trailing types that stand out. The exception is 'Pin-up'; its large, red-edged, pure-white single flowers make this a fine plant for tubs, where it will softly call the attention of dreamy passers-by. If you prefer visitors to faint clean away, 'Pin-up Flame', a red and yellow version, should do the job.

In baskets, boxes and large tubs the trailing types are superb; they're vigorous, bold, yet not so chunky and solid as to be totally smothering. 'Happy End' has relatively small, double and semi-double flowers in four colours, and a determinedly trailing habit. It works well in a basket by itself. The Illumination Series in a similar habit comes in separate colours; the apricot with its orange buds looks especially good with *Helichrysum petiolare* 'Limelight'.

The Panorama Series is less insistently trailing in habit and has the extra benefit of deep bronze or bronze-veined leaves in some colours. This is the most adaptable of all varieties, suiting both baskets and raised, timber-edged garden beds. The pastel Show Angels Series is a little more lax and a little less uniform in its doubling and in colour but, at their best, the flowers are fully double with contrasting picotee edges.

Some tuberous begonias are available as tubers, but many, in both groups, come only as seed. Check the general advice on page 175 but buy pelleted seeds if possible. Don't firm the compost, sow the seed as evenly as you can and don't sieve compost over it until after germination. If you have shaky hands or poor eyesight get someone else to do the job. Cover the pot with cling-film, and keep it at 21°C/70°F out of direct sun. Never let the seeds or seedlings dry out and be sure to treat them against damping off disease.

# *Bellis* English Daisy

Would you rather have a daisy in your border or a bellis? Well exactly: 'daisy' says weed and 'bellis' says class – which is why catalogues tend to list them as bellis. All are derived from the little English lawn daisy.

Cultivated forms, especially doubles, have been known since at least the seventeenth century. The early herbalist John Parkinson, in his *Paradisus Terrestris* of 1629, illustrates some fully double sorts which, even allowing for the usual artistic over-enthusiasm, are very striking. He also features a double hen-and-chickens form which appears to be extinct; only the single-flowered 'Prolifera' remains. These and the more modern double daisies collected by Margery Fish from cottage gardeners are all propagated by division, but virus infection has, unfortunately, weakened them, making them less easy to propagate.

But seed-raised bellis have improved greatly in recent years. Plants are more prolific, the flowers are more fully double, they last longer before revealing their yellow eye and they are also a little more uniform in their colouring. Like dahlias and perennial chrysanthemums, the genetic make-up of bellis is unusually complicated, and creating cultivars in uniform colours is more difficult than in most plants – though this is not necessarily a disadvantage.

Bellis can be divided into two groups: large-flowered sorts producing relatively few flowers and the more prolific small-flowered types. Large-flowered cultivars – with names like 'Monstrosa', 'Goliath' and 'Radar' (the latter has flowers fully 5cm/2in across . . . yuk) – are big, blowsy and not at all elegant. They also age disgracefully, starting off as fat and flowery pompoms, although sometimes rather dishevelled, and eventually revealing a garish yellow eye as the petals curl back,

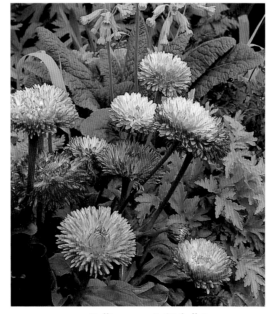

Bellis perennis *'Robella'*

making the flower look even more ragged. Some, though, are more than acceptable. The award-winning 'Robella' is an attractive one-off, whose large flowers last well before the yellow eye finally appears.

The uniquely coloured Habanera Series is an exciting development. The white is pure white but the other three shades are all bicolours. 'Habanera Rose' is white with the petal tips stained pink; 'Habanera Lipstick' (also known as 'Habanera White with Red Tips') has more of the petals stained, this time in bright red; in 'Habanera Red' almost the full length of each petal is bright red, with just a little white at the base. The four colours combine unusually well in the mixture but the chunky flowers of *griegii* or *kauffmaniana* tulips best balance the impact of the large daisies.

Of the smaller-flowered types, 'Galaxy' can be ruled out; the flowers open with a yellow eye which looks especially unpleasant in the pink form. The rest are all delightful and highly engaging. Some, like 'Pomponette', 'Button' and 'Tasso', have quilled petals creating tight button-like flowers; 'Carpet' has flat petals. Reaching little more than 15cm/6in in height, all these are excellent in containers with dwarf bulbs like muscari or small daffodils; just make sure you choose the colours carefully.

'Carpet Pink' is especially attractive and it looks lovely with the white form of *Muscari azureum*. Its colour can vary slightly and a few plants usually feature white petals stained red on the backs; the overall effect is pinkish but look closer and it's clear that, as the tissue of each petal becomes thinner towards the edge, the red from the backs shows through. What's more, in the centre of the flower the petals roll inwards, showing off their red colouring. The effect is dazzling – even on such a small flower.

LEFT  *This delicate spring planting shows that biennials can be used to create the sort of satisfying tapestry which snobbish plantspeople believe is possible only with esoteric woodland flowers from China. With 'Primrose Monarch' wallflower behind, Bellis 'Pomponette White' has been slipped in alongside Milium effusum 'Aureum', Bowles' golden grass. This too is grown as a biennial, but there is rarely a need to do anything but lift it in autumn from where it has self-sown and slide it in where it will look best.*

# Brachyscome *Swan River Daisy*

That 's' in *Brachyscome* is always perplexing; where did it come from? People think you're mad if you leave it in. The botanist Cassini, who coined the name in 1816, first called them all *Brachyscome* but by 1825 he had changed his mind and was calling them *Brachycome*. His second choice became widely used but the original is correct.

Swan River daisies, as they are less confusingly known (the Swan River is in Western Australia), have seen much improvement recently. They've not lost their fresh-mown-hay fragrance, but their habit has become less straggly and unstable without becoming excessively dumpy (the ultimate misdemeanour) and the colours are fresher, clearer and more diverse.

Once there was only purple and a range of watery tones. Then 'Summer Skies' added some deeper colours and white, together with some pretty and distinct blue- and lilac-tinted whites. 'Bravo' refined them in a different way: it comes in four clear colours (dark blue, pale blue, violet and white), each with either a black or a white eye.

Brachyscomes are relatively hardy (they can even be sown outside in many areas), they grow strongly and they are usually in flower at planting time. So you can choose from the eight colours of 'Bravo' or the slightly less predictable but more subtle shades of 'Summer Skies'.

The white with a black eye could go in a black and white planting with *Nemophila* 'Pennie Black', also known as 'Total Eclipse', *Dianthus* 'Black and White Minstrels' and the white 'Giant Hyacinth Flowered' candytuft. In a container or small, richly fed bed the pale blue with a white eye could go with *Petunia* 'Fantasy Sky Blue' in a similar shade.

The blue forms are invaluable in blue and white plantings. 'Blue Star' or both the pale and the dark blue from the Bravo Series could merge into *Ageratum* 'Blue Horizon' or the bicoloured 'Bavaria'; their finely cut, fresh green foliage would contrast well with the dark and lustrous leaves of *Heliotropium* 'Marine'. *Salvia farinacea* 'Victoria' would make a harmonious presence in the background while in the front alongside the brachyscome, *Nemesia* 'KLM' would start bright, then fade away as the season advanced, its space to be occupied by the spreading brachyscome and heliotrope.

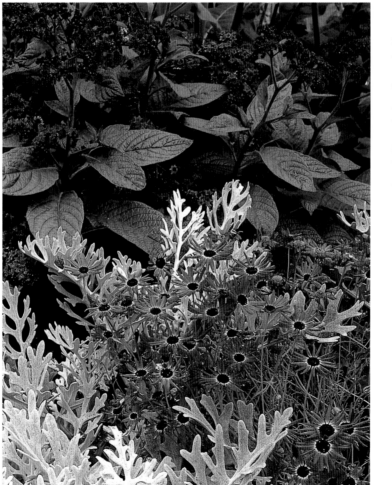

LEFT *Using dark-flowered brachyscome with the silver-leaved* Senecio cineraria *'Silver Dust' is a familiar yet effective combination, and the white ring in some of the brachyscome flowers, especially those of the older varieties with their narrow petals, creates both harmony and contrast at the same time. In the background is the seed-raised* Heliotropium *'Marine', less highly scented than cuttings-raised types, but more prolific.*

# Brassica *Brassica*

Goodness, how the humble cabbage and kale have come up in the world recently. Even people who should know better still scoff at the idea of including cabbages or Brussels sprouts in ornamental plantings; please, ignore these sceptics. Brassicas are amongst the best of all foliage annuals, and not necessarily those developed exclusively for their supposedly ornamental qualities.

'Ornamental' cabbages and kales should be used with discretion. Often, thoughtful reflection (or, indeed, the more common instant emotional reaction) will lead you to eschew some of them altogether. No one wants a garden replication of the roundabouts packed with the flat heads of ornamental kales in pink, white and green, like some bizarre commemorative exhibition of the tackiest of tableware. Individual plants carefully chosen for colour – that's very different.

The 'flowering cabbages' and 'flowering kales' bred for their coloured foliage are not for summer schemes. Their colour develops best as temperatures decrease, so they should be sown in early summer and planted in late summer for brightening the autumn garden. Cultivars developed for their culinary use are generally more acceptable and effective as summer ornamentals.

Conventional red cabbage, with a smoky blue cast to its leaves, is a fine summer foliage plant and looks superb with blue or pink petunias or *Chrysanthemum segetum* 'Prado'. The older open-pollinated types like 'Red Dutch' and 'Red Drumhead' are better than modern $F_1$ hybrids; the newest cultivars tend to have few outer leaves, yet it's this outer foliage which is the most effective ornamentally.

Red Brussels sprouts like 'Rubine' or especially 'Falstaff' are ideal for a bolder statement, although they may need staking. With trails of canary creeper or the silky blue of *Ipomoea* 'Heavenly Blue' scrambling amongst them and producing a constant succession of flowers, they spark both joy and surprise.

Two recently introduced kales are outstanding ornamental foliage plants. 'Redbor' is a winter hardy yet summer sumptuous dark purple-leaved curly kale. It's splendid in combinations with the sharper purple of *Verbena* 'Homestead Purple', a blue-bracted *Salvia viridis*, the slender purple-blue spikes of *Salvia farinacea* 'Victoria' or even scarlet 'Rambo' salvias. *Petunia* 'Purple Wave', which will scramble up through it given a little encouragement, makes a startling companion.

'Nero di Toscana' is quite different but no less striking. A traditional Italian variety, sometimes known as 'Black Tuscany', it has a more open habit that allows neighbours such as the grey-leaved *Eucalyptus globulus* or magenta petunias to sneak their stems in amongst its long, rumpled blue-green foliage, creating a wild blend of associations.

These summer brassicas appreciate root space in the early stages. Sown in mid-spring, then pricked out into 9cm/3½in and then 12.5cm/5in pots, they should have enough room to develop without the combined risk of drought and starvation, which will prompt the lower leaves to drop.

Once you plant brassicas, cabbage whitefly, flea beetle and caterpillars can cause trouble, but the latter two seem less of a problem on 'Redbor' than on all the others. And at the end of the summer you can eat them!

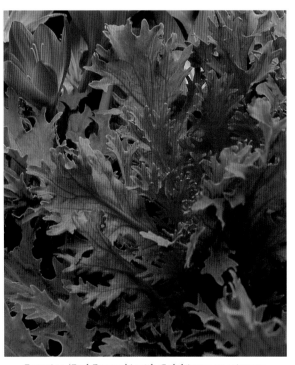

Brassica *'Red Peacock' with* Colchicum speciosum

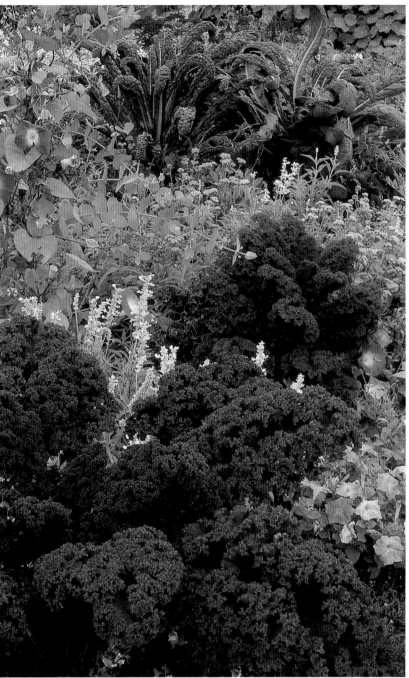

ABOVE LEFT *The Black Tuscan kale, correctly known as 'Nero di Toscana', may not actually be black but it's surely one of the most impressive foliage plants for summer bedding. Here, the aptly named, cuttings-raised Verbena 'Snowflurries' mingles with it, creating a bold contrast, with Nemesia denticulata and the foliage of a black coleus filling in the background.*

ABOVE RIGHT *Vegetables can be beautiful too. In the front, the curly red kale 'Redbor' makes foaming mounds of lava-like foliage which is impressive from planting time right through to the following spring. At the back, the chunky blue-green fountains of 'Nero di Toscana' stand out boldly amongst the blue ageratums, petunias and ipomoeas which tie the display together, sparked by white spikes of Salvia farinacea 'Cirrus'.*

# Calendula *English or Pot Marigold*

Calendula is the first of the misnamed marigolds. Neither French nor African marigolds saw a hint of their supposed homes until gardeners grew them (both originate in South America), and English marigolds grow wild in the Mediterranean.

Like the other colourful native southern European annuals, calendulas grow naturally as cornfield weeds. Breeders have broadened the calendula colours, developed their flower forms and, as you might expect, reduced their height. Unfortunately, little has been achieved in the continuing battle against powdery mildew. And this is one of the two reasons why the very dwarf calendulas like 'Bon Bon' and 'Fiesta Gitana' are unsatisfactory; the other, of course, is that they can be so very ugly. Their congested growth restricts air circulation among the plants, with the result that, although they were selected with mildew resistance in mind, the disease prospers in such close conditions, often disfiguring plants in their prime. The overcrowding of stems and foliage also prevents thorough spraying – so mildew is almost guaranteed.

However, in their taller forms, calendulas are both invaluable and consistently endearing. They bring a colour range similar to that of African and French marigolds but with no tendency to the grossness of the former or the unnatural congested dumpiness of the latter. The introduction of a small number of more pastel, even pinkish,

Calendula *'Double Lemon Coronet'*

Calendula *'Kablouna'*

Calendula *'Touch of Red'*

tones increases their versatility. Their habit is another feature that marks them out. They have a natural angularity of growth and a branching habit, both of which prevent all the flowers from being held in a flat plane at the top of the plant; this not only makes them easy to dead-head but leaves the dead-headed plants looking as if they never needed attention in the first place.

In annual borders, calendulas generally occupy the middle ground. The subtle colouring of varieties like 'Indian Prince' and 'Touch of Red' with chestnut or mahogany backs to the petals is best appreciated at close quarters. However, it's inevitable that the lower parts of the plant become a little ragged, and so they need a place where slightly shorter plants like bushy blue echiums, bronze-leaved *Hibiscus acetosella* 'Red Shield' or dark-eyed *Cosmidium* (correctly, *Thelesperma*) 'Brunette' can effect clever cover-ups.

In perennial borders, this masking is easier to achieve. Calendulas are especially good when grown as specimens or groups in autumn borders where dark-leaved asters, particularly forms of *Aster lateriflorus* such as 'Prince' and 'Horizontalis', can hide those bare stems with their sympathetic colouring, then take centre stage as the calendulas finally fade. Asters also help with support.

As with so many members of the daisy family, calendulas show intriguing variations in the form of their flowers. The

RIGHT *Sultry red, orange, yellow and gold make an unbeatable combination of colours. This all-dark selection from the bicoloured Coreopsis 'T&M Originals Mixed' is about to be overwhelmed by Tropaeolum 'Forest Flame', which will need to be kept in order to prevent it from taking over the whole flower bed. Calendula 'Indian Prince', the backs of whose petals echo the colour of the coreopsis, also connects with Rudbeckia 'Toto' in the front. The rich olive foliage belongs to Haloragis 'Wellington Bronze'.*

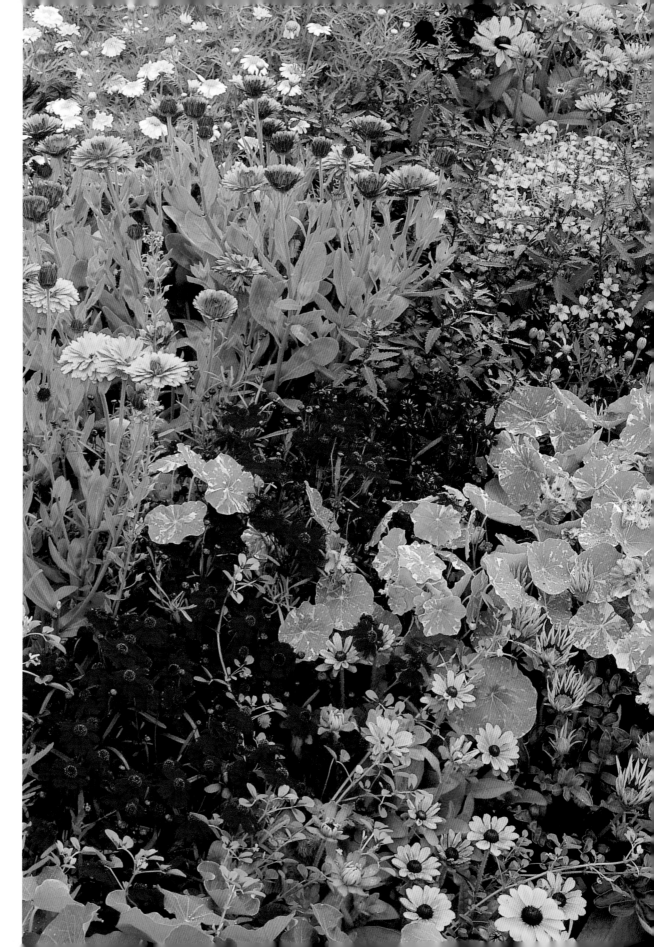

delicate simplicity of the wild single-flowered types may be essential in annual meadows. By contrast, the unexpected sophistication of the anemone-centred Kablouna Series is delightful and it makes an invaluable cut flower; unfortunately it is also difficult for the seed grower to keep the plant true to type.

From the radiant, perhaps impossibly garish, 'Radio' (great with *Dahlia* 'David Howard') to the variable 'Pacific Mixed', the full doubles are the most familiar. All eventually open to reveal the eye of the flower; the more fully double, the longer it takes – but keeping them fully double takes the seed grower time. So the most reliable seed for doubles is likely to be the most expensive.

Almost every year, individual colours from one series or another, such as 'Double Lemon Coronet' or one-offs like 'Campfire', are released. Many of these are very beautiful, either in the purity of their pale shades or the delicacy of their bicolours. But frankly, they tend to be transient, so those you enjoy one year may vanish from catalogues the next. Mixtures, like the old 'Art Shades' and 'Pacific Mixed', and the more recent

Kablouna-style 'Princess Mixed', often include colours rarely seen separately, but the quality and uniformity may vary between suppliers.

All the double forms make excellent cut flowers. The stems may not be long but the individuality of the flowers can at least be enjoyed in small arrangements. Cut them just before the flowers are fully open, plunge them immediately into water, then remove the leaves and recut before arranging them.

Seeds of calendulas are intriguingly curved and bristly, and sufficiently large to be easily sown by hand where they're to flower. Space them widely from the start and thin quickly so that they branch. Although calendulas often behave as winter annuals in the wild, in gardens the soil may be too heavy and the season too wet – so the survival rate can be poor. You can move seedlings without too much disruption in spring, but for more careful positioning it's better to sow calendulas in cool conditions (a cold frame or cold greenhouse rather than a heated propagator), pricking them out into trays, then individual 7cm/3in pots, and plant before the roots become crowded.

LEFT *Two hardy annuals, calendula and borage, both with a naturally open habit, mingle contentedly. The white form of borage, Borago officinalis 'Alba', will soon be as widely grown as the blue form – it self-sows as enthusiastically and often needs thinning out. Calendulas self-sow too and, unless carefully rogued, lose their double flowers in favour of the more natural single forms of their wild ancestors.*

# *Callistephus* *Aster*

There's something warming and uniquely comforting about asters. The very word sparks a nostalgic feeling which speaks of between-the-wars country houses. A late breakfast of kedgeree waiting under silver lids on the sideboard; the boys about to go back to school for the autumn term; an uneasy mix of concern and confidence about developments in Europe in the evening smoking room . . .

Perhaps it's the softness in the colouring of end-of-season asters, a dull glow which, throughout the colour range – a range wider than that of most annuals – allows a mellowing of any potential harshness. And their fixed place as late-season flowers, gently marking the end of summer, looking back on a brighter season, on the brink of a chillier change . . . it all fits with the nostalgic mood.

But sales of asters were fading for years, for decades. Gardeners developed a taste for brighter flowers and, at the same time, the increase in aster wilt disease ensured that asters were frequently unsuccessful, especially in small gardens. The wilt problem is still with us; trials have proved that there are no wilt-resistant asters – whatever the catalogues say. But the softness of their colouring does have a stronger appeal to modern gardeners.

Taller and medium-sized asters fit well into mixed borders. Forget the shortest types, like the appalling 'Starlight Rose' which, at about 15cm/6in, flowers in a single brief burst before it shrivels. The medium and taller asters are splendid companions for perennial asters, late pokers, sedums, grasses and other autumn perennials.

'Florette Champagne', reaching about 60cm/2ft, is a gorgeous soft champagne shade with a touch of pink in its long slender petals; set it amongst the dark stems of *Aster lateriflorus* 'Prince'. The slightly taller 'Apricot Delight' could go behind rustier pink autumn sedums and a dwarf blue perennial aster like 'Professor Anton Kippenberg'. The 'Prinette' mixture with pale centred flowers and needle-like petals is a prolific blend of richer shades; the restricted colour mix allows it to be used in perennial borders where broader mixtures could jar.

Separate colours in asters are still the exception. Mixtures prevail, although this is fine if you grow them for cutting; cut just as the flowers are opening and be sure to remove the lower leaves. The frilly 'Ostrich Plume', the neater 'Riviera' with its long stems and 'Duchess' with flowers like incurved chrysanths are all worth growing. But the colour blend may vary with the supplier, so if you feel you have too few colours, try the same variety from another supplier the following year.

Callistephus chinensis *'Prinette Mixed'*

The Modern Japanese types, like the Matsumoto Series and Fan Series, are different. These are bred for upright growth and to branch well from the base so that, instead of cutting single stems, the whole plant is cut just above soil level: one plant makes a bouquet. Don't be afraid to do exactly that.

Aster wilt remains a problem. Wilt is a soil-borne disease and growing asters in the same place two years running is a mistake. To avoid attack, plant asters in a different space in the border each year or, if you grow them for cutting, rotate them around the vegetable plot or the cutting-garden. To grow a few for cutting in infected soil, plant them out from 12.5cm/5in pots to provide each with a kernel of wilt-free soil.

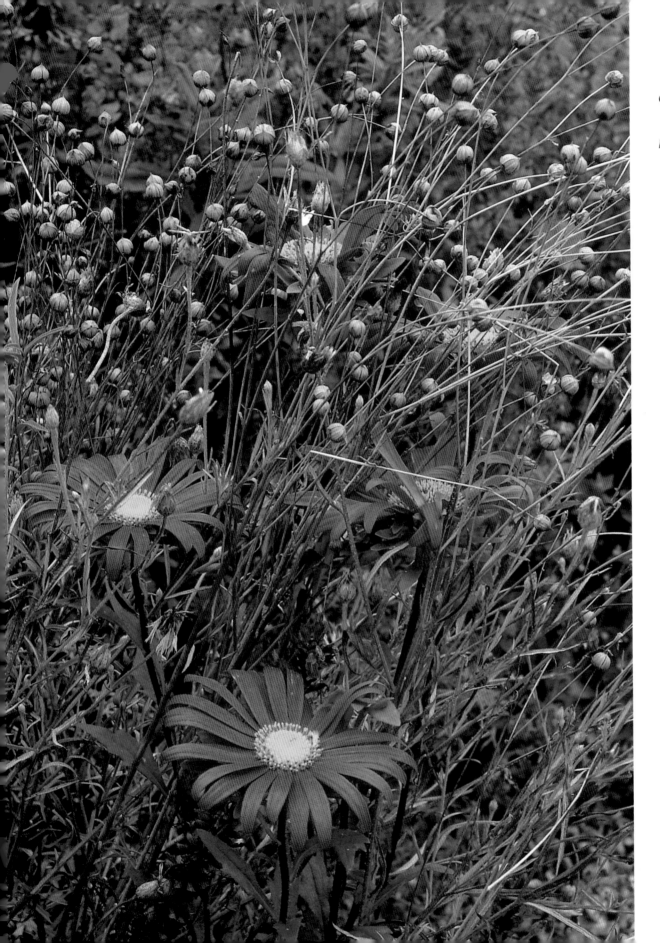

LEFT *The original wild form of* Callistephus chinensis *is a simple and elegant plant. In naturalistic plantings it's far more sympathetic in form than more highly bred types which are often too bold or blowsy. Here, with the neat seedheads of* Gypsophila elegans, *it makes an attractive late-season combination.*

# *Campanula* **Campanula**

How, as they say, are the mighty fallen. In the days of the great English country houses biennial campanulas were a crucial and spectacular element in staged indoor displays. *Campanula pyramidalis* was the main choice, and was even known as the chimney bellflower from its most frequent position in the house in summer. Now it's rarely grown, but is still worthwhile outdoors as a border biennial in milder areas where its vast quantities of smaller flowers are often less combative in their appearance than the chunkier bells of *C. medium*. In cold areas and heavy soils it may not survive the winter.

The Canterbury bell, *C. medium*, also has a history as a display plant for the grand country houses and, given large pots and rich feeding, can be truly spectacular – as well as long lasting. Sown in early spring, moved on so plants never become pot bound, kept cool while they're under glass and fed – well, they can be astonishing. These days, it's easier to prick them out into 9cm/3½in pots, line them out in a row in the garden, then move them to their flowering places in autumn.

Their natural form is the simple bell, in blue, pink or white. The cup-and-saucer forms, with their enlarged and coloured calyx, are more dramatic and altogether more colourful, but they can be too overpowering alongside more demure neighbours in mixed borders. Semi-double forms are also sometimes listed in catalogues. All tend to be named descriptively: 'Cup and Saucer Mixed', 'Double Mixed' and so on. For containers and for smaller gardens, 'Ring of Bells' is a dwarf, 38cm/15in, cup-and-saucer type in the usual colours plus lilac; 'Bells of Holland' is a slightly taller, bell-flowered

Campanula medium *'Single Rose-Pink'*

equivalent, also in four colours, at about 45cm/18in. Most unexpected is 'Russian Pink', at 38–45cm/15–18in, which can be grown as a half-hardy annual or a biennial and comes only in this soft rose shade. It is said to flower in just sixteen weeks from a spring sowing. A better show from more elegant plants comes from overwintering. This makes a splendid container plant.

The dainty *C. patula* on its wiry stems is registering an upsurge of interest and is certainly the pick for most gardeners, although seed remains difficult to find in catalogues.

The seed-raised forms of *C. carpatica*, in blue and in white, are valuable in pots. This is an underrated biennial, unusual in combining neat growth with a poise uncommon in dwarf varieties. Grow 'Blue Clips' with dwarf narcissus like 'Jumblie', or in both colours with *Muscari azureum* or with *M. botryoides* in the same two shades.

Summer-flowering *C. isophylla* had a few heady years as a popular trailer for summer pots, raised as a half-hardy annual; however, its brittle growth habit has relegated it not quite to the obscurity from whence it came, but it's now less easy to find. The Stella Series is the one to look for, but it needs an early sowing to flower from July.

LEFT *Canterbury bells,* Campanula medium, *have traditionally been grown as specimens for indoor decoration, for greenhouse display, as bold displays in cottage gardens and sometimes in large pots by the door. More frequently, now, they're slipped into mixed plantings, as here with white violets. The 'Bells of Holland' mixture reaches only about 45cm/18in in height, ensuring that this approach is more manageable in smaller gardens.*

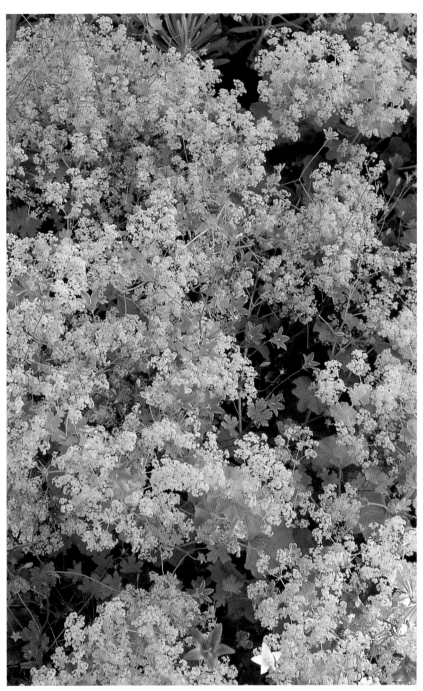

ABOVE *The smaller campanulas are much under-used spring container plants, bringing both colour and character to what can be predictable displays. Planted in spring from plants in flower, or almost so, 'White Clips' and 'Blue Clips', both seed-raised forms of* Campanula carpatica, *snuggle up to* Primula *'Wanda Supreme Blue',* Anemone blanda *'Atrocaerulea', boldly splashed variegated ivy and white hyacinth 'L'Innocence'.*

ABOVE *The delicacy of the British native* Campanula patula, *a rare biennial, is perfect here, where it has sown itself into a gap between plants of* Alchemilla mollis *in its clouds of pale green foam. The only problem with this delightful combination is that when the time comes to cut back the alchemilla to prevent it throwing sheets of self-sown seedlings, the campanula may also be cut down when its seedlings would be valuable.*

# Centaurea *Cornflower*

The cornflower is one of the four cornfield weeds that every child once knew, every farmer once despised yet secretly enjoyed, and which are now sown intentionally – both in our 'historical' cornfields and in gardens. Of these weeds, the corn cockle (*Agrostemma githago*) has recently become more widely grown in gardens since the introduction of 'Ocean Pearl', the large-flowered white form, but is becoming increasingly rare in the wild as its seed is so short-lived. The corn marigold (*Chrysanthemum segetum*) is a fine garden plant in its own right while the corn poppy (*Papaver rhoeas*) has produced the Shirley poppies and more recently 'Mother of Pearl' and 'Angel's Choir'; it's also more common in the English countryside than it has been for many years.

The cornflower (*Centaurea cyanus*), however, has been the subject of the most attention from breeders, who've worked in two directions: they've reduced its height and developed its bushiness to create a more acceptable bedding plant, and they've also increased its colour range and basal branching to enhance its potential as a cut flower – and as a border plant.

The Midget Series is simply too small and squat to be taken seriously but the Florence Series, at about 30–35cm/12–14in and in six colours, five of which are Fleuroselect Award winners, is quite something. The plants are impressively prolific; sometimes the heads of the plants are almost too packed with flowers but no

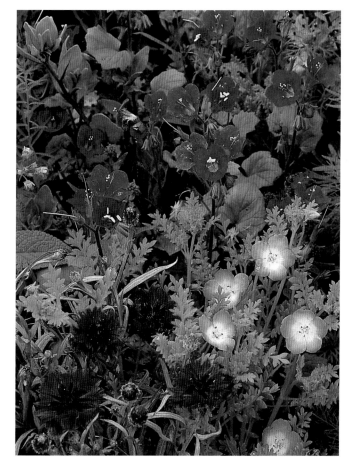

more so, I suppose, than a dwarf Michaelmas daisy. The Florence Series flower for a long season and snipping a few shoots out for small bouquets goes entirely unnoticed. However, they make such dense plants that pugnacious companions are needed to break them into less solid blocks. *Helichrysum petiolare* again comes to the rescue, its silver shoots insistently surging through; they look especially comfortable in 'Florence Lavender' and 'Florence Pink'.

There are some interesting forms in taller cornflowers. The 'Frosty' mixture, whose white petal tips create an altogether lighter look, sparkles against dark-leaved shrubs like the deep purple-leaved *Cotinus coggygria* 'Notcutt's Variety', even in the full mixture of blues, purples and pinks. Separate colours are not available in the 'Frosty' type but the Boy Series of tall varieties for cutting, for the back of annual borders and for mixed borders now comes separately in black (in truth, more of a deep rich purple), white (sometimes called 'Snowman'), red and the usual cornflower blue. I suspect this is

LEFT *Blue may be an uncommon colour in hardy annuals but these three species from a blue-themed hardy annual mix make a sparkling combination. The deep blue* Phacelia campanularia *is one of the quickest hardy annuals to flower and later gives way to other varieties. The wild cornflower,* Centaurea cyanus, *stretches and continues to flower as the weeks pass, while the softer* Nemophila menziesii *with its white eye has a long season unless allowed to become dry.*

the same as the Ball Strain sometimes listed.

Here is a case where the setting is crucial, for these are tall plants that can be lost, highlighted or made partners by their background. 'Black Boy', against silver *Elaeagnus × ebbingei*, stands out well – in fact the result is truly beautiful; against a purple beech hedge the effect is entirely different, but as impressive in a heavy, sultry sort of way; but against a laurel hedge the light and shade of the laurel's large leathery leaves detract from the cornflower display.

'Snowman' works against the same two backgrounds for the opposite reasons: against the elaeagnus it harmonizes, against the beech it stands out brightly. 'Red Ball' looks superb against the fresh green of a thuja hedge. 'Blue Ball', sown a little late and set in gaps in a late summer and autumn border, provides electric sparks amongst crocosmias and pokers against a yew hedge.

All these taller types are best planted from pots, the better to allow their roots to develop and to allow them to become substantial plants before being set amongst permanent plants which would overwhelm smaller specimens.

Mildew can sometimes cause problems in dry summers, although the congested growth of the Florence Series seems unexpectedly, though not totally, resistant. Spraying against mildew, dead-heading and cutting for the house have a noticeably beneficial effect on staying power.

The taller types require support. Branching as they do, simply looping string around the clump usually proves unsatisfactory: the plants lean more and more heavily over the string. Stretching 15cm/6in mesh pea-and-bean netting horizontally between canes, at about 45cm/18in above ground, supports the stems more effectively.

RIGHT *The spreading growth of* Geranium × riversleaianum *'Mavis Simpson' sprawls amongst the tall shoots of 'Black Boy' cornflowers, which are flopping adrift from their supports, with occasional shoots of the white-tipped* Salvia viridis *'Claryssa White' peeping through. The geranium spreads so much that it requires wide spacing, but well-established plants of the cornflower and salvia can be set into this space to grow away and not be overwhelmed by the tide of geranium growth.*

# *Cerinthe* Honeywort

I've lost count of the number of times I've read that cerinthes grow wild in New Zealand. Where this nonsense came from I cannot imagine, but nonsense it is. Cerinthes are annuals or short-lived perennials which originate in southern Europe and can be seen by tourists taking a spring holiday in the Med. This also gives you some indication of the conditions they prefer in gardens.

*Cerinthe major* var. *purpurascens* is the one which has taken plantsmen by the scruff and demanded to be grown in their gardens. In addition to its entirely unexpected blue-purple colouring it has the great benefit of often lasting through the winter in many areas – well, through one winter at least. 'Kiwi Blue' looks very similar – named because the seed was originally sent to Britain from a gardener in New Zealand, but it is completely different from the plant growing there in the wild.

Spring-sown plants will flower amongst blue agapanthus; a dusting of white *Gypsophila elegans* is a glittery companion. Overwintered plants will flower with irises; with the almost outrageous blue-tinted black 'Dusky Challenger', they are simply astonishing.

But there are others. *Cerinthe major* itself has brown-tipped yellow flowers with noticeable, white-spotted leaves. This is the more typical Mediterranean form and it is a wonderful, autumn-germinating, dry garden plant. The young leaves are long, rounded and pale and distinctively spotted in white. Then, provided they are given the space, the young plants will naturally branch well from the base, developing relatively few stout branches as they mature. The flowers hang, partially hidden by bracts, from arching spikes, so plants are best sown, or allowed to remain, near a path where the flowers can be examined close up.

Better still is the stunning *C. retorta*, which is bold enough to make an impact from a distance. My seed was sent to me out of the blue, having been collected, with permission I might add, from the garden of the British Embassy in Athens. This is another winter annual. The bracts around the flower, bluish in *C. major* var. *purpurascens* are deep purple in *C. retorta*.

Seed of all three plants tends to be relatively short-lived, but the large nutlets can be collected from the base of the flowering stems while the topmost flowers are still open. Sow them at once, or simply allow the plants to self-sow – which they will do readily on gravel in a sunny place.

Cerinthe major *var*. purpurascens

# *Chrysanthemum* Chrysanthemum

It's a relief to realize that these innocent yet exciting Mediterranean chrysanthemums have so little in common with the cheerleader's pompons seen on showbenches. So little, in fact, that botanists have given those we grow as annuals not one but five genera all to themselves (see page 184). For, while those show chrysanthemums may be truly remarkable, they're as distant from anyone's idea of a companionable garden plant as a prickly pear cactus. And while the showbench chrysanthemums are known (and loved or despised) for their size and perfection of form, annual chrysanthemums boast other qualities more suited to the garden: adaptability and sparklingly original colour.

Colour in annual chrysanthemums is unique in two ways. There's a purity in the buttercup colour of wild *C. coronarium*, and in its pale semi-double form 'Primrose Gem', which is rare and refreshing. 'Primrose Gem' brings out the richness in *Salpiglossis* 'Chocolate Pot' and the coppery undertow of *Antirrhinum* 'Sonnet Bronze'.

In the wild, the pure buttercup yellow is the dominant form, but in many areas there's a small, more or less constant, proportion of a yellow-eyed white form, var. *discolor*. This persists in gardens, creating occasional refreshing surprises, as in the wild.

In *C. carinatum*, purity of colour is just one attraction – and the purity is by no means universal. Muddy shades have crept in, but it's still the sparkling colour combinations which are so surprising, so exhilarating. However, now that we're mostly reduced to 'Court Jesters' and similar fling-all-the-colours-in-together-

Chrysanthemum coronarium *'Primrose Gem'*

Chrysanthemum carinatum *'Polar Star'*

type mixtures, hunting out separate colours like the very clean 'Polar Star' and the newer red and yellow bicoloured 'German Flag' is proving more difficult. But more of these single colours are coming.

Like so many bicoloured flowers, the colours of 'Polar Star' make valuable links with neighbours. The dark eye connects with the foliage of *Hibiscus acetosella* 'Red Shield'; the yellow ring could be picked up in 'Sonnet Yellow' antirrhinums, and the white in silver foliage or *Lavatera* 'White Cherub'; trained on a fence or wigwam of canes behind, the lemon and white climber *Mina lobata* 'Citronella' would pick up both colours.

There are also doubles, which are daintier and altogether more interesting than the more familiar double florist's chrysanthemums – or rather, there were. Usually seen under the name of 'Dunnettii', these are now hardly listed in catalogues, although they were once available in separate colours. When the doubles are derived from forms with ray florets in two or three bands of colour, the result can be delightful. Unfortunately, the doubles are even more rare than the name 'Dunnettii', for this name is sometimes now used to cover an unpredictable blend of both singles and doubles.

There are two other annual chrysanthemums which demand attention. The corn marigold, *C. segetum*, was once a familiar cornfield weed in Europe but has declined dramatically since herbicide use became so common. This species is a useful and long-flowering garden plant, while 'Prado', with black-

LEFT *This sharp yellow planting features close harmony in the flower colours and basic flower form, with just enough contrast in the other aspects to make it interesting. The naturally dwarf sunflower 'Pacino', with its slightly ragged ring of petals, is surrounded by the contrastingly finely cut foliage of a wild-collected* Chrysanthemum cornarium *from the Greek islands. In front, a not-very-rustic example of* Rudbeckia *'Rustic Dwarfs' is infiltrated with* Bidens *'Golden Eye', also with dissected foliage and the yellow-edged leaves of* Pelargonium *'Charity'.*

centred bright yellow flowers, is the form most often listed. Adding *Antirrhinum* 'Black Prince' and *C. multicaule* around the base makes a bold grouping. The lower, looser habit of *C. multicaule* enables it to sprawl around the base of taller plants, and under African marigolds it successfully tones down their brashness. 'Gold Plate', in bright butter yellow and the paler 'Moonlight' are the most readily available; there's rumoured to be a white.

The two most widely grown chrysanthemum species, *Chrysanthemum carinatum* and *C. coronarium*, both originate in Mediterranean regions. One of the most obvious aspects of the way that annuals adapt to the Mediterranean climate is that most germinate in late summer and autumn. They then develop as the temperature cools and the rainfall rises, continuing to grow through the winter and making an extensive root system which then sustains the plants as the temperature rises again and rainfall drops off in spring.

Plants which are well established when temperatures rise will continue to grow, making larger and more impressive plants and flowering for many weeks even in high temperatures. In addition to chrysanthemums many other native Mediterranean annuals, including poppies and larkspur, behave in this way. We replicate this adaptation in the garden by sowing in autumn.

However, away from the moist, mild winters of the Mediterranean and similar climates, colder, wetter winters combined with a heavy soil reduce the chances of overwintering. Sowing indoors in early spring, growing cool and potting on before the pots become crowded with roots is then the right approach.

Chrysanthemum carinatum 'Court Jesters'

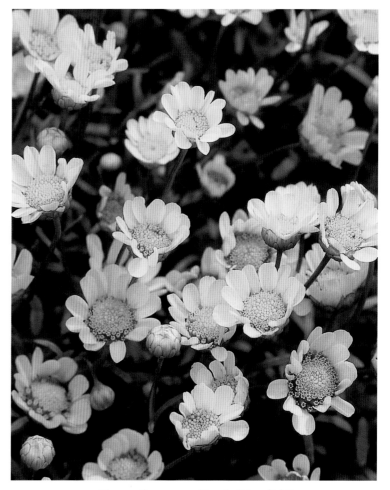

Chrysanthemum multicaule 'Moonlight'

# *Clarkia* Clarkia

Long known as a vital ingredient of children's seed mixtures into which the cheapest – and lowest-quality seed – was often dumped, the clarkia is unjustly undermined by such disparaging treatment. This slight on a truly delightful flower came about in a familiar way.

Until the 1920s, new clarkias were being introduced in exquisite individual colours. Then as it became more expensive to maintain a high level of consistency, they faded away and only mixtures were left. Mixtures command a lower price, so there's even less incentive for seed companies to keep the quality high – and the downward spiral continues.

But the quality of mixtures is now being improved, so the colours in *Clarkia* 'Love Affair' can be said confidently to be red, crimson, rose, salmon, pink, purple, carmine and white because seed of each colour is grown and harvested separately then blended together. However, the colours in 'Double Mixed' are far less distinct and the balance is far less predictable.

The colours grown for these formula mixtures are also now listed separately, so we have 'Chieftain', in clear mauve, and the unambiguous 'Appleblossom' and 'Salmon Queen', the latter two first listed in the 1920s.

These all make excellent cut flowers – cut when the first two or three flowers on the spike are open to ensure that the whole spike lasts well. It's well worth sowing a row of 'Love Affair' or the similar 'Rhapsody' between cabbages, and even clumps in a border amongst shrubs will not miss a few stems cut for a display in the house.

In mixed borders, 'Appleblossom' looks good with the bold spikes of *Agastache foeniculum* 'Alabaster', while the stronger-coloured 'Salmon Queen' makes a tasteful, if unexpected, neighbour for Oriental poppies in similar shades; just let the clarkias self-sow in autumn – they will overwinter and flower with the poppies.

All this so far refers to *Clarkia elegans*, correctly known as *C. unguiculata*; the other long-standing species grown is *Clarkia pulchella*. This is less bold in habit, far more bushy and at 30cm/12in only half the height. The white, 'Snowflake' or 'White Lace', is the pick and, falling into smaller variegated hostas like 'Ginko Craig', it looks just right. 'Passion for Purple', the other separate colour usually available, is a lovely surprise amongst dark-leaved heucheras like 'Stormy Seas'.

*Clarkia bottae*, which has recently migrated from the woodland clearings and chaparral of California to the seed catalogues, is the one species which you see listed under both *Godetia* and *Clarkia* – depending on the catalogue. The pretty upward-facing flowers in various shades of bluish purple come with names like 'Amethyst Glow', 'Lady in Blue' and 'Lilac Blossom'. Their relatively open habit allows them to mingle well with annual phlox and antirrhinums, hardy geraniums and low campanulas; we eagerly await a white form.

All these clarkias can be sown direct where they're to flower; if you raise them in pots as half-hardy annuals, grow them cool and make sure that you never let the pots become overcrowded with roots.

Clarkia bottae 'Amethyst Glow' with the pinks from Limonium sinuatum 'Pastel Shades'

RIGHT *The plant of* Clarkia pulchella *'Snowflake' at the top, with its divided petals, is the true form of this cultivar although occasionally plants with broader, undivided petals appear. This reversion often takes place when plants are allowed to self-sow over a number of years without the off-types being removed.*

*In either form, there is a clean purity of the colour that really sparkles, as here against the slightly greyish leaves and rose-pink flowers of* Geranium **x** riversleaianum *'Mavis Simpson'.*

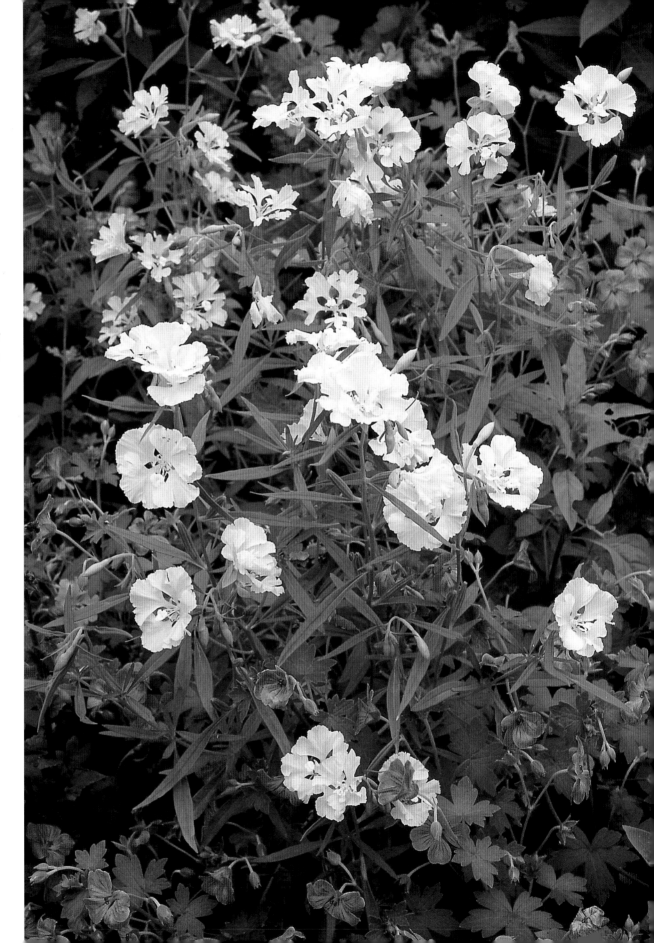

# Cleome *Spider Flower*

'What on earth are *they*?' So goes the reaction from the visiting innocent gardener to a bed full of cleomes. Four petals like the ears of a demented pantomime rabbit stand up from the end of each stem in the head of flowers, with the four thread-like stamens hanging below and a rocket-battery of darker buds standing upright in the top of the spike.

The effect is unashamedly exotic. Individual plants reach 1.2m/4ft high, or more from an early sowing, and branch impressively if pinched. This exoticism is enhanced by the bold foliage, a valuable feature in itself in early summer. Recent introductions from the wild feature unusually dark foliage but a late flowering season, useless in cooler regions at least. Bringing these characteristics together with existing forms in a simple breeding programme could be rewarding.

The names, and the consistency of the colouring in the different cultivars, leave something to be desired. As with many open-pollinated varieties which have been around for decades yet are not important economically, the seed producers have been less than thorough in their attention to ensuring that the plants stay true to type. Hence the flowers of 'Violet Queen', never exactly violet in the first place, vary from altogether mauve to opening mauve then ageing to blushed white. 'Cherry Queen' is more consistent yet no more cherry than 'Violet Queen' is violet; 'Pink Queen' is, at least, pink while 'Helen Campbell' is certainly the purest white.

The mixture usually entitled 'Colour Fountain' is more valuable than many. The flowers are in a sympathetic colour range that harmonizes well without culling; plants from the mix are ideal as a feature in themselves planted through an autumn border. Fronted by and mingled amongst the developing foliage of asters and hardy chrysanthemums, the reckless spidery flowers make a splendid precursor to the main business of the border. In a long swaying mass fronted, perhaps, by 'Operetta' asters in similar shades with their distinctive, quilled balls of spiky colour, your jaw will drop. The same idea can be translated to a round bed where cleomes make a sufficiently relaxed centrepiece not to emphasize the formal shape.

Another, less common, use for cleomes, is in containers – but not in the mixed plantings of petunias and lobelia seen alongside porches everywhere; the scale would be farcical. Start them off in early spring, keep moving them into individual pots and pinch them to encourage the characteristic lurching branching, then move them into their final containers in a cold greenhouse or tunnel for a couple of weeks before moving them outside. The result will be substantial plants which create a combination of drama and fascination set in a group of three or four outside the front door. But beware: do not place them so close to the

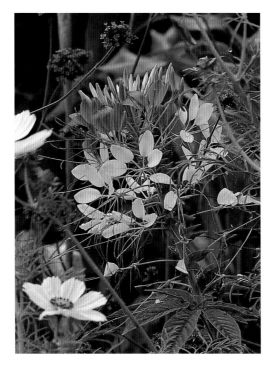

LEFT Cleome *'Violet Queen' may not be especially violet in colour but its two-tone flower heads fit well with, at one end of their spectrum, the tall purple flowers of* Verbena bonariensis *and, at the other, white cosmos. Earlier in the season, before the flowers erupt, the dark, bronze-toned foliage of the cleome makes a fascinating contrast to the green leaves of the comsos.*

RIGHT *Mixtures and single colours can, occasionally, work well together. In front of these ancient espaliered apples, the bold and bright* Nicotiana sylvestris *gives solidity to the mixed plantings, and the cosmos and cleome work especially well together as their colour palette is similar, ensuring a natural harmony.*

pathway that they're constantly brushed, for each leaf has a sharp and painful spine at the point where the leaf joins the stem. Cleomes also attract bees – too many, perhaps, for inclusion in children's gardens.

It's also possible to manipulate the height of cleomes a little by starting them later than usual. This not only avoids the requirement for good heat early in the season but allows them to be grown in small gardens at the front of the border. Late sowings will not wait until they've reached the height seen at the first flowering of early sowings. Instead, they will flower on shorter stems, but with little branching and perhaps without the staying power of those sown earlier.

ABOVE *This sumptuous but rather unlikely subtropical-style planting features the yellow-striped leaves of* Canna 'Striata' *fronted by the spiky ripples of the blue-grey* Melianthus major *and at the back the bold, dark leaves of* Catalpa x erubescens 'Purpurea', *which is cut back each spring to produce the most dramatic leaves. Running through, and somehow not clashing horribly with the cannas, is* Cleome 'Violet Queen'.

Plant breeders have attempted to create consistently dwarf and naturally branching types but without noticeable success and I suspect – what a relief – that it may never be possible to marigoldize them genetically. Cultural techniques, as described above, provide the best options for adapting them to garden situations.

# Cobaea *Cathedral Bells*

Vigorous and spectacularly exotic, *Cobaea scandens* is neither a difficult plant nor a rare one. Its seeds are large and easy to sow, it climbs strongly, and a single plant will cover a large area . . . yet relatively few gardeners grow it.

Perhaps its need for a high germination temperature, not less than 20°C/70°F, is a deterrent. But most of us need so few plants that four seeds split between two 9cm/3½in pots on a windowsill is plenty. Sow each large flat seed, on edge, just under the surface of the compost and cover with clingfilm. Germination can be irregular, but remove the film when the first seedling is through or, better still, peel it back halfway. Leave the seedlings to develop at their own pace then pot each up individually in 9cm/3½in pots, moving them later into 12.5cm/5in pots. Keep them growing on at 12–15°C/60–65°F, then harden them off carefully before planting out after the last frost.

*Cobaea scandens* needs support. The desperate tendrils at the end of every divided leaf ceaselessly search for it. They need to be supported in their pots, where they can be tied to a single cane in their early stages, then pinched soon after their move into large pots and trained up three more canes spaced evenly around the edge. They can, there is no doubt, be difficult to manage in their early weeks and are apt to strangle their neighbours on the greenhouse bench.

In the garden, trellis is the most effective support system: wire or especially plastic netting can sag under the weight of what, in warm areas, may be a large volume of growth unless it's fixed securely to a wall at regular intervals. On a sunny wall, and with good support, growth of 4.5–6m/

Cobaea scandens

15–20ft in one summer is possible, so guiding the growth through a shrub is usually impractical.

Cobaea looks impressive given a large space on a wall of its own, as it enjoys in the garden at Sissinghurst in Kent, but in cooler areas may only thrive with the extra cosiness that a sunny wall provides. In warmer areas it will even make a wild and rambling hedge of growth on a wire fence . . . the warmer the summers, the more situations it will relish.

A problem can occur when cobaea is grown on a wall – the lower growth may not be well covered by foliage and flowers. The trick is to plant another, less vigorous climber to cling to the lower reaches of the cobaea. Canary creeper, *Tropaeolum peregrinum*, is a good choice; it covers well and looks ravishing as it mingles into the purple flowers of the cobaea.

A bushier alternative is *Mina lobata*. This unlikely relative of the convolvulus appreciates the same warm conditions as the cobaea and its bushier growth brings the whole planting forward into the border a little so that it will integrate better with its neighbours. Its flowers start in warm red, then mature through orange, yellow and finally white. Can you imagine it with the deep purple cobaea bells?

There's also a less common white form of *C. scandens*, 'Alba' (the two forms look good mingled together), and this is better underplanted with the pretty lemon and white bicoloured *Mina lobata* 'Citronella' to make an altogether cooler, sharper sun-loving association.

Many years ago there was also a variegated form, rare then and unheard of now. I recall that it was raised from spring cuttings; I wonder if it still exists?

# *Convolvulus* Convolvulus

For many gardeners, the association between these hardy annual convolvulus and the dreaded bindweed with its racing roots is simply too much – banishment from the garden is total and rarely reconsidered unless the enlightenment of experience overcomes prejudice. But just look at what they're missing!

In cooler climates in particular, the flared convolvulus trumpets (for once the word 'trumpet' really does describe the shape of the flowers) are a real treat. The blue is of a depth and richness unknown in any other annuals and in almost any other flowers of a comparative size. When gardeners see convolvulus at their best they almost always seem surprised and delighted, yet as soon as they hear the name, their enthusiasm wanes.

Annual convolvulus fall into two groups: bushy types based on *Convolvulus tricolor*, which are covered here, and climbers based on what used to be called *Convolvulus major* but which is now more correctly known as *Ipomoea purpurea* – these will be found under *Ipomoea* (see pages 102–103).

The star of them all is 'Royal Ensign', sometimes called 'Blue Ensign'. With flowers like a petunia, only a little smaller, the throat is like the chuckling sun on the Teletubbies – but a great deal less irritating. A slightly ragged white star then splays into the rich blue outer edging.

In a border which is focused tightly on blue flowers, with *Lobelia* 'Blue Wings', *Salvia farinacea* 'Victoria', *Salpiglossis* 'Kew Blue' and *Phlox* 'Blue Beauty', the bright spark from those yellow throats just makes the blues seem even more intensely blue.

Red, rose and white are also available separately (all have that same yellow throat and white star) and mixtures occasionally feature a very

pretty and desirable palest sky-blue form which I've not yet seen listed separately.

The white, with its creamy throat, is ideal as a petunia substitute in cool and damp areas, and shines like satin, even on dull days. The red can be a little variable but at its best has a hazy maroon tinge; the rose is perhaps the least successful as the colour can be murky. The mixture may be listed as 'Ensign Mixed' or 'Flagship'.

The Ensign Series is just the right size. Bushy enough for the front of the border, or even as a low cover in the middle ground, it's also lax enough for baskets and other containers, where the colouring and habit of 'Royal Ensign' can be invaluable. 'Royal Ensign' is pushy enough to insinuate itself amongst other plants yet not so dominant that it smothers them. 'Blue Flash' and the 'Dwarf Rainbow Flash' mixture are less than half the height and so less adaptable.

It would be a mistake to stretch the comparison with petunias too far, but convolvulus do have the advantage of larger, more manageable seed and seedlings which are also robust enough to handle more easily. They germinate well at much lower temperatures than petunias but, unfortunately, they still lack the colour range.

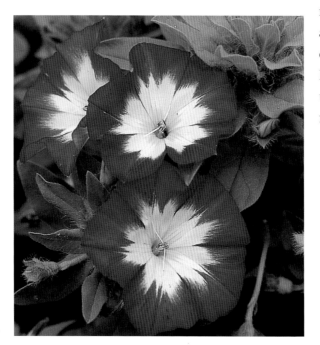

Convolvulus tricolor *'Royal Ensign'*

RIGHT *Even the pugnacious habit of* Salvia viridis *'Claryssa White' and 'Claryssa Pink' allows the persistent trails of* Convolvulus *'Royal Ensign' to peep through. Although both salvia and convolvulus are tough enough to be sown in the open ground in many areas, if you're planning a border careful sowing in a cool greenhouse and pricking out into individual pots allows more precise planting.*

# *Coreopsis* *Coreopsis*

The catalogues do us a disservice. In some, the *only* coreopsis in the list is 'Early Sunrise'; but, while this is useful as a perennial that flowers prolifically in its first summer, to list only this is to ignore the invaluable and truly annual sorts. This will not happen here.

The 'coreopsis' group is something of a botanical bombsite, filled with the debris resulting from the demolition of *Leptosyne*, *Bidens*, *Calliopsis* and *Cosmidium*, as well as *Coreopsis*. The convenient convention of listing the true annuals under *Calliopsis* and the perennials under *Coreopsis* seems to have been abandoned. Cultivars of *Coreopsis tinctoria*, sometimes listed under *Calliopsis bicolor*, are highly prolific, sparsely bushy annuals in yellow, chestnut and almost scarlet. These sparky, long-season daisies are invaluable companions to marigolds; in the same general colour range, their lighter air and slender foliage create a quiet contrast.

There are two main groups. The taller reach 60–90cm/2–3ft in height and are mainly represented by 'T&M Originals' – hardly variable enough to be called a mixture, the flowers differ largely in the size of the mahogany centre on the deep yellow petals. The closely related *Cosmidium* (correctly *Thelesperma*) 'Brunette' is similar, but more uniform. Both are superb mixed border annuals, although they require twiggy brushwood as support against rainstorms. Both are delightful amongst crocosmias such as 'Rowallane Yellow', and with solidagos or in front of dark-leaved cotinus.

Most coreopsis are shorter,

Coreopsis *'Mahogany Midget'*

ranging in height from 20–30cm/10–12in. 'Mahogany Midget' has none of the ugly squatness of some dwarf annuals, while 'Gold Star' is self-descriptive; 'Dwarf Mixed' is usually a blend of the two and 'Treasure Trove' definitely is. 'Mahogany Midget' is excellent with *Linaria* 'Fantasia Yellow'.

More rarely seen, but first introduced from Arkansas in 1823, 'Tiger Stripes' is a mix derived from *C. radiata*, with slender petals in various patterns of orange, mahogany and yellow. Invaluable in 'marigoldments' – blends of flowers in the chestnut, mahogany, rust, lemon, yellow, orange and gold shades of marigolds – its slim petals are a refreshing contrast to double French marigolds. 'Mardi Gras' is a modern dwarf equivalent.

But I glossed over 'Early Sunrise' . . . This cultivar, and the similar 'Sunray', can also be treated as biennials. Sown in summer and planted in autumn, they will make larger plants and flower more prolifically.

Finally, there are two species, which, as I write, are not listed in catalogues but which I mention by way of encouragement to order them, should they ever surface. *C. maritima* is a very bright, noticeably succulent plant which develops enormous tubers, where it grows as a sprawling perennial on its native Californian shoreline. In gardens, it's a bright annual for sowing direct and reaches about 45cm/18in in height.

*Coreopsis douglasii* is shorter, its deeply cut dark green foliage being rather bushy, and its slender-stemmed, bright yellow daisies standing up well; the whole plant reaches about 30cm/12in.

# *Cosmos* **Cosmea**

*Cosmos* . . . a name hinting at star quality and quite rightly, too. These plants are currently undergoing a powerful revival; in recent years plant breeders have been turning their attention to these relations of the more flamboyant dahlias, with noticeable success. Two things have been on their minds: reviving some of the wonderful lost colours and flower forms from the past, and making advances which enable the use of cosmos in more ways. And this is one of those cases where the introduction of new, more dwarf varieties has been no bad thing.

The two main groups of cosmos are noticeably different and both have seen improvements or revivals. *Cosmos bipinnatus* is naturally a tall plant, reaching about 1.2m/4ft, with large but simple daisy-like flowers. In most forms its fresh green, finely cut foliage is valuable from soon after planting time, although some seed stocks develop sparse leafage which reveals too much stem and provides a poor background for the flowers.

Tall, single-flowered forms in reds, pinks and white have been available for many years and have been grown commercially for cutting. Developments for this market have led to the revival of semi-double types such as 'Psyche', with fluffy groups of shorter petals in the centre of the flower, and the unique 'Sea Shells', with each petal rolled into a tube. In single colours we now have dark-eyed types like 'Daydream' and pale flowers with magenta lacing like the rather variable 'Picotee', and 'Pied Piper Red'.

All these have proved invaluable plants in mixed borders, their loose open habit being much more companionable with perennials and shrubs than chunkier annuals. And enough single colours are available to make carefully planned colour schemes possible; 'Purity' in a clean white is an especially valuable form.

With 'Sonata', the height was reduced to around 60cm/2ft. The first plants of the award-winning 'Sonata White' were unusual in being strangely flat-topped with most of the flowers set in a single plane above the foliage. More recently, plants of 'Sonata' have grown a little larger and developed a slightly looser, more rounded habit – an improvement to be sure, but perhaps the result of the seed growers being less than rigorous in keeping it to its original specification.

'Sonata White' is a wow planted with bronze-leaved forms of *Pennisetum alopecuroides*, as is 'Sonata Carmine'. In the larger sorts, matching 'Purity' with *Buddleja davidii* 'White Profusion'

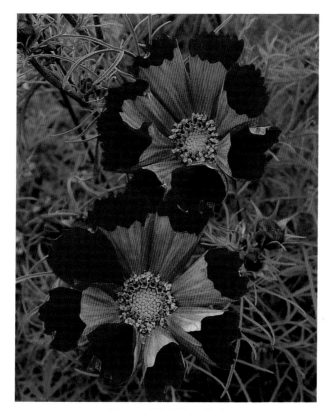

Cosmos *'Pied Piper Red'*

OVERLEAF *The reduced height of* Cosmos *'Sonata White' allows it to mingle intimately with other plants in this small garden setting. Here, it's settled in alongside the slender vertical spikes of* Salvia farinacea *'White Victory' and* Nicotiana *'Lime Green'.*

*If the 'Sonata' cosmos is only available as a mixture, as is so often the case, then move the plants on into 12.5cm/ 5in pots and the first flowers will be open at planting time. You can then separate the whites from the pink and carmine shades, which can be planted in situations that better suit their colour. Notice how the finely dissected cosmos foliage makes a fine background for the broader leaves of the zinnia seedling.*

or 'Picotee' with a dark-leaved cotinus guarantees a sharp intake of breath. 'Dazzler', in its rich velvety crimson, stands out boldly in front of a silver-leaved shrub like *Elaeagnus* 'Quicksilver'; in front of *Physocarpus opulifolius* 'Diablo', it blends to make a richly sumptuous planting. Perillas and heucheras in the foreground could complete the picture.

Well-established plants provide the best show. It's advisable to start the seeds no later than mid-spring and move the plants on into 12.5cm/5in pots for planting out. The first flowers are often opening at this stage so rogues can be segregated and individual plants selected from mixtures. In many areas, you can also sow seed outside, where it's to flower, in late spring.

Although *Cosmos bipinnatus* and its forms are true annuals, they can be rooted from cuttings, a process probably of little interest to gardeners but an enormous help to plant breeders. The other group, based on *C. sulphureus*, are true perennials and are more closely related to both the chocolate-coloured and chocolate-scented *C. atrosanguineus*, and to dahlias.

The tallest of these is about the height of the shortest of the *C. bipinnatus* types, around 60cm/2ft. All are much less suitable for cooler summer conditions and are rarely successful in Britain except in containers and cosy conditions in rich soil. The colour range is limited to reds, oranges and yellows, but most are semi-double and more dependably so than forms of *C. bipinnatus*.

Raising forms of *C. sulphureus* by sowing outside is much less successful, partly because seed is more expensive and packets usually contain fewer seeds. And in cooler areas especially, growth of *C. sulphureus* may not be sufficiently rapid for good flowering-sized plants to develop from a late-spring sowing.

The Ladybird Series, reaching up to 30cm/12in, and the more vigorous Sunny Series, growing to twice that size or more, come in just red, orange and yellow. There may be a little variation in the shades of each colour and in the degree of doubling but not sufficiently to prove uncomfortable to the gardener. They're all great sun lovers, with the shades harmonizing well; all sparkle with *Helichrysum petiolare* 'Limelight' arching through them.

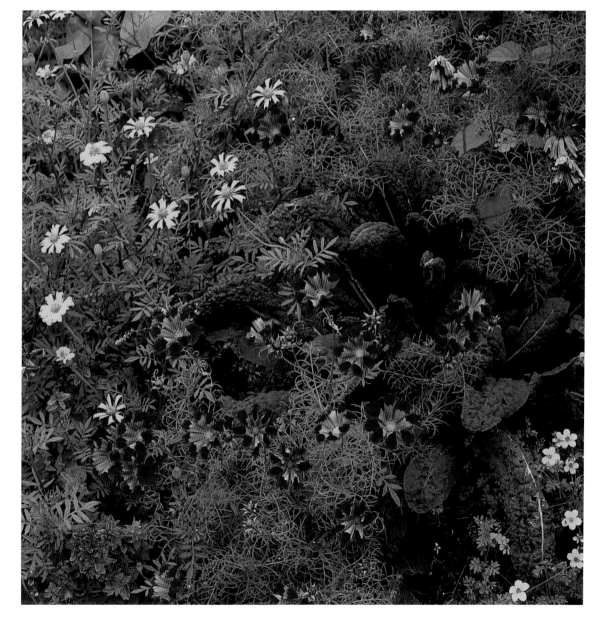

LEFT *At Wave Hill in the Bronx, New York, this dramatic variegated* Canna *'Striata' is fronted by the dense feathery domes of* Bassia *(formerly* Kochia*) scoparia – the burning bush, well known for transforming itself into a rich mound of fire in autumn. Sprawling through is 'Sunny Orange-Red', a semi-double form of* Cosmos sulphureus, *which needs the hot New York summers to give its best.*

RIGHT *The feathery foams of the cosmos foliage threaten to overwhelm the 'Nero di Toscana' kale, but this is a tough plant which can hold its own against most competition. 'Pied Piper Red' is the first of a new series of sea-shell- style cosmos in single colours. Alongside is one of the old, rediscovered Victorian striped French marigolds adding to the freshness with green leaves as well as two-tone flowers.*

# *Delphinium* **Larkspur**

Two, indeed three, very different plants fit here – and only one is a true annual. It is possible to grow the herbaceous border delphiniums, hybrids of *Delphinium elatum*, as annuals; sow very early, grow on strongly and plant out in early summer. For the back of an annual border, the Southern Series has proved outstanding – as long as their early season absence is tolerable. The slim spikes, considered old-fashioned by delph buffs (but that's beside the point), actually fit in better with annuals than the fatter spikes of the slightly earlier-flowering, but altogether less dependable, Pacific Giants.

But it's the truly annual larkspurs, now correctly classified as *Consolida*, which have been such a revelation to me in recent years. It's the less familiar of the group that have proved so valuable, but let's dispose of the more traditional types first.

The densely packed spikes of 'Hyacinth Flowered' and the Imperial Series often have a crude, unfriendly habit – a long way from *Consolida ambigua* from which they were developed. Stiff and upright in growth, the taller mixtures and some of the delightful single colours are nevertheless invaluable as cut flowers. They're also very attractive when dried. The exquisite blue and white bicoloured 'Frosted Skies' and the intriguing 'Earl Grey' in dusky pink are the pick; grow them in rows where they'll brighten the rhubarb. In the border, however, they sit uneasily, unless acting for perennials in a very traditional herbaceous planting.

But there's a less well-known, less developed group, closer to the *Consolida regalis* from which they're derived, that has an airy and relaxed demeanour; these are indispensable. The two featured most often in catalogues are 'Blue Cloud' and 'Snow Cloud'. The flowers are single, five-petalled and, massed on a well-developed plant, they truly have the look of a cloud of inky or milky butterflies, fluttering prettily on the breeze. The plants branch repeatedly, the flowers keep coming and the growth is never so dense as to crowd out neighbours. Although the 45cm/2½ft plants are not thoroughly self-supporting, neither are they so dense as to smother their neighbours if they flop. In fact, the most delightful and surprising associations can come about when antirrhinums, verbenas, dianthus, godetia, salpiglossis and other determined annuals find their way through the clouds of colour. And as the larkspurs lean, new flowering shoots emerge from the leaf joints along the stem to add to the intimate confusion.

Although they are happy sown direct, it is best to raise these varieties in cool conditions indoors and plant them out from 7cm/3in pots in thoughtfully planned positions to create the most effective intermingled plantings. Interplant them amongst and alongside other annuals rather than in a fat block, remembering that they may reach over 60cm/2ft in height and spread.

With 'Sonnet Rose' antirrhinums, the quivering billows of *Consolida* 'Snow Cloud' are like spume from the ocean around besuited bathers languidly rolling in the surf. The more upright cuttings-raised verbenas like the mauve 'Lila' or 'Pastel Pink', rather than the flatter-growing Temari and Tapien series, also make good companions.

*Delphinium grandiflorum* is the other species grown; it is a perennial though one which requires good drainage to ensure its winter survival. 'Blue Butterfly' is a gorgeous royal blue, 'Sky Blue' is self-descriptive. Both will sulk and may fade away if overwatered in their pots.

Consolida ambigua

RIGHT *In this bold grouping, the powerful magenta of* Lychnis coronaria *and* Consolida 'Blue Cloud' *larkspur make a startling and unlikely association. While the magenta and blue create a contrast, a more robust white larkspur amongst the silver lychnis leaves helps it all come together.*

RIGHT *The stray white wands of* Consolida 'Snow Cloud' *fall into the foreground while green-edged midnight foliage of* Solenostemon *(coleus)* 'Black Heart' *fills the background. This sets off that most valuable, yet underused, grey foliage plant* Plecostachys serpyllifolia.

RIGHT Trachelium 'Passion in Violet' was bred as a bushy pot plant but it makes a valuable outdoor annual from an early sowing, its mauve, but perhaps not violet, umbels throwing repeatedly, and ever taller, all summer. Here, Consolida 'Blue Cloud', with the matching blue of Anchusa capensis 'Blue Bird' (at 45cm/18in twice the height of 'Blue Angel' and so more useful), strikes boldly through the centre to open its vibrant flowers.

BELOW The Exquisite Series of larkspurs is intended for use as cut flowers and can develop rather overcrowded spikes for an informal planting. Here, once the spike of 'Exquisite Salmon Beauty' has begun to lean under the pressure from neighbours (in this case the autumnal foliage of Lysimachia ciliata 'Firecracker'), small side shoots emerge which are less crowded and more delicate, and which peep through the foliage creating interesting associations.

# Dianthus Pinks and Sweet William

Garden pinks are amongst the best-loved of perennial flowers for their old-fashioned charm, their scent and their long flowering season, so why are the annual pinks and their various relatives not equally popular? It's true that some, like 'Raspberry Parfait', combine a squat habit with garish and smudgy colouring in a way which endears them to few; many even lack scent as a redeeming feature. Chiefly, though, gardeners are disappointed to find that these are not annual versions of perennial pinks. This frustration prevents recognition of the value of the wide range of forms and colours in annual dianthus.

The annual pinks developed from *Dianthus chinensis* and *D. superbus*, and some with blood from the sweet William, *D. barbatus*, are all single-flowered and closer in style to a traditional bedding plant than a border pink. They make well-branched, twiggy little plants with flowers concentrated towards the top. They flower early and long but may rest in the heat of the summer when they can be snipped back and soaked to promote new flowers.

The Telstar, Princess and the thirteen-colour Ideal Series are the most widely available and some individual colours are superb – although mixtures are more frequently seen in catalogues. There are many combinations you could try. 'Telstar Crimson', with deep red flowers and dark foliage to match, is good in front of *Cosmos atrosanguineus* or *Dahlia* 'Bednall Beauty'. 'Ideal Deep Violet' is uniquely rich in colour with a pale edge to its petals, and is warm and sultry with *Solenostemon* (*Coleus*) 'Rob Roy'. 'Telstar Picotee' (red with a white edge) is the choice when you need a bicolour with a little

Dianthus barbatus *cultivar*

more style than those in the Parfait Series – try it alongside *Pelargonium* 'Venus'. 'Princess White' is a clear, pure shade, effortlessly impressive with 'Sonnet Rose' antirrhinums or 'Delft Light Blue' larkspur. 'Telstar Colour Magician' is unique with flowers which open pink and fade to white – a plant association in a single plant.

The Feather Series, in red and in white (sometimes listed as 'Crimsonia' and 'Snowdonia'), is rather different and, sadly, very hard to find. They have a loose, open, airy habit, with large deeply fringed flowers and, if planted in boxes or baskets, they trail enticingly and blend well with trailing lobelia and even with petunias. In beds and borders their habit and persistence allow them to mingle intimately with other plants to create striking and endearing associations.

Seed-raised carnations have developed in two absolutely opposite directions. The taller Chabaud types, carrying names such as 'Chabaud Giant Double Mixed', 'Floristan', 'Luminette' and 'Champion', make superb cut flowers – especially 'Champion', blooming prolifically in their first year from seed. The colour range is unexpectedly broad and includes pretty picotees as well as pure colours, including yellow. All are well scented (some intoxicatingly so). While a mixed planting may

Dianthus '*White Feather*'

look a little too jazzy in a herbaceous border, single colours are occasionally available, and the mixtures are unrivalled in rows in the vegetable or cutting garden.

At the same time, carnations have been developed as pot plants: the Knight, Lillipot and Monarch Series stand out. In sheltered places, these also make good plants for containers and in warm

RIGHT *The unique suitability of the Feather dianthus for informal plant groupings is shown in this intermingled summer planting. The slender upright flowering shoots of 'Red Feather' rise from its spreading stems through the dark foliage of purple-leaved beetroot and 'Breakaway Red' geraniums. Behind is* Amaranthus *'Hopi Red Dye' with the cuttings-raised* Verbena *'Temari Red' behaving the same way.*

gardens thrive in the open ground. The Monarch Series, in seven colours, is the pick, with strong scent and good performance in tubs; there they need neat companions like the smaller coleus, 'Inky Fingers' for example, or silver *Helichrysum petiolare* 'Goring Silver' to prevent their being smothered.

Sweet William, *D. barbatus*, can be difficult to use in the garden. The problem is that other than a few justifiably difficult-to-find varieties such as 'Roundabout' which have been turned into dwarf annuals, these are uncomfortably late-flowering biennials. This means they're often still at their best when summer annuals are waiting to be planted and there's an understandable reluctance to tear them out.

The answer is to grow them not in exclusively temporary spring plantings, but in spaces in perennial and mixed borders. However, then the problem is that the captivating single colours with their old-fashioned picotee and bicoloured flower forms are so hard to find. You may find only the admittedly irresistible 'Sooty', in the deepest blood red with a ring of white specks in the centre and foliage which deepens to crimson as the plant develops. This is a wonderful plant and probably the same as 'Nigrescens' and 'Dunnet's Dark Crimson'. It's at its best towards the front of the border, surrounded by fresh green foliage where its deep colouring can be best appreciated.

LEFT *White foxgloves are superlative biennials for shady glades. Here, with grasses, columbines and* Dicentra spectabilis, *they stand pure and upright, gleaming in the green glade. They will self-sow freely, often flowering most impressively in their first year then tailing off noticeably.*

# *Digitalis* Foxglove

The foxglove of the English woods and Scottish hills has long been cultivated in gardens. Ever since cottagers were first inspired to move plants from their natural habitat closer to their homes, the better to enjoy their beauty more constantly, foxgloves have been grown around houses. And once this began, selection, change and development were inevitable, as individual plants appreciated for their special beauty were preferred over the more commonplace.

In some wild populations, up to a third of all foxglove plants may be white, but otherwise they vary relatively little. Whites may be spotted or unspotted, although those without bold markings often feature a tawny ghosting where the spots might have been. Ugly forms known as 'Monstrosa' or 'Peloric Form', in which the topmost flower is opened from its familiar tubular shape to a large flat saucer, have been known for centuries and are still occasionally seen in the wild. Interesting curiosities, they have little else to recommend them. Foxgloves have developed more impressively in terms of stature, colour, spotting and the arrangement of the flower spike; these features can be related to the way in which plants are used in the garden.

In their natural forms and colours, sweeps or scatterings of foxgloves are at home in shady naturalistic plantings with other natives like male fern (*Dryopteris filix-mas*), weeping wood sedge (*Carex pendula*) and nettle-leaved bellflower (*Campanula trachelium*). White foxgloves are perfect plants for woodland planting. But their bold rosettes, while attractive in themselves, are pugnacious

and pushy, shouldering out more delicate neighbours. Choose carefully which plants to retain; the rest can go for compost.

Foxgloves will usually self-sow with all too much enthusiasm, so it's important to dead-head the spikes as they fade. Watch them carefully, for the lowest seed pods will be ripe and dropping their seed while the upper flowers are still at their best; it may be necessary to sacrifice a few days' flowers to prevent the appearance of sheets of self-sown seedlings, most of which must be removed. Leave just a few exactly where they will best show themselves.

In such wild situations, the more highly developed forms look out of place. New colours, including yellow and the gorgeous 'Sutton's Apricot', have come from centuries of selection and breeding; in 'Giant Spotted' and 'Glittering Prizes' spots have merged into bold blotches, while 'Excelsior' carries its flowers all round the spike rather than elegantly on one side as in the wild forms. These forms may be unsuitable when used in wild gardens, but look like improvements on the wild species if you use them in colourful and sophisticated borders.

There are practical difficulties associated with using foxgloves in borders. Although all these forms of *Digitalis purpurea* often behave as short-lived perennials, the first flowering season is their most spectacular; and the larger the plants the greater the spectacle. Traditionally, you sow seed outside in midsummer, thin and then transplant seedlings into their flowering sites in early autumn, by which time they've reached a substantial size.

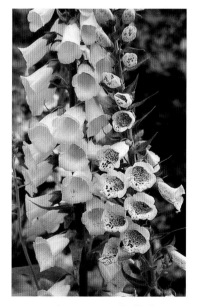

Digitalis purpurea *f.* albiflora
*(two forms)*

Digitalis *'Giant Spotted'*

But few gardens have room to raise such large plants and in today's crowded borders, with so many more autumn flowers now used, there's little space into which to set the plants; and the later they go out the less impressive the show. Additionally, in poor garden soil much of that soil may be lost from the roots in the transplanting process, thus retarding development and reducing the spectacle.

Raising them in pots can solve the problem. Sow in late spring then move the plants into 9cm/3½in, 12.5cm/5in and then 4l/8in pots as they grow. The result will be large, luxuriant plants; and you will probably need fewer than you expect – they can be set out 60cm/2ft apart. Because they have such a tight and undisturbed rootball they can be planted later, when there is more room in the autumn border, and still make a staggering succession of spikes from the leaf joints in the rosette. Any left-overs can be moved on into tubs to make impressive doorway displays.

Like hollyhocks and sweet Williams, foxgloves have also been turned from biennials into annuals – to no one's great advantage. 'Foxy' is reckoned not only to be substantially shorter than the 1.2m/4ft plus of most varieties, but is supposed to flower in its first summer from an early spring sowing. When it was first introduced this was actually true – its choice as an All-America Selection seemed to reward its uniform dwarfness. Its deterioration is revealed most clearly in its height: when I first saw it the plants looked very fine, if a little odd, at just over 60cm/2ft; more recently 1.2m/4ft has been seen; treated as a biennial they almost match the towering 'Excelsior'.

LEFT *The slim and startlingly upright spikes of* Digitalis parviflora *stand erect amongst the more languid growth and big pale bells of* Campanula takesimana. *Like most foxglove species, this is actually a short-lived perennial which produces a good plant when sown in summer as a biennial and will then self-sow in any reasonably sunny well-drained soil. It seems as happy there as in damper conditions in partial shade.*

RIGHT *The crushed raspberry and cream colour of* Digitalis × mertonensis, *a hybrid between* D. purpurea *and* D. grandiflora, *demands a careful choice of companions and, in this town garden, white works unexpectedly well. The pure white form of* Campanula persicifolia *is as likely to self-seed as the foxglove. The back of the garden gleams brightly with white* D. purpurea.

# *Eccremocarpus* Chilean glory vine

Forsythias make a bright and buttery splash in early spring but goodness, aren't they dull in summer? Viburnums, weigela, flowering currants . . . none have anything to offer for many crucial months. Well, here's the answer: all are perfect hosts for climbers and in particular for eccremocarpus.

The Chilean glory vine, *Eccremocarpus scaber*, makes a great deal of bushy growth and because of this it needs stout support. The tendrils cling securely but it pays to plant on the shady side of the shrub so that the shoots snake their way through to emerge into the sun; in this way the whole shrub supports the climber. (Since growth tends towards the best light, if you plant on the sunny side, the shoots will lurch away from where support is provided.)

In cool areas planting on a sunny fence or wall is preferable. Eccremocarpus will cling well to trellis or wire mesh fixed to the wall, or a wall-grown evergreen ceanothus such as *Solanum crispum* makes a good host. In such situations this naturally woody climber may well survive the winter in gardens where otherwise it might be killed. When it does survive, only a brutal spring pruning of old woody growth will ensure another prolific display.

The fat inflated pods burst with flat, shiny black seeds and seedlings may spring up, especially in gravel and often some distance from the parent plant. The soil under wall-grown specimens can be dense with bright, fresh seedlings in late spring. These seedlings are vigorous enough to flower in their first summer in all but the coldest gardens and flowers may unexpectedly appear from the foliage of shrubs acting as surprise hosts.

Mixtures are most often found in catalogues. They have names like 'Tresco Hybrids', 'Anglia Hybrids', 'Fireworks' and 'Carnival Time', but they pose a problem to the thoughtful plant arranger: young plants are rarely in flower at planting time so there's little opportunity to select separate colours from the mixtures for special positions. If only mixtures are available, plant individual plants in their own positions, cross your fingers and hope for the best!

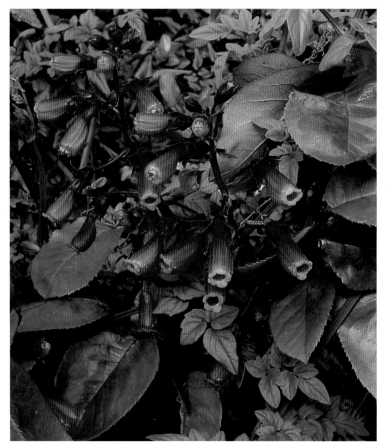

Eccremocarpus scaber

The wild species, in orange, is also often listed and this sits best against plain green foliage, although I've also seen it growing up into *Fremontodendron* 'California Glory' – a startling combination; the yellow goes well with a ceanothus like 'Puget Blue'; 'Tresco Cream', in almost white with a hint of yellowish orange, would make a fitting partner for white cathedral bells, *Cobaea scandens* 'Alba'. The pink, and the dusky red of 'Tresco Crimson', are better seen in close-up on a pillar or the side of a sunny doorway as their colours have little penetration and make less impact from the back of a border.

# *Eryngium* **Miss Willmott's Ghost**

The most important single element in successful gardening is learning to see. Being open to seeing and understanding the landscape of the garden and how it affects you physically and emotionally is crucial – as is being sharp to the garden's details, the plants.

*Eryngium giganteum* is a biennial familiar to many gardeners and is often wrongly thought to be a thistle by the less observant, even though the flower head, flowers and seeds are all entirely different in structure. So, by association, it's often burdened with the reputations of unrelated plants like the bold, statuesque but unstable thistle *Onopordum nervosum*, and the entertainingly named *Silybum marianum*, with its pretty silver-veined foliage, overwhelming mass of growth and invasive self-seeding. (The latter is still worth growing, if only for the entertainment of imparting its generic name to more straight-laced garden visitors.) *Eryngium giganteum* is better behaved than either. It's known as Miss Willmott's Ghost because seed surreptitiously scattered by the great, turn-of-the-century gardener bloomed ghostly-silver, marking her passing, months after she had visited a garden. Many gardeners grow it and it's always the same; or at least it was . . .

Botanist Martyn Rix has a good eye. On a trip to Trabzon in Turkey he saw a variety of *E. giganteum* which was different from the familiar form. He collected seed and introduced

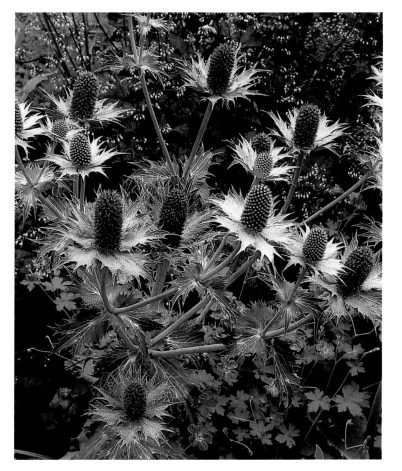

it to our gardens. Now known as 'Silver Ghost', the silvery bracts which make up so much of the flower's attractiveness are larger than in the usual form and their dissections are different; the flowers also last longer and are carried in larger heads.

Tramping about in the wilds of Turkey few of us would have spotted this distinction. But this is just one of many cases where opportunism and 'being open to seeing' has led to the introduction of a good new plant.

This species is a genuine biennial. If you have enough seed, simply copy Miss Willmott and fling a handful through any border which would benefit from silvery exclamations. The seedlings make an impact from an early age with their broad, stiff silver leaves, glinting in the sunlight – so ensure that they're not overwhelmed by their neighbours. Otherwise, sow in pots in early summer, move the seedlings on into 9cm/3½in pots, then plant in sun or partial shade in carefully chosen sites before the roots become too congested. In the years that follow, the seed sowing will take care of itself.

LEFT *The flower heads in the dramatic branching structure of* Eryngium giganteum *open successively over a long period and here are offset very effectively against* Heuchera 'Palace Purple', *itself an excellent spring bedder when raised from a good stock of seed. The questing stems of* Geranium x riversleaianum 'Mavis Simpson' *clamber in from below.*

# *Erysimum* *Wallflower*

Wallflowers are a peculiarly British phenomenon. Originally native to our seaside cliffs, they're still largely a staple of British gardens where their relaxing colours and sharp scent are an integral feature of both traditional and more modern displays.

These spring-flowering biennials have two, no three, great attractions. Their colour, for a start. Few plants cover their range, from deepest blood reds and purples, to golds through primrose, peach and other pastel shades to almost white. Their enjoyably ragged spikes of slightly floppy-petalled flowers are not only colourful but unexpectedly endearing (like cheerful urchins, extras in a BBC Dickens dramatization). And then there's that scent – nothing can compare with the fragrance of just a few wallflowers after a spring shower.

Their third attraction is that they're so easy to raise. In truth, wallflowers are dwarf shrubs; some varieties are even raised from cuttings for planting in informal Mediterranean-style gardens and sunny borders.

More traditionally, wallflowers flower prolifically the following spring from seed sown in summer. The seedlings are thinned then transplanted into nursery rows outside; in autumn the plants are dug up and moved to their flowering sites. They can be very leafy at this stage and, as this is combined with a tendency for the soil to drop off their sparse roots in the moving process, it's easy to understand why sometimes they fail to settle.

Amazingly, wallflowers are still sold in bundles of a dozen or twenty plants, almost invariably in mixed colours only and with all the soil shaken from the roots. They're pulled from a bucket of murky water and wrapped in old newspaper – the better to soak your car seat on the way home. Do not buy these plants. Wallflowers deserve better; in particular, retaining soil on the roots is crucial (and is this not a basic prerequisite with all plants?) Alternatively, plants are sold in packs of ten – plants so small that they never achieve their natural boldness. Do not buy these either. Buy them grown in large pots, or, better still, raise your own.

Wallflowers germinate well in cool conditions and you can sow them in a cold frame, or even in pots outside in summer, then prick them out directly into 7.5cm/3in pots. From here they can go in nursery rows in the traditional manner and from there to their final homes. Alternatively, you can move them on into 12.5cm/5in pots, although watering more than a few may prove exasperating. Wallflowers benefit from spending at least part of their lives in pots. When finally planted in autumn their root-balls hold together far better than those of plants raised in the traditional way.

There are three groups of varieties. The five-colour Prince Series, from Japan, is the smallest. These

Erysimum 'Ellen Willmott'

RIGHT *Traditionally, wallflowers are used in bedding schemes but here they work well in a mixed planting. Under shrubs and amongst perennials, 'Purple Queen' wallflowers blend with 'Recreado' tulips to create a dark but hardly sombre association. The remains of the tulip foliage will disappear amongst the spreading perennials and the tulips can be left in place, as the shrub roots dry the soil out sufficiently in high summer to suit the tulips.*

are best suited to raising in pots and also to planting in containers, especially with dwarf tulips, hybrids of *T. greigii* and *T. kauffmanniana*. The habit of the Prince Series can be rather flat-topped and in the open ground plants may perform poorly; when other, softer colours become available it will be more tempting to overlook its shortcomings. Where a short variety is needed in the open, the four-colour Bedder Series is more dependable.

However, it's amongst the tallest types that the best colours – twelve altogether – are found. The sultry 'Blood Red' makes a bold contrast with 'White Triumphator' tulips or in a closer colour companionship with *Tulipa* 'Queen of Night'. The rich-coloured wallflower 'Purple Queen' ('Ruby Gem' is always given as a synonym but it is, actually, purple) is a wonderful shade, while the least common is also one of the prettiest: *Erysimum* 'Ellen Willmott' is rarely listed but its pale peachy tones are both unexpected and gorgeous. I like it on its own, in a small bed, perhaps by the front door, where its colour can be admired and its fragrance savoured.

Taller tulips are also most effective in mixed borders: they have a natural looseness of habit which allows them to blend well. 'Cloth of Gold' wallflowers, for example, look good with cream and green 'Spring Green' tulips and with blue sparks from one of the taller forget-me-nots planted out at the same time. A similar effect in a mixed border comes from planting the wall-flowers around the perennial *Brunnera macrophylla*.

LEFT *This spring planting in a small suburban garden shows how wallflowers can be integrated into naturalistic designs without looking out of place. The whole arrangement is yellow and deep purple. Lysimachia ciliata 'Firecracker', with its deepest purple, almost black leaves (there are yellow flowers in summer) and 'Ravenswing', the dark-leaved form of the British native Anthriscus sylvestris, set the dark tones. Narcissus 'Petrel', with its many-flowered heads of creamy flowers, and the flowers of the anthriscus sit at the other end of the spectrum with the pale yellow of 'Primrose Monarch' wallflowers and the yellow leaves of feverfew adding sparks. 'Mellow Yellow' columbines, with yellow leaves and white flowers, neatly take in both of the paler colours.*

# Eschscholzia *California Poppy*

One of the great joys of writing this book has been that again and again I find I can say that the plants are easy to grow – and so it is here. Too often, enthusiasm for growing a plant so fulsomely praised by an author and covetously desired by the reader is dampened by the long and detailed description of its very particular cultural requirements which follows. Not so here.

To begin: even the most mean-spirited seed companies provide a generous fill of seeds in packets of California poppies – two or three hundred is common – in contrast with the six geranium seeds some companies supply. Germination of California poppy seeds is trouble-free and speedy, given at least some sunshine, from a direct sowing at any time from spring to midsummer. Flowering continues for weeks, and their own self-sown seedlings may start to flower at just the time the parent plant starts to run out of oomph. In mild areas they can be sown in the autumn.

So, they grow like weeds . . . surely there's more to it than that? Of course. California poppies are simply the most exquisite of all the genuine annuals. Whether setting the whole landscape afire in their native habitat or as a single plant growing by a gravel driveway, their simplicity is captivating. The harmonious variations in the rippling of their petals, the delicate intermingling of shades, their flower colours (sparky or soft and now including more pretty pastels), the fine foliage, with greys becoming more widespread than the usual green . . . their list of attributes is endless. And the altogether happy conjunction of flower and foliage is delightful, the broad petals contrasting with finely dissected leaves.

The wild California poppy, *Eschscholzia californica*, is generally yellow, sometimes with orange spots at the base of the petals, although more than ninety wild forms have been described by botanists. Breeding has widened the colour range impressively, shortened the height, added doubling and fluting to the petals and silver shades to the foliage; 'Rose Chiffon' is recognizably an eschscholzia but clearly different from the wild progenitors.

Taller cultivars like the creamy 'Milky-white', 'Purple Gleam' and 'Red Chief' at about 45cm/18in are now available. They also appear in invaluable colour-themed mixtures where, in spite of their height, they're often the first to flower.

Most recent improvements mirror the developments of the early years of the nineteenth century. Sutton's Seeds were the first, with dwarf cultivars such as 'Sutton's Flame' as well as some with fluted petals like 'Sutton's Gaiety' and 'Sutton's Frilled Pink'. 'Sutton's Gaiety' was also very striking in its dramatic bicoloured flowers; the insides of the flowers were pure white, the outside brilliant red – what a combination. These have long since vanished and, with the present vogue for ever shorter varieties, are unlikely ever to return. However, we may well see these colour combinations on dwarf plants – perhaps even with silver foliage.

The revival of the old fluted types is evident in the 'Thai Silk' mix with single flowers, while the flowers in the 'Ballerina' mix (sometimes called 'Prima Ballerina') are double, in various degrees. But it's the single colours which have made a mark in recent years and they really are captivating.

The best varieties are those which combine silvery foliage and fluted flowers in various shades. The names include 'Apricot Bush', 'Apricot Chiffon', 'Apricot Flambeau', 'Rose Bush', 'Rose Chiffon' and 'Sugared Almonds'. It

Eschscholzia *'Rose Chiffon'*

has to be said that some of these may be synonyms – although it's not clear which! 'Rose Chiffon' is especially gorgeous. Its yellow eye lifts it from a familiar pink and silver pastel combination into something more special. That additional colouring makes it ideal to scatter in pale yellow and beige pea-gravel (rather than grey grit) – and that's all you need to do: scatter the seed. After the first rains the seed will germinate. The early silvery leaves look delightful against the pebbles from the moment they unfurl. 'Rose Chiffon' is also entrancing, emerging from the low silver of *Lamium maculatum* 'Pink Pewter'.

I was amazed when 'Apricot Chiffon' sowed itself into the ground-hugging *Veronica reptans* 'Sunshine', whose flat carpet of yellow leaves (and absence of blue flowers) sneak slowly across gravel; this makes a stunning combination.

Rather different from all these is *Eschscholzia lobbii*, known colloquially in California as 'frying pans'. The plant reaches only 15cm/6in and the flowers are the smallest of the cultivated eschscholzias, often just a quarter of the size of the California poppy, and bright yellow in colour. It's superb for crevices in a sunny stone terrace. Trickle the seed along the cracks and it will soon be in flower. The rich yellow *E. caespitosa* is a bushy little species, large in growth and significantly larger in flower than *E. lobbii*. 'Sundew', its paler lemony form, will grow happily in the cracks of an old limestone wall where just enough seedlings should reappear each year to maintain the display.

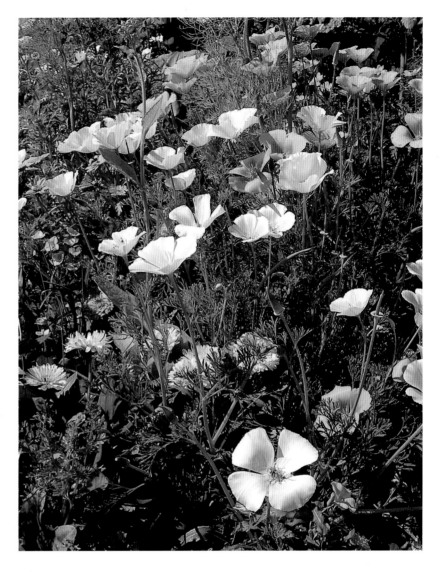

LEFT  *California poppies have an endearing ability to self-sow in the right places and this vegetable garden proves the point. Here, a few orange seedlings bring sparks of colour amongst the cabbages, shallots and parsley, but unless dead-headed, or pulled out ruthlessly, they will cover the whole vegetable garden the following year.*

ABOVE RIGHT  *California poppies like this 'Milky-white', together with yellow forms closer to the wild type, are important constituents of yellow colour-themed mixtures which are so valuable in new gardens. Here, the pale Calendula 'Lemon Pygmy' and a camissonia add to the blend.*

RIGHT  Eschscholzia lobbii

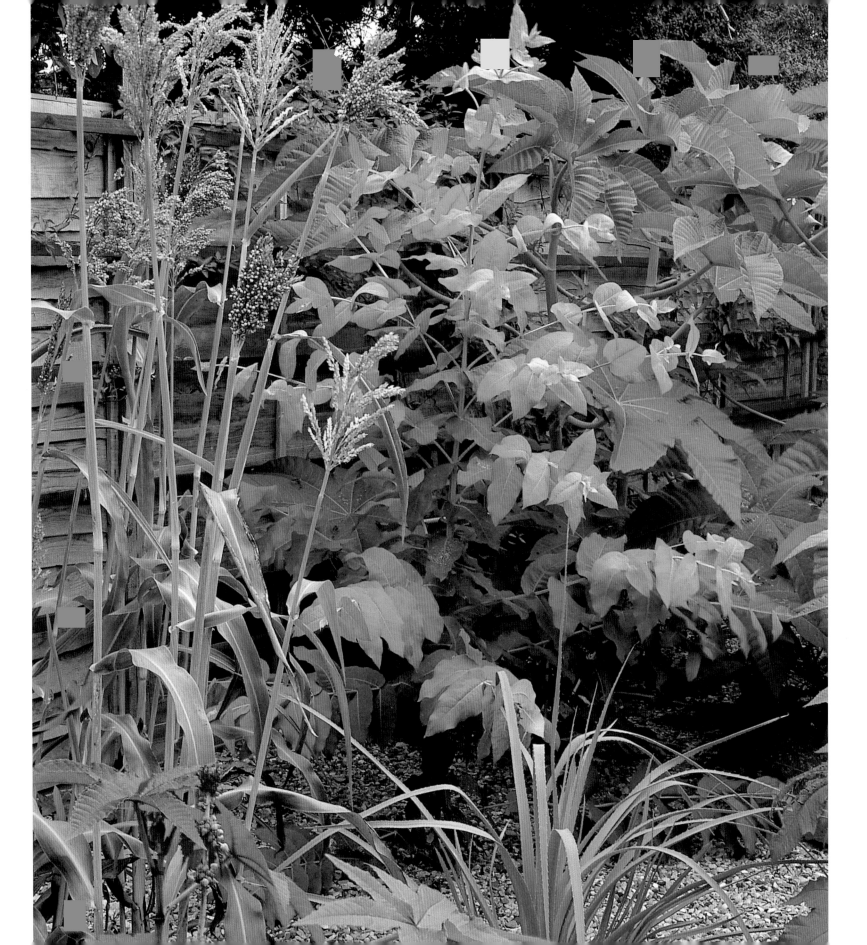

# *Eucalyptus* Eucalyptus

In the wild and in warm gardens, eucalyptus make enormous trees, some with spectacular flaking bark, shimmering silver foliage and spidery white, yellow or red flowers. It may sound as if they have no place in this book but the ability of a few species to reach 1.8m/6ft in their first summer from seed is invaluable.

Back in the nineteenth century, eucalyptus were great favourites; in British seaside resorts of the 50s and 60s they re-appeared as features in formal bedding schemes. Now they have new roles as valuable partners in contemporary mixed borders, as silver highlights in subtropical schemes in cool gardens and as ingredients in more informal summer annual plantings.

The blue gum, *Eucalyptus globulus*, with fat and strong stems and large, soft, blue-grey leaves, is outstanding. Sow it in spring at about 21°C/70°F, prick it out first into 7cm/3in pots then move it on into 12.5cm/5in pots or even larger ones. The crucial clue to growing a luxuriant specimen in the garden is not to let the roots become pot-bound before planting. This can easily happen if you sow the seed in winter in the hope of developing a sub-stantial specimen for planting out – but the plant may become restricted in a small pot. In the cosiness of the green-house, growth of both shoots and roots is rapid; if the pot is too small the roots curl round inside. Then, after planting, the leafy top growth catches the wind like a sail and constantly loosens the roots, which struggle to grow from their tightly curled rootball. Even if you knock in a stake for sup-port, because it must be placed close to the stem, the stake rav-ages the rootball on its way to more solid soil below. A large pot, on the other hand, gives the roots space to develop freely in their early stages, prevents their becoming pot-bound and so allows them to grow out more freely after planting. An occasional drench with liquid feed encourages strong growth after planting.

Eucalyptus are essential ingredients in the pastel, pink and silver schemes still so popular. Try them with sweet peas, such as the striped lilac and white 'Pulsar' or the peachy 'Champagne Bubbles' (both temptingly scented), falling into them from a fence or wigwam of canes alongside or behind. Try them with the irresistible two-tone, pink and white *Salvia coccinea* 'Coral Nymph', tall enough to grow up into the lower branches; or with the pale lavender-rose *Petunia* 'Pearly Wave', bred for baskets and as ground cover but a great scram-bler through the branches, given a little early help.

With blue too, *E. globulus* is special – and top of the list of companions must be *Ipomoea* 'Heavenly Blue', in soft and silky sky blue; silver foliage is the per-fect foil. Plant the ipomoea at the base, check that it climbs the eucalyptus and refrains from surging off in another direction, and it will look superb. *Ageratum* 'Blue Horizon', the blue and white *Salvia farinacea* 'Strata' and more silver in *Senecio cineraria* 'Silver Dust' can go around it.

*LEFT The blue gum,* Eucalyptus globulus, *is the most widely used eucalyptus for single-season effect. Here, it mingles with a specimen plant of* Ricinus *'Zanzibariensis'; both reach over 1.8m/6ft high in their first summer. To the left is the plant catalogued as 'annual sugar cane', a form of* Sorghum vulgare, *which is most striking in flower, and in front is the perennial* Eryngium pandanifolium, *which in its second year makes a statuesque flowering plant.*

Eucalyptus gunnii

# Gazania *Gazania*

Most gardeners would give gazanias rather a mixed reference. Undeniably colourful, their sparkling flowers have the unfortunate reputation of closing in dull weather – a reputation which, in the case of older varieties, is entirely deserved. This has led some gardeners simply to pass them by, turning to boring old marigolds when they need plants in this colour range.

Two things have happened which should dissuade all but the most stubborn from this view. The first is that with the Talent Series we have plants with soft grey foliage so that even when the flowers are closed the plants still have great value.

The second event of significance in the development of seed-raised gazanias is that a plant breeder in California started visiting his gazania trials in the middle of the night. This was not a sign that in his quest for the ever-open gazania he had finally abandoned control of his own reason – on the contrary.

In their native South Africa, gazania flowers close up in poor weather to protect the pollen from moisture. This mechanism is triggered by low temperatures, poor light or a combination of the two. Older varieties like the 'Sunshine Hybrids', 'Sundance' and 'Harlequin' were effective outside only in bright sunny weather and on the rare occasions when they were brought into the house as cut flowers and the constant warmth ensured the flowers remained open. Plant breeders have been working intensively on developing gazanias in which this mechanism is less prominent, allowing the flowers to stay open longer in cooler, duller climates.

Visiting the gazania trials in the middle of the night revealed individual plants which closed up just that little bit less than their neighbours. These were then checked during

Gazania × hybrida *'Mini Star'*

Gazania *'Talent'*

daylight hours, and the best incorporated into the breeding programme. The result was the Daybreak Series, whose flowers really do stay open longer than most other gazanias.

'Daybreak Red Stripe' is especially startling, recalling the best of 'Sundance' and 'Harlequin' in its boldly striped flowers, but with the addition of a newly introduced long flowering habit. It makes an impressive planting with the cuttings-raised *Oenothera* 'African Sun' alongside, or *Bidens* 'Goldie'; it's important to plant gazanias with low-growing neighbours as they flower so much less well when overshadowed.

The colour range has broadened too, although I see little point in growing the pinks and cream which have now appeared in the Chansonette and Mini-Star series; they always look slightly dirty. The more familiar yellows, orange shades, chestnut and gold, in some cases striped in contrasting shades or with contrasting marks at the base of the petals, are far more effective.

Although gazanias make splendid mixers in sunny containers and in intimate plantings in small sunny corners, they also make spectacular ground cover. On sunny banks along the drive or at the front of a property facing a road, sweeps of 'Talent' gazanias may cause passing drivers to swerve in shock and astonishment – so avoid this planting if you live on a bend.

RIGHT *The fiery tones of Gazania 'Sundance' on trial at Unwin's Seeds in Cambridgeshire. Most of the larger seed companies hold trials in which they not only assess potential new introductions but grow the same seed that they put in the packets as a quality control.*

# *Godetia* Godetia

The godetia is a sadly devalued flower. From its inclusion in children's seed mixtures and its popularity as a promotional give-away it has become . . . perhaps not derided but certainly passed over. This is unjust. It's true that, as with many hardy annuals, some stocks can be poor but others can be both prolific and colourful – so let's think positive.

Godetias have two special qualities. The satiny sheen on their petals is unrivalled; even on dull days it shimmers and flickers, and as you look into the flowers with their slender stamens and divided style it's as if a ballroom dancer had fallen on her bottom and kicked her legs in the air (allowing for some licence in the details of human anatomy). And godetias come in such colours – no yellows and no genuine blues, it's true, but amongst the purples, reds, pinks and white there's a unity of tone which allows even the mixtures to harmonize; there are also some unique colours and bicolours. And all are very easy to grow.

Like nasturtiums, which have suffered from much the same tainted reputation, godetias were once very popular and available in a wide range of colours. In the 1880s Suttons listed 10 varieties, in the 1920s it was up to 23 and even in the 1950s catalogues listed between 10 and 20. Then they declined; by the 1980s many catalogues listed but three or four. Now a revival is taking shape and some catalogues again list a dozen varieties.

The revival began with the $F_1$ hybrid Grace Series of tall cut-flower types,

Godetia *'Salmon Princess'*

Godetia *'Schamini Rose'*

which are exceptionally prolific and come in seven separate colours; they're superb in borders with perennials or as cut flowers and can produce fifteen stems per plant. Cut them when about a third of the flowers on the stem are open and the remainder will open in the vase.

The dwarf, eight-colour Satin Series followed. These plants are incredibly prolific with some gorgeous individual colours, but in some catalogues the seed is over 200 times the price of older cultivars! Its arrival increased interest in godetias but less in these expensive $F_1$ hybrids and more in the old cultivars. 'Sybil Sherwood', in salmon orange with a white edge, is perhaps the only old cultivar which never quite disappeared. Now 'Salmon Princess' has returned, the tall, semi-double 'Schamini' type has been reintroduced, and individual colours like 'Rembrandt' in red with a white edge and 'Duke of York' in carmine with a white centre have come back.

Mixtures like 'Bornita' and 'Improved Dwarf' have been upgraded, new introductions like 'Precious Gems', which is blended from individual colours, have taken the mixtures to new heights . . . everything is looking up for the godetia. Except that the botanists have scrapped the name and merged them into the clarkias; catalogues still list them as godetias, and so do I.

In the garden, single colours like 'Salmon Princess' and 'Schamini Carmine' fit well into mixed plantings with perennials and can be sown as late as early summer and still flower well. Interplanted or backed with forms of *Salvia coccinea* and taller forms of *Salvia farinacea*, the effect is striking and the contrast in flower forms very appealing.

The unusually speedy Satin Series can even be sown direct to follow sweet Williams, which are usually still at their peak at planting time for summer bedding. However, this seed is expensive and perhaps better cosseted in pots.

ABOVE *The bronze-purple foliage of* Heuchera *'Palace Purple' makes the perfect companion for a plant from Godetia 'Improved Dwarf Mixed'. Individual plants were raised in pots and planted in the most appropriate places in the border when the first godetia flowers showed their colour.*

# *Helianthus* **Sunflower**

In 1888 Vincent van Gogh was living in Provence, in the Yellow House at Arles, and during the summer of that year he painted a series of pictures of orchards, gardens and sunflowers which he used to decorate the house for the visit of Paul Gauguin. He wanted this decoration to create 'effects like those of a stained-glass window in a Gothic church'.

During this time he looked forward to a new life in which people would 'live in nature as though they were flowers'. The sunflower came to be the symbol of van Gogh's conviction that an artistic renaissance could only take place in the sun.

For the gardener, even the briefest look at his vibrant sunflower pictures reveals something unexpected. Few flowers arranged in that familiar cream and yellow vase resemble today's idea of a typical sunflower. The ray florets of some are slim and shaggy; in others they have almost vanished and the flowers resemble fat orange buns.

Catalogues from the late 1880s show few such variants. There's a tall single yellow, a primrose yellow single which was new in 1889, a dwarf form reaching about 90cm/3ft, a tall double orange and a shorter, well-branched, small-flowered form. Those shown in van Gogh's paintings were probably grown in gardens from home-saved seed where variations would often occur or, perhaps as likely, plants raised from bought seed which were inherently variable.

Since then, the colour range has widened. There are more doubles like 'Orange Sun', shorter cultivars suitable for small gardens and for cutting have appeared, and so-called 'pollen free' cultivars, which don't shed pollen on the furniture when cut for the house, have also been introduced. Amongst those in unusual colours, the tall 'Velvet Queen' is a deep and sumptuous velvety reddish brown at its best, but in my garden has proved variable. 'Prado Red', sometimes called 'Ruby Sunset', is more uniform in colour and, at 1.2–1.8m/4–6ft, a little shorter. 'Valentine' is a lovely creamy yellow with a black disc and 'Moonwalker' has attractively branched, pale heads with rather a frilly look.

There are still relatively few doubles and some are less than immediately appealing. 'Teddy Bear' reaches about 60cm/2ft with yellow, rayless pincushion flowers. The rather gross 'Sungold' with big double flowers on 1.8–2.4m/6–8ft stems is also occasionally listed. Dwarf types are slowly becoming more widely available. 'Holiday' reaches 1.2m/4ft and branches strongly from the base. It was bred for cutting but also makes a wonderful border plant, especially with dark-stemmed *Aster lateriflorus* crowding in alongside. In a pot, 'Big Smile' keeps to just 38cm/15in; 'Pacino' can be even smaller.

In gardens, the taller sunflowers make a superb screen around the vegetable garden, or to divide it; 'Valentine', 'Prado Red' and 'Prado Yellow' would be ideal. Along new boundaries they can make a spectacular show. If space allows, grow three or four cultivars, one behind the other. If not, a row of 'Valentine' or 'Pastiche' mixture could go at the back with 'Teddy Bear' or 'Music Box' mix in front. In mixed plantings 'Moonwalker', 'Velvet Queen' or 'Sunbeam' are an elegant back-of-the-border presence, especially in the first year after planting when tall perennials may not make their full height. But even in later seasons their colour and poise reliably continue to give full value.

Helianthus *'Velvet Queen'*

Helianthus *'Orange Sun'*

LEFT *Dwarf sunflowers can be difficult to integrate into mixed plantings, but by careful choice of variety and of neighbouring plants you can create attractive combinations. Here, 'Pacino' is set against the slender foliage of Bowles' golden grass, Milium effusum 'Aureum', while in front are two almost perfectly matching annuals. Viola 'Universal Primrose Shades' has a slightly darker lip but the upper petals match almost exactly the crinkled flowers of the 'Primrose Gem' nasturtiums. The broad, bold leaves of 'Bull's Blood' ornamental beet fill the foreground with contrasting deep bronze.*

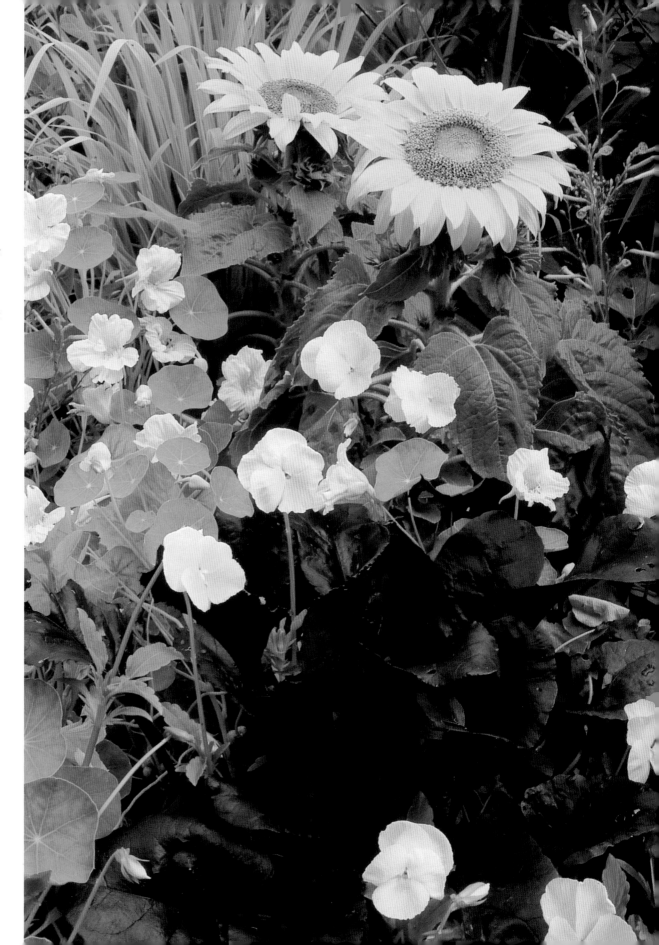

# *Helichrysum* Strawflower

Best known as attractive dried flowers (wire the stems to keep the heads from drooping), helichrysums are strangely neglected as fresh cut flowers and as annuals for summer borders. But their colour range is now unexpectedly impressive and the newer, taller types, like the King Size and Sultane series, come in intriguing pastels as well as the old-style fiery shades.

All, naturally, keep their colour for an unusually long time and, in habit, many fit with perennials especially well. Only the relative difficulty in finding the separate colours with which to plan effective plant associations has undermined their progress; now this is being remedied.

Although helichrysums are tough enough to be sown outside in many areas, treating them as half-hardy annuals and raising them in pots is more dependable and ensures earlier flowering. This technique is especially useful with plants chosen from the newer, taller types with their wider range of colours, such as the King Size and Sultane series . Raising them in pots, finishing at 12.5cm/5in, allows them to be positioned more precisely in borders.

For many years 'Bright Bikinis' were the only dwarf type and, at first, made good bedders; 'Hot Bikini' in fiery orange red was the only widely available separate colour and this certainly looked the part with beetroot, 'Malibu' lettuce or other reddish foliage. But seed stocks deteriorated and the plants seemed taller each time I grew them. Now the invaluable Chico Series in five colours is supplanting them and although plants can be rather squat they have the advantage of spreading surprisingly well. The seed is more expensive than that of 'Bright Bikinis' so you'll find far less in the packets, although the quality is more dependable.

Oh, finally, just one more thing: helichrysums may seem inexplicably absent from some reference books. The truth is that the botanists now place them in the genus *Bracteantha* – try there. But the various forms of *Helichrysum petiolare*, relations of the strawflowers, remain helichrysums.

LEFT *'Chico White', one of five colours in the dwarfest series yet seen, sits neatly amongst 'Lemon Gem' tagetes with 'Malibu' lettuce in the background. For more intimate tapestry plantings the Chico Series is ideal, although when grown in poor soil it can look depressingly dumpy; rich conditions and no lack of water give it a slightly more open and uneven look. I've found that regular dead-heading prolongs the flowering season significantly.*

# *Hesperis* Sweet Rocket or Dame's Violet

'Among the most desirable of hardy flowers' wrote William Robinson in *The English Flower Garden* in 1883. Well, sweet rocket, sometimes called dame's violet, is indeed delightful, and desirable, especially the white form, *Hesperis matronalis* var. *albiflora*, which has a purity of colour that makes it invaluable both as a tall, informal ingredient of spring bedding schemes (with *Allium* 'Purple Sensation' – wow!) and as a dependable self-seeding woodlander.

Sweet rocket's endearingly relaxed habit of growth, which fits well into mixed borders of all kinds, is useful not only in shady sites, where it's most often seen, but in sunnier sites too. Flowering as they do in early summer, their clouds of small flowers are perfect when allowed to self-sow amongst the strong shapes of inter-planted Oriental poppies and bearded irises. With self-sown 'Mother of Pearl' poppies, sweet rocket can fill a whole border with refreshing colour.

This combination works exceptionally well, especially if sweet rocket is restricted to the white form – when the mauve appears alongside some Oriental poppies and irises, the resultant colour combinations can be a little too disputatious. Choosing varieties of poppy and iris

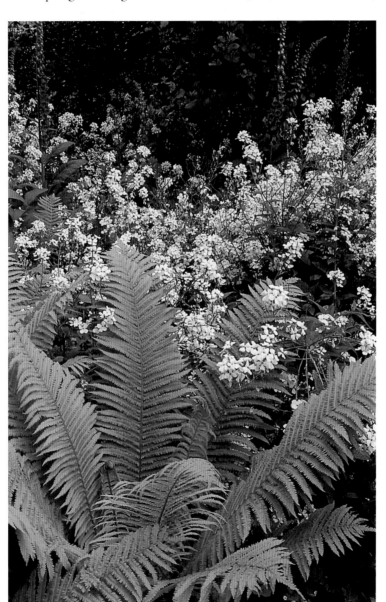

carefully creates more comfortable groupings with the mauve form; white, pink and purple are more suitable than orange, scarlet and bright yellow.

Apart from the purity of its white and the softness of its mauve colouring, its other irresistible quality is the scent – it is, after all, called sweet rocket. (This name derives from a comparison with rocket the vegetable, which does not have sweetly scented flowers. It also goes by the mysterious name of 'close sciences'!)

As evening falls, the scent of the sweet rocket is powerful and soft, intoxicating in the best sense of the word. Just a few plants bring fragrance enough to a small garden.

LEFT *In woodland situations, white sweet rocket,* Hesperis matronalis var. albiflora, *is perfectly at home, its clean white flowers bringing light to shady borders. Here, it makes a bright combination with the freshly unfurled fronds of the shuttlecock fern,* Matteuccia struthiopteris. *As sweet rocket has relatively sparse foliage, hellebores, aconites and other early flowers growing underneath will not be smothered.*

# *Impatiens* Busy Lizzie

The first I saw of busy lizzies (why *are* they called that?) was in the damp light of an early summer morning in the London suburbs. A huge plant filled the window of a Victorian house where, as a lad, I delivered newspapers, its clay pot tottering on the inside windowsill. Bare stems were its most striking feature, the leaves were sparse and pale, and the scattering of brash pink flowers seemed insufficient to redeem the situation. When it suddenly disappeared, I noticed a few stray leaves peeping out of the dustbin. I then forgot about busy lizzies for ten years.

Now the impatiens, as it's mostly called, is the best-selling bedding plant in the world, transformed by plant breeders, for both better and worse, into a dwarf and prolific plant which tolerates a wide variety of conditions. In rich soil and plenty of moisture, plants develop an open, companionable habit which suits the intimate, intermingling schemes which are ideal in today's small gardens. Neglected, and in poor soil, an inelegant tightness of habit reduces their appeal.

The familiar bedding impatiens can be difficult to distinguish: the Expo, Tempo, Super Elfin and Accent series include more than twenty different colours each and the nuance in shades can be very useful when planning small-scale plantings with the precision they deserve.

There are also two interesting smaller series. The Swirls, which partner the Super

Impatiens *'Bruno White'*

Elfins, are delightful with their dark picotee edges to the paler flowers; the two Mosaic colours have a delicate patterning of speckles which may not show up well in mass bedding but is captivating in containers.

The best advice is to scour the catalogues for separate colours which exactly suit the effects you wish to create. Mixtures, as usual, predominate, but don't buy them. There are twenty-seven colours in the 'Tempo' mixture and forty seeds in a packet; what are the chances of actually getting one plant in each colour? Combine red, orange, purple, pinks of all kinds and cerise (some with white starry patterns) in one bed and the result can be spectacular . . . spectacularly lurid.

Impatiens *'Mosaic Lilac'*

But from so many colours some wonderful colour-themed blends have been created. 'Super Elfin Mother of Pearl' is the pick, a meld of pastel pinks, lilacs and white which is outstanding and, as impatiens thrive in moist shade, can bring true light to the darker areas of smaller city gardens. In brighter sites with silver foliage like *Senecio cineraria* 'Cirrus' or the compact *Helichrysum petiolare* 'Goring Silver', these soft shades seem almost fashionable again.

The Bruno Series has brought unexpected benefits for the gardener: the seeds are larger than those of other impatiens and the seedlings more vigorous, making them

Impatiens glandulifera *'Candida'*

far easier to handle. The plants are also more open in habit, the flowers larger, and both petals and foliage are thicker, so they thrive better in hotter, drier conditions than other cultivars.

Of course, there are other annual impatiens. One which has caused a particular stir, mainly for the wrong reasons, is *Impatiens glandulifera*, the Himalayan balsam. Known in Britain, from the shape of the flowers, as policeman's helmet, this name will mystify anyone who knows the NYPD better than the British bobby. The pods pop as they ripen and fling seeds far and wide; the succulent seedlings germinate by the thousand and soon smother their neighbours. This tall, moisture-loving species has become a pest in some parts of Britain, colonizing river banks where it's as familiar to fisherman as the boot full of water and the mosquito. The white form, 'Candida', is especially beautiful and, even as I write, the sweet and distinctive balsamic smell comes back to me. Although it's valuable for its speed in reaching back-of-the-border size, just be aware that the seeds will come up everywhere.

The bedding types are trickier to raise and are best sown at about 21°C/70°F but certainly no warmer than 23°C/75°F. They're also best with some light; this does not mean full sun, rather that a dusting of vermiculite as a covering is more suitable than a sifting of seed compost. Never water seeds or seedlings with cold water.

Cover the seed pot with clingfilm to keep the seeds moist and, after pricking out, avoid sudden fluctuations in temperature (especially cold spells); plants which have endured this inter-rupted growth develop unevenly with a mix of short and long shoots and may not establish well once planted.

RIGHT *Using a mixture of plants in different colours needs careful thought. Here, although there are nine different genera in and around this terracotta chimney-pot, the colour range is sufficiently restricted to ensure harmony. Impatiens 'Accent White' is close in colour to the pale edges of the pansy flowers, the light tips of* Helichrysum petiolare *'Limelight', the variegated ivy and the variegated felicia and also the pale lime nicotiana flowers. The lobelia, petunia and dark pansy are all in the same colour range so the contrast with the impatiens and other pale colours is a soft one.*

# *Ipomoea* Morning Glory

Sorry, I must sit down . . . it makes me go weak just to think about the silky sheen on those delicate petals . . . like caressing . . . 'Heavenly Blue' ipomoea is essential; no one with a soul can resist it once they've seen it. Like the most captivating of lovers it's not perfect but is nevertheless both irresistible and deeply satisfying – the perfect combination.

This may all seem a little excessive. But to see those buds poised in the afternoon sun, rolled like strange sea molluscs, ready to unfurl the next day before even the photographer deputed to record them is awake and out in the garden in the best of the first light . . . They have so much allure with so little pretension. Confidently gorgeous in the privacy of the best light, in the suffocating heat of the day they close up and there's nothing to see – except tomorrow's potential.

'Heavenly Blue' is the best, but its growth depends on the summer weather. Given warmth it will thrive, even in a short season, luxuriating and flourishing, covering fences with foliage and exquisite flowers. In cooler gardens or seasons, growth is less rapid, especially in the early stages when the foliage and growth tips may develop yellow streaks; this is a plant whose response to warmth is striking.

There are other shades in this group, based on *Ipomoea tricolor* and *I. nil*, but they need more warmth. Many of these are descendants of the Imperial morning glories which gripped Japan in the mid-nineteenth century in much the same way that tulipomania swept Europe.

Ipomoea purpurea

£5 per seed is known to have been paid by the lustful and the avaricious.

Japanese catalogues still list an unexpectedly wide range of unusual ipomoeas; few are listed in the West, although 'Chocolate', in a strange milk-chocolate shade with a dash of rose, is sometimes seen. Doubles such as 'Double Blue Picotee', the 'Early Call' mixture in scarlet, white, orange, pink and purple, and the repulsive 'Roman Candy' with its white splotched leaves (which I cannot discuss further) tend to require warmer conditions even than 'Heavenly Blue'. In many areas they are more dependable as conservatory or greenhouse plants – red spider mite will probably ruin them, but not before you've enjoyed them for a few weeks.

There is also a group of hardier sorts based on *I. purpurea*, once known as *Convolvulus major*. Sow these outside where they're to flower ('Heavenly Blue' and its allies need a greenhouse start). They are usually available only in an irritating mixture including purple, pink, red, cerise and white, although separate colours are occasionally listed. These include what purports to be *I. purpurea* the species; 'Crimson Rambler' in more of a cerise colour with a clear white eye; the brighter 'Scarlet O'Hara'; and the best, the wonderfully rich and vivid 'Grandpa Otts', which is both dependably leafy and prolific. Grow this, or the very similar 'Star of Yelta', up through a dark buddleja like 'Black Knight' for a uniquely sultry display.

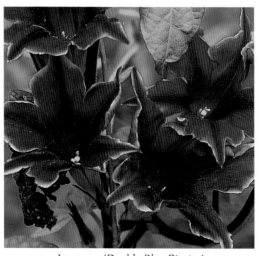
Ipomoea *'Double Blue Picotee'*

RIGHT Ipomoea 'Mini Sky-blue' is only slightly smaller in flower than 'Heavenly Blue' but is certainly less vigorous in growth. This allows it to be set on the flat to twine through its neighbours, in this case Salvia farinacea 'Blue Victory', without smothering them, and its tempting trumpets spark joyful surprise. Its tendency to develop creamy marks in cool conditions, which can just be seen here, is the more easily masked when it snakes amongst leafy neighbours.

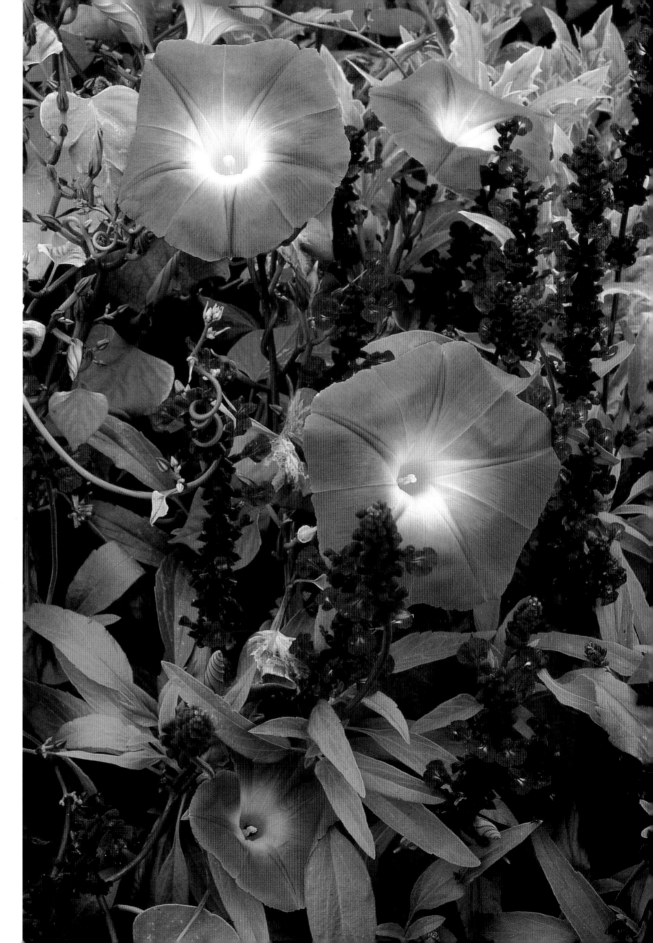

# *Lathyrus* Sweet Pea

Sweet peas have been the subject of oscillating fashions over the years yet, while they may not have quite regained the extraordinary popularity they once enjoyed, sweet peas are the one annual which non-gardeners love and which even prejudiced gardeners exclude from their otherwise sweeping derision directed against annuals.

The intoxicating fragrance of sweet peas, which is at its most penetrating on warm dry days, delights everyone from chintzy grandmothers for whom the sweet pea inspires powerful, if rather vague, warm nostalgia, to toddlers surprised by the scent. Bees and pollen beetles like them too. It's especially refreshing that enthusiasm for sweet peas not only extends across the whole spectrum of gardeners but also encompasses almost the whole range of styles of sweet peas themselves, from wild species and old cultivars to the latest introductions.

Whole books have been written on the chronological history of sweet peas but let me summarize. The wild sweet pea, *Lathyrus odoratus*, originates in Malta and was sent by the monk Franciscus Cupani to England in 1699. This was probably the magenta and purple bicolour we now grow as 'Cupani'; its scent is overpowering, the colours rich but the flowers small. By 1800 five colours had appeared including, in 1726, 'Painted Lady', the pretty pink and white bicolour which still looks good twining up through *Lavatera* 'Lisette'.

Two leaps forward took place towards the end of the nineteenth century. Henry Eckford, from Shropshire (who had previously bred new calceolarias and verbenas) developed the Grandiflora sweet peas, with (comparatively speaking) larger flowers, in a better shape and a wider range of colours; these still retain the fragrance, strength and freedom of flowering of their predecessors.

These Grandifloras were neglected for decades, although their remarkable fragrance has again made them increasingly popular at a time when more modern types are less dependable in their perfume. They're also used to make up mixtures with names like 'Old Spice' and 'Old Fashioned Scented Mixed'. There are even new cultivars in this group such as the white 'Vanilla Ice' and the scarlet 'Philip Miller' with its blue flecks. All are best grown where their relatively small flowers can be appreciated: by a gate or on one side of a doorway where the scent will waft through tantalizingly to the other side.

In 1901, everything changed. In three different gardens the pink Grandiflora 'Prima Donna', one of Henry Eckford's most popular introductions, sported a new flower form. It happened with Henry's own plants, it happened in the cut-flower nursery of William Unwin near Cambridge and it happened at Countess Spencer's family home at Althorp in Northamptonshire (now well known for very different reasons). In all three places, sports appeared with much larger flowers, a more open shape and a noticeable wave in the standard (the upright part of the flower). The Althorp type was introduced by head gardener Silas Cole as 'Countess Spencer' but proved rather variable; the slightly smaller-flowered Unwins type was introduced as 'Gladys Unwin' and was much more uniform. The two came together as the Spencer sweet peas.

Sweet peas in this style are the most widely grown today but a few years before the first Spencers appeared, in California in 1894, a very different

Lathyrus odoratus *'Sunsilk'*

Lathyrus odoratus *'Helen Thomas'*

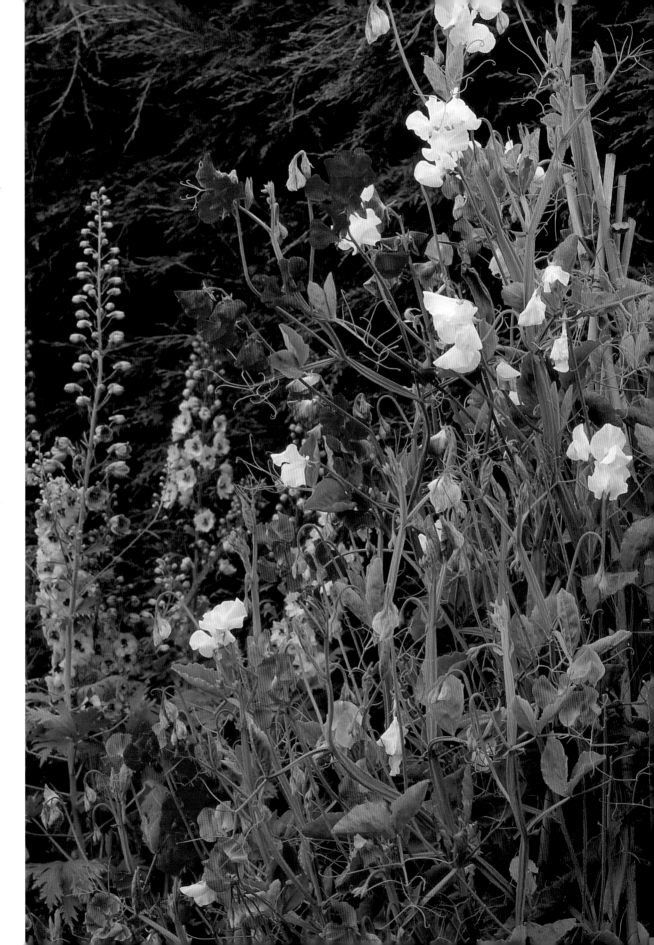

RIGHT *Training sweet peas on a wigwam of 2.4m/8ft bamboo canes is the simplest way to grow them for cutting. Push the canes at least 60cm/2ft into the ground and tie them securely at the top. The whole mass of stems should also be tied in loosely as they develop, or they may collapse away from their support – as they're starting to show signs of doing here. Set against the dark green of the yew, this colourful mixture stands out well although a colour-co-ordinated blend such as 'Rosemary Verey' in pinks and cream would blend more happily with the delphiniums alongside than this multicoloured mix. Although flowers will be picked for the house from this planting, it will still look well in the flower border as there should still be enough blooms to give a bright display in the garden.*

ABOVE LEFT *Hazel branches make splendid plant supports of all kinds. Here, in a mixed border, the hazel is a discreet support for the modern favourite 'Beaujolais' sweet peas.*

ABOVE RIGHT *Long, straight, newly cut hazel poles are bent into an arch and the flat, fan-like tip growth is used to fill the gaps around the sides, the better to support the old-fashioned 'Cupani' sweet peas. This looks elegant from the moment it's set up and, as the sweet peas continue to clamber, its character still shows through.*

type was discovered: a small-flowered, very dwarf, slightly spreading cultivar christened 'Cupid'. Like the Grandifloras, this too all but disappeared but has now been revived to the extent that pots of 'Cupid' are sold in garden centres for windowboxes.

Over the years other dwarf types have appeared, though none quite so remarkably prostrate as 'Cupid'. The 60–90cm/2–3ft 'Snoopea' mixture is probably the best known. Its silly name may have deterred as many gardeners as it attracted. It has no tendrils, unlike the 90cm/3ft 'Jet Set'; which is admirably self-supporting but sadly no longer available in the delightful separate colours as it once was. More recently, 'Explorer' has appeared, a non-tendril type with seven colours in a brighter, sharper colour mix than the eight more pastel shades of 'Jet Set'.

New colours and colour combinations have also been added to the Spencer sweet peas. The flowers have become larger, with a greater certainty of individual stems carrying four or five flowers but they're less dependably scented; some are hardly scented at all. Other recent developments have included some striking bicolours from New Zealand known as 'Romance', 'Love Match', 'Hammett Bi-colours' or 'Kiwi Bicolour Mixed'. Striped cultivars have returned, first as 'Unwin's Striped', then in the Ripple Series, then in the Heavenly Series and more recently in 'Rosy Dawn', the first striped version of a Spencer sweet pea with orange-red patterning on white. 'Helen Thomas' is a striking picotee, 'Sunsilk' a shimmering orange-pink.

Most seedsmen who specialize in sweet peas concentrate on the Spencer varieties, and there's an increasing feeling amongst non-specialist gardeners that new introductions are too similar to earlier varieties. The seedsmen's urge to introduce *something* new every year often overwhelms the necessity to ensure that new introductions are genuine improvements. This has prompted a wariness of new varieties and an inclination to look back to older types, even to wild species.

Wild types other than those derived from *Lathyrus odoratus* have increasingly been taken up. Forms of *L. tingitanus* with unexpectedly large flowers in shades of red and pink, plus bicolours, are ideal growing through stout cistus or brooms in Mediterranean-style plantings. *L. chloranthus*, with picric yellow flowers on vigorous plants makes you gasp as it sprawls through one of the blue-leaved euphorbias like 'Blue Hills'.

Growing sweet peas is, as the saying goes, like sex and playing the guitar: easy to do badly. Sweet peas will survive and flower from a sowing at almost any time and in most conditions; but to thrive they need sunshine, rich soil, plenty of water and regular attention to either picking the flowers or dead-heading. Sow them in pots in autumn and keep them ticking over through the winter before planting in spring, and you will have the most robust, longest-flowering plants.

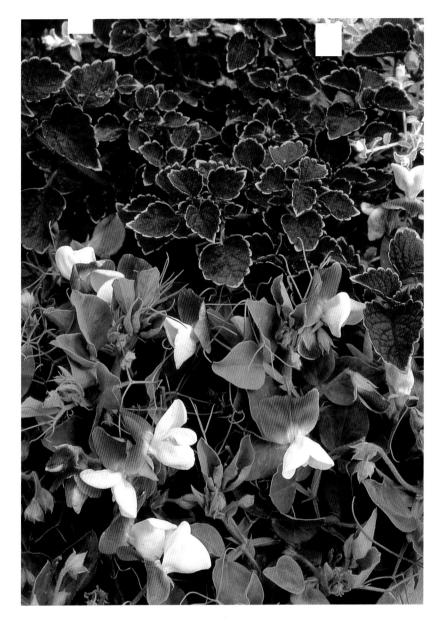

ABOVE *'Cupid' is a variety from the late nineteenth century, revived and reintroduced almost a hundred years later. It hugs the ground very closely and spreads to no more than 23cm/9in across, its pretty two-tone flowers appearing over a long period all summer. Here, it creeps over blue-stained edging boards from under an old cuttings-raised coleus, 'Rob Roy'. A few silvery wands of* Plecostachys serpyllifolia *peep into the top of the picture.*

# *Lavatera* **Lavatera**

The satiny sheen on the petals of a lavatera is unique amongst annuals: sheer and tempting, open to delicate caress, apparently fragile but reassuringly tough – like a flapper out on a date. Few annuals mix such allure with such easy availability!

That sheen combines with the constant profusion of flower, and a good price, to bring us one of the most valuable of all annuals – and one which has shown how a neglected species can be improved.

'Silver Cup', one of the early Fleuroselect Silver Medal winners, showed what could be achieved by careful selection in what had been a relatively undeveloped species. In addition to their sheen, the petals are broad and they overlap to create a more substantial flower. The markings on the petals are bolder and more distinct, and there are more flowers on each stem than in older types.

And 'Silver Cup' was the right plant at the right time. Mixed borders had become commonplace, yet the short and bushy annuals which were still the norm looked out of place in such plantings; the two styles of plants looked uncomfortable together. 'Silver Cup' had not only the quality but also the stature and the style to look well alongside, say, *Aster* x *frikartii* 'Mönch', in front of silvery elaeagnus or pyrus or behind the crowded glaucous stems of autumn

Lavatera *'White Cherub'*

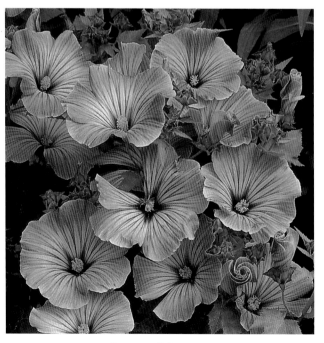

Lavatera *'Silver Cup'*

sedums. So it was an instant success; annuals which associate well with shrubs and hardy perennials are invaluable.

In succeeding years additional varieties appeared occasionally: 'Mont Blanc', white, with exceptionally dark foliage, and its pink counterpart 'Mont Rose'; 'Ruby Regis' in carmine pink; then more recently the Beauty Series in two veined pinks, white and a carmine; then the even more prolific 'White Cherub', shorter and a little more crowded in the flower head but retaining its ability to integrate.

Another feature of lavateras which has enabled them to fit well into changing styles of gardening is their adaptability. They can be raised as hardy annuals, sown directly and thinned to about 30cm/12in; they can also be raised indoors and pricked out into pots or even trays; and they have the ability to recover from a period of less than ideal growing conditions and still give a good display.

Recently, however, a problem has arisen. Lavatera leaf-spot disease first attacks plants at ground level and then attacks the foliage, causing plants to collapse unexpectedly and dramatically, which ruins the display. Most commercial seed is treated against the disease if it's found when tested by the seed company; plants grown from home-saved seed are more vulnerable.

RIGHT *Colour-themed mixtures can include a wide, if unpredictable, range of varieties in a narrow colour range and here, among the pinks, the salmon and rose shades are flowering together. Lavatera 'Pink Beauty' dominates; the colour is simply so powerful. The rosy bracts of a pink Salvia viridis pick up the same shade while Clarkia 'Appleblossom' fills in delicately behind the bold pods of the opium poppy Papaver somniferum.*

# *Linaria* **Toadflax**

An old favourite and a series of impressive newcomers are bringing linarias to new prominence in the annual border, rescuing them from their former obscurity.

*Linaria purpurea* has often been treated almost as a weed. Its particular purple colouring is not a sympathetic one and it self-seeds all too determinedly. The rose-pink 'Canon Went' redeems its reputation in bucketfuls and the slightly shorter 'Springside White' is also proving valuable. Both flower well in their first year from seed and their slender spikes add a bold upright accent to mixed borders and spacious annual plantings.

But then, from Japan, comes the Fantasia or Fantasy Series. First, like mimulus, they can flower in as little as six weeks from sowing. They then develop dense clouds of tiny flowers which, although carried on short plants, nevertheless retain a charm lacking in so many dwarf varieties. They meld well with the shorter annual phlox, impatiens and *Helichrysum petiolare* 'Roundabout' and 'Goring Silver'.

Eventually, the flowers fade. The kitchen scissors then have a job to do, snipping the whole plant back by half. A precautionary soak with liquid feed, perhaps another soak from the watering can if the weather is dry, and they soon burst into flower again. Unfortunately seed of Fantasia is very expensive so it's best to raise it in pots where there will be fewer losses. But it's worth the extra cost.

Seed of traditional annual linarias, such as the 'Fairy Lights' mixture, is cheap and comes in vast quantities, and you can sow it outside where it's to flower. These older linarias come only in mixtures, but in gaps or cracks in paving they can be delightful; and the colour range can be manipulated by purposeful dead-heading. New, in a similar style, comes 'Gemstones'. Its greyish foliage and slightly floppy growth carry a succession of long-spurred flowers in red and orange shades. Ideal in a small container in a sunny place, it will flower again in its second year as long as its roots are not left too sodden in winter.

LEFT *At Nori and Sandra Pope's unique garden at Hadspen House the familiar* Linaria purpurea *'Canon Went' is an invaluable feature of the long border. Although a true perennial, this flowers prolifically in its first summer and here blends with the rich foliage of* Atriplex hortensis *var.* rubra *and the vibrant* Dianthus carthusianorum *in the foreground. The linaria is, though, a rampant self-seeder; even dedicated dead-heading will usually leave a few seeds to produce seedlings for the following year.*

# Lobelia *Lobelia*

For most gardeners there's only one species of annual lobelia, *Lobelia erinus*. Within this species there may be two types for different uses, the bushy for bedding and the trailing for baskets, but both are in decline. Yet it would be a blinkered gardener who accepted this sad fact and simply let lobelia stagnate; there's scope for some creative planting here. Fortunately, I've found a new way of growing them for bedding and there's a relatively unrecognized group of cultivars deserving our wider attention.

Traditionally, bushy lobelia has been grown as an edging plant around formal bedding schemes, while trailing lobelia has been grown in hanging baskets, windowboxes and other containers. The dividing line has always been a strict one but I've always found 'Crystal Palace Compacta', 'Mrs Clibran' and the other bushy bedding types rather contrary: they're too dumpy and squat yet they often collapse in heavy rain. So I tried planting trailing varieties like 'Blue Cascade' on the flat, and the result was a much lighter, more airy look. The lobelia intermingled attractively with neighbouring plants and created an easy blend with the natural informality of perennials and relaxed annuals.

The older Cascade and Basket series are genuinely lax in habit, but the more recent Regatta Series is far superior. The plants branch more determinedly from the base, growth is a little more dense, there are far fewer wispy trails and the whole plant seems to remain a little less unfocused. The result is a series of eight colours which are ideal for informal summer schemes and which also bring an increased richness and denseness of colour to baskets and containers.

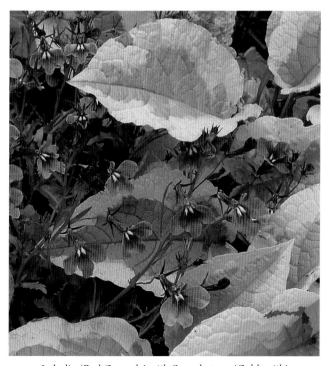

Lobelia *'Red Cascade'* with Symphytum *'Goldsmith'*

What's more, a glittering new colour appeared as part of the Regatta Series – a blue and white bicolour. This is simply spectacular: it is sparkling, light and far more effective than other new shades such as the watery lilacs. *Lobelia* 'Regatta Blue Splash', planted on the flat, with blue, white and other blue and white bicoloured flowers will bring you up with a start. Try a blend of 'Regatta Blue Splash', *Salvia farinacea* 'Strata', *Phlox* 'Bobby Sox', *Lathyrus sativus* and *Ageratum* 'Bavaria', with *Ipomoea* 'Mini Sky-blue' twisting through them all and the occasional cool pool of silver foliage.

Lobelia mixtures are a disaster. Now that there are up to eight different colours in a mix, colour compatibility has become an issue. Blending together dark and light blues, white plus various carmine and washed-out lilac shades creates a peculiarly offensive result. Seed companies should formulate the colours into two mixtures: a combination of all the blue shades plus white, and a mix of the carmine, rosy and lilac shades plus white. Both would be valuable in different situations and indeed would make attractive baskets without other companions.

The Regatta Series of bushy trailers and the 'splash' type in both the Regatta and the ball-shaped Riviera Series have been significant recent improvments in lobelias; the other has been the development of $F_1$ hybrid perennial lobelias which are making an increasing impact as summer annuals.

The great breakthrough was the $F_1$ hybrid Compliment Series, now in three separate colours (the mix has additional shades). This was

LEFT *Seed-raised perennial lobelias, like this* Lobelia *'Queen Victoria', develop quickly enough to make a first-season impression. Here, in front of the rich yet sparkling blue flowers of* Salvia guaranitica *'Blue Enigma', the lobelia brings the eye forward from the fading sanguisorba in the background and its beetroot foliage sets off the blue salvia flowers well.*

RIGHT *White baskets are cool in every respect. Here,* Lobelia *'White Cascade' mingles in a simple planting with* Impatiens *'Accent White' to make a basket which is both soft and neat in its appearance. This corner site is ideal: both plants do well – in fact, they probably grow best – in a little shade. White lobelia never comes 100% white, hence the few blue flowers from a single rogue plant.*

bred primarily as a cut flower, with 90cm/3ft unbranched stems produced in good numbers – four is common in the first summer. The shorter Fan Series followed, in five colours; the plants branch from the base to produce an astonishing number of spikes just five months from sowing.

The pick of these are 'Compliment Scarlet' and 'Fan Scarlet' – the latter with strongly red-tinted foliage. As yet there's no white in either series and none with the beetroot-coloured foliage seen in vegetatively propagated cultivars. These plants are superb as first-year flowerers for the new perennial border, and for summer annual planting schemes where an impact is required from a tall, upright plant which retains a little elegance. Try 'Fan Scarlet' with *Nicotiana langsdorffii* alongside and a billowing of *Consolida* 'Snow Cloud' around them both, plus *Convolvulus* 'Red Ensign' in front with coleus 'Red Velvet' and *Nemesia* 'Innocence'.

There's yet another reason for growing these seed-raised perennial lobelias. Not only do they flower prolifically as annuals, but many vegetatively propagated perennial lobelias are badly infected with virus, so the seed-raised types, which do not carry virus infection, are becoming indispensable.

Raising lobelia from seed can be a tricky business for many gardeners. At 25,000 per gram the seeds really are minute; so they're difficult to sow, the seedlings are tiny, they have a tendency to damp off and they're very tricky to handle singly when it comes to pricking out. The standard recommendation is to prick out in patches of seedlings – which are easier to handle. With mixtures this ensures you achieve a well-integrated blend of colours, and you will always find plenty of seeds in the packet – as many as 2500.

But this is bad practice in two groups. White-flowered bedding lobelias always carry a small percentage of blue-flowered plants, which can ruin a carefully planned display. If you prick out seedlings singly you can eliminate any blues before planting. And packets of the Compliment and Fan series may contain as few as fifty seeds which, allowing for the inevitable loss of many tiny seedlings, can leave you with all too few. The answer is to sow all lobelias very thinly, at a minimum of 20°C/70°F, keep the seed moist, cover very lightly and allow the seedlings to remain in the seed pot a little longer than usual; then they will be large enough to handle individually.

# *Lobularia* **Alyssum**

People can be so unfair. Just because alyssum seed is usually cheap, and because it's so easy to grow, and because it self-seeds, and because for years it was a case of 'any colour as long as it's white' . . . well, alyssum was not exactly despised but simply sidelined; it was not considered a serious plant.

This attitude also seemed to infiltrate the seed companies. Although maintaining high-quality standards for other seeds, somehow it seemed less critical with alyssum. So, for example, 'Carpet of Snow' produced a carpet that looked as if every cat in the street was asleep underneath.

In recent years, plant breeders have worked hard to change the situation. Plant habit is more predictable and, in particular, there are now many exciting new colours. The seed companies have responded not only by promoting alyssum but also by ensuring that the seed in their packets gives good-quality plants.

Until the 1920s alyssum was white. Now there are also cream, various pinks, shades of mauve, apricot, red, deep purple, lemon and some very pretty bicolours where the flowers in the centre of the spike open in one shade and then age to another.

Alyssum is an unusual case in which the mixtures, especially those like 'Aphrodite' and 'Easter Bonnet' with the widest possible range of colours, can be very effective. But not if grown in traditional ways. Sowing the seed direct and thinning to 10–15cm/4–6in gives results that are too unpredictable. Sowing indoors, pricking out, then planting out individually at 15cm/6in creates a jarring series of colour blocks.

The way to create a really pretty tapestry of intermingling shades is to sow indoors in cool conditions but to sow in cellpacks (see page 176). Sow four or five seeds from the mixture in each cell and leave them unthinned. Plant them out without breaking up the

individual cells of compost. The individual plants, in their separate colours, will knit together and spread out, and as they come into flower all the colours will meld and be more evenly distributed over the whole planting.

Amongst all the new colours, the best are the purples like 'Violet Queen', which is both surprising and effective sneaking out across paving from under blue-leaved hostas, and 'Creamery', which looks perfect under and in front of 'Coral Reef' annual phlox in similar tones. This, and newer richer tones, also looks just right creeping out from under golden hostas. Of the pinks, 'Golf Rose' is good in containers with geraniums. I've found the apricot shades rather weak and the red such a strange, almost dirty, shade that it seems to fit well with nothing else except other alyssum.

All alyssum, I should say, has some degree of scent but 'Sweet White' is the best, giving a lovely sweet honey fragrance even in partial shade.

Having tried to show that alyssum should be taken a great deal more seriously than its reputation suggests, I must confess that it can be disappointing. In hot dry conditions it suffers from powdery mildew and flea beetle, and its flowering period can be cut short. Rich soil and plenty of water ensures a longer display but also a slightly more open habit. In cool, moist conditions with no shortage of nutrients in the soil alyssum will often come back quickly after trimming, but in poor, hot, dry conditions you will be left with toasted twigs.

Allowing the plants to self-sow, while initially seeming an attractive and easy option, is sometimes a mistake. Over the years the clear colours of the more unusual shades are soon watered down and the habit of the plants becomes more and more straggly.

RIGHT  *In a little shade, white alyssum is less likely to suffer from the powdery mildew which can be so troublesome in full sun and dry air. Here, under old espalier pears, these self-sown plants derive from a mixture sown long ago and have mostly reverted to white. The occasional mauve-flowered plant, the blue lithodora and the ranunculus add highlights and rhythm.*

LEFT  *An old favourite and a relative newcomer. 'Carpet of Snow' is a long-established alyssum, although it makes less of a flat carpet than some more modern varieties. Nemophila 'Pennie Black', correctly N. menziesii subsp. discoidalis, is an intriguing little annual closely related to the more familiar baby blue eyes (N. menziesii). It dislikes dry conditions and is rather fragile so can be damaged in exposed, windy gardens, but its deep purple-black flowers edged in white are perfectly partnered here, as they intermingle with the white alyssum.*

# *Lunaria* Honesty

Honesty is one of those plants that is always appreciated but rarely used to its full potential. True, it is valued as a dried flower – for its silvery seed heads – and for the wild garden, especially in its delightful but underused white form. But as a spring bedding plant, honesty tends to be ignored. Perhaps because gardeners are locked into the preconception that spring bedders should be a great deal shorter than honesty's 75cm/2½ft.

In shady wilder gardens, many seedlings can simply be left to develop where they sow themselves. But in woodland borders which feature more delicate plants, it's important to be selective about which honesty seedlings are left in place. Plants like delicate woodland ferns, anemonellas and hepaticas may be overwhelmed by the surly growth of honesty's rough rosettes.

For bedding, raise honesty in pots in the same way as foxgloves (see page 79), but plant out from smaller pots; their root systems are relatively sparse and there's even more possibility that soil will fall off the roots than with foxgloves. Space the pots well to encourage the plants to develop a full crown. These will throw more flowers than plants which have been crowded in their youth.

The purple honesty looks excellent with 'White Triumphator', or yellow 'West Point' tulips, or splits of the rich pink perennial *Silene dioica* 'Minikin' – this makes a powerful combination; the white finds a perfect partner in the sultry 'Queen of Night' tulip.

But there are two varieties that will deceive you: variegated forms, spectacularly anaemic and gross, which, when their seedlings first appear, are as green as their unvariegated relations. But they break out in blotches – irregular creamy splatts; andperhaps I should just mention pigeons . . . 'Variegata' and 'Alba Variegata' are the names to avoid.

Honesty does have a problem or, more accurately, a plague: turnip mosaic virus. The usual symptom is white streaks in the purple honesty flowers. It also attacks wallflowers; brassica crops like turnips, cabbages and sprouts can also be badly affected. A few misguided gardeners admire the streaky effect but do not be tempted; burn the plants at the first sign. Burn any infected wallflowers as well.

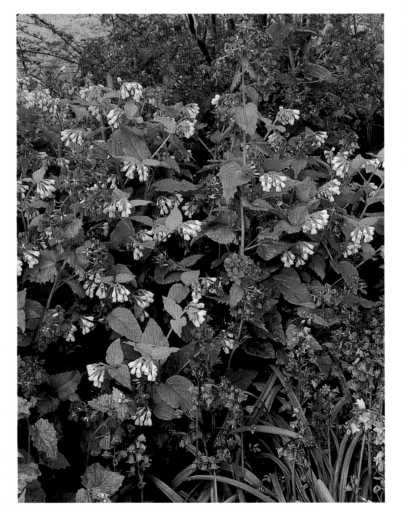

LEFT *Testimony that self-sown seedlings can place themselves perfectly amongst perennial plants. The pure-white comfrey,* Symphytum orientale, *is fronted by Spanish bluebells,* Hyacinthoides hispanica, *while behind, in front and weaving through, are the purple flowers of honesty,* Lunaria annua. *Of course the gardener can take a hand in the look of this planting by removing self-sown seedlings from inappropriate positions and moving them to more advantageous ones.*

# Matthiola *Stocks*

Desirable though they may be as cut flowers, stocks remain deeply unfashionable as garden plants. Nevertheless, there are glints of light in the world of stocks which should set the sensibilities of gardeners stirring. But first, let's just forget about all those stocks with bewildering names: Trysomic, East Lothian, Selectable Column. They're either fiddly to grow, difficult to overwinter or discreditably fleeting in flower. There are, however, others which deserve attention.

One is not actually a *Matthiola* but a *Malcomia*, *M. maritima* to be precise. Available only as mixture, the esteem in which it is generally held is indicated by the usual cultivar name, 'Mixed'. This is a plant whose status has long been low but sow it in cracks in paving or in gravel, choose the shade you like best from the mix which appears and each year pull out all the rest until you have an effective uniform stand in just one colour.

The wild Mediterranean species, though, are in a class of their own. The splendid *Matthiola tricuspidata* makes a rounded shrub of greyish leaves with spikes of heavily fragrant, rich pink flowers; it's excellent in dry plantings where it self-sows and with *Lathyrus chloranthus* scrambling around, it makes an arresting combination – but seed is hard to find.

The night-scented stock, *Matthiola bicornis*, is usually consigned to empty spaces behind taller plants because although the penetrating scent is intoxicating, the flowers (which have always been rather dowdy) only open at night. Even so, it's indispensable, but now there's 'Starlight Sensation' with bolder, brighter colours; it was a top-seller in its first season.

Finally, while most breeders have concentrated on short double-flowered stocks, from Holland come stocks intended to have single flowers. Ridiculed by professional growers, their colours and the scents may yet cause a revival of interest.

Some catalogues have tried to persuade us that their dumpy double stocks like 'Cinderella' are good for bedding outside. Sadly, this isn't the case, but in containers, 'Cinderella' can be charming.

Rarely is it suggested that cut-flower stocks such as 'Goldcut', 'Anthony', 'Cleopatra' or 'Sentinel' (which occasionally turn up in catalogues) are used in borders, but in my small experiment with 'Sentinel', I found that they were very effective.

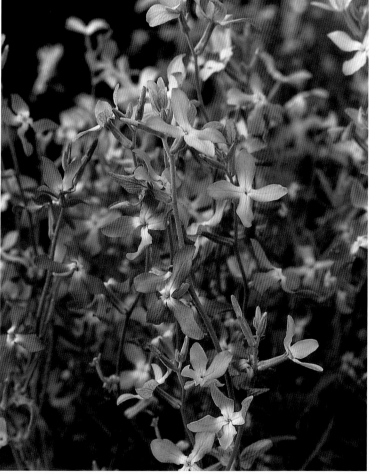

Matthiola bicornis

OVERLEAF *This new peachy single-flowered annual stock, 'Apricot', here mingles with the slightly rosier spikes of* Linaria purpurea *'Canon Went' and the dark-eyed* Potentilla x hopwoodiana *in the pink section of that magical border at Hadspen House in Somerset. Even paler, the rarely seen* Collomia grandiflora *sneaks into the picture along with lime-green nicotiana.*

# *Mimulus* **Monkey flower**

And to think that some people have never even grown them . . . they don't know what they're missing! But the virtues of the mimulus are not the usual ones of elegance and a long season. The plants themselves are not especially refined and their season can be short, especially if they are grown in unsuitable conditions. No, mimulus have other qualities.

Firstly, modern dwarf mimulus can flower in as little as six weeks from sowing. This makes them invaluable plants with which to remedy any mistakes, perfect when you see a gap looming in the border or empty space in a forgotten container, – or for a flying start in an early spring, as they are unusually hardy too.

All this is fine . . . but if the flowers themselves were un-interesting such virtue would be worthless. Yet the flowers are delightful.

The most widely available Magic Series boasts twelve different plain-faced colours, a few slightly spotted, the colours blending with each other harmoniously. The colours have great subtlety (though you could argue that is like saying some colours are a little too similar!). Unfortunately, the absence of the separate colours from most lists means that plants from 'Magic Mixed' or 'Magic Pastel Mixed' must be pricked out individually into 7cm/3in pots, and then you should select the individual colours

Mimulus '*Viva*'

as they come into flower.

The slightly taller, slightly larger-flowered 'Calypso' comes only as a mixture, but the flowers are powerfully dusted with spots in contrasting colours; 'Viva' comes in just the one shocking colour . . . bright yellow with the boldest of mahogany blotches. Wow!

And there's more: mimulus enjoy damp and shady condit-ions, which most annuals do not. In containers on shady patios in town gardens, they're invaluable. True, the converse of this is that in hot and dry seasons they shrivel and die, but who cares? We have plenty of other annuals for such situations. Mimulus make splendid companions for other damp-loving plants such as smaller hostas in yellow or with cream or yellow variegations. Choose from the seven colours in the off-white to deep yellow range, some of which have contrasting throats or speckles.

And there's another virtue to these British-bred but American native annuals: they make wonderful plant-ings on their own, either as a mixture or in single colours. Now I can't quite pin down why this is, but it's true.

Mimulus '*Magic Peach*'

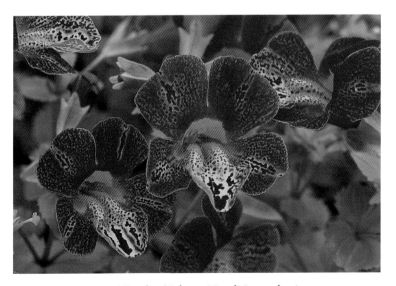
Mimulus '*Calypso Mixed*' *(one colour)*

# *Myosotis* Forget-me-not

Forget-me-nots – there's no getting away from it – are blue. While pink and white forms are available, it's the blues which retain that clear-eyed glint, that sharp sparkle, which so enlivens the spring garden but which is never gross or overdominant. The pinks, sad to say, are usually a little murky in colour and the whites, especially the dwarf forms, age disgracefully.

There are two other factors to take into account: size and habit. The name 'Blue Ball' says it all; its short, congested, rounded form lacks elegance, so I recommend you go for taller cultivars. While for tiny spaces a modest habit may be useful, the general demeanour of myosotis is so restrained that they're never overpowering.

The name 'Royal Blue' tells you its colour, a little over-optimistically, but not that it can reach 40cm/16in in good soil. This is an ideal size both for associating with tulips (most of whose long stems are hidden) and for intermingling in more permanent woodland plantings.

In large containers, interplanting with yellow 'West Point' lily-flowered tulips creates an uplifting combination but, please, not by the bedful as is sometimes still seen in parks. In a large spring planting, break up the border by associating myosotis with wallflowers, polyanthus and other spring biennials, and use tulips to overlap the individual groups. 'West Point'

tulips could straddle the boundary between 'Royal Blue' forget-me-nots and 'Primrose Monarch' wallflowers; another lily-flowered tulip like 'White Triumphator' could be set alongside 'West Point' in the myosotis and run into 'Blood Red' wallflowers.

The oddly named 'Blue Basket' and also 'Blue Spire' are shorter at about 30cm/12in and a little less rich in colour. 'Victoria Blue' is a little more dwarf still at about 25cm/10in, as is the unusually large-flowered 'Music'; all need tulips just a little taller so that the tulip flowers are held above the blue foam.

There are, however, situations where the shorter varieties are welcome, which is a relief as the taller cultivars are more difficult to find in catalogues. In semi-shaded woodland plantings, where myosotis are slipped in amongst hardy geraniums, tiarellas and woodland phlox, they will stretch out more than they do out in the open sun and lose their congested habit. Even so, 'Blue Ball' will never develop the more relaxed airiness of 'Royal Blue'.

You may be tempted by the other colours: of the pinks,

LEFT *The nodding white flowers of* Symphytum orientale *are here accompanied by the intense blue of 'Royal Blue' forget-me-nots, self-sown amongst comfrey from the previous year. Allowing forget-me-nots to self-sow often turns up happy associations like this, but over successive generations the flowers may decrease in size and mildew become more prevalent.*

121

'Rosylva' at 20cm/8in, with flowers in a clearer rose-pink than most, is certainly the pick; the myosotis listed simply as 'White' is, at 30cm/12in, taller than other white forms.

It has been traditional to sow myosotis outside in short rows, then thin and transplant them to their final homes. But seed of some of the newer cultivars like 'Rosylva' is relatively expensive, so you may not find much in the packet. Sow it in pots outside or in a cool, well-ventilated greenhouse in summer and prick out into 7cm/3in pots or into trays.

Powdery mildew is the one disfigurement which will be obvious and it can severely limit growth and reduce flowering. It can be especially troublesome in hot, dry springs and as summer approaches, when conditions are naturally encouraging. The taller, more open cultivars are less susceptible owing to the better airflow through their more widely spaced shoots. But in some seasons 'Blue Ball' becomes 'Grey Ball'.

LEFT *Myosotis 'Blue Basket' creates a sky-blue foam through which 'White Triumphator' tulips emerge. Behind, the white is repeated in the flowers of* Lunaria annua *'Alba Variegata' in an informal spring bedding.*

BELOW *The loose airy sprays of Myosotis 'Royal Blue' intermingle prettily with* Geranium asphodeloides *and gently tone down the intensity of the geranium flowers. Both thrive in the same dappled shade.*

Nemesias are on a roll; plants go though cycles of fashions and nemesias are definitely on the up. And don't they deserve it, for they rival pansies in their range of colours and colour combinations and in both the glints and softness of their bright and pastel colourings.

The first hint of a revival was the reappearance of some Victorian varieties. True, their history was masked by the seed companies christening them with new names, but revivals they certainly were.

This was the case with the dainty red and white bicoloured cultivar first known as 'National Ensign', then, after gaining an Award of Merit in the 1950s, 'Aurora'. It reappeared as 'Mello', then 'Mello Red & White' and also 'Danish Flag'. Its blue and white counterpart, now universally known as 'KLM', was originally 'Twilight'. At least the white-eyed 'Blue Gem' kept its name.

At the same time, some of the old larger-flowered forms in single colours like the self-explanatory 'Fire King' and 'Orange Prince' reappeared along with the 'Tapestry' pastel mixture from which individual shades are now being selected. Indeed, one look at a planting of the 'Tapestry', 'Carnival' or 'Triumph' mixtures shows how many gorgeous colours and bicolours there are to be pulled out and developed as separate shades. For nemesias cover as wide a spectrum as any annuals, and with bicolours too there's enormous potential for the development of invaluable shades and combinations.

The problem with nemesias has always been that they're unable to thrive in hot dry conditions and tend to have a relatively short flowering season. But this makes them especially useful in cooler, damper areas where they not only come into flower quickly but last well. They're also valuable as early starters, planned with the intention that latecomers will spread out into their spaces as they fade away.

'Sundrops', in a mix of five groups of shades which between them will yield plants in at least twenty different colours, attempts to resolve these problems. Over twenty years in development, this is a very short-growing mixture which when it first flowers does so with an unusual, not-very-nemesia-like flat-topped habit. It then stretches a little, especially in rich conditions. My delight at its long season is tempered by disappointment in its initially inelegant habit.

'KLM', however, is a lovely partner for *Nemophila menziesii*, especially as both enjoy the same cool conditions, and their growth habits complement each other so well. 'National Ensign' is more difficult to place, but with 'Horizon Picotee' geraniums and *Salvia* 'Salsa Scarlet Bicolour' it creates a bold and sparkling show. Blend it with 'KLM' amongst *Salvia farinacea* 'Strata' and *Phlox* 'Buttons White with Red Eye' to give a new meaning to red, white and blue. In a softer, more intriguing style try it with *Viola* 'Bowles' Black' or 'Blackjack'.

Seed of nemesias is a little particular in its requirements. Temperatures above 15°C/ 60°F will impair germination, so if you sow it in summer as a quick filler, a cool place outside is preferable to the warm greenhouse. Fluctuating temperatures can also reduce germination, so in spring it is best to use a thermostatically controlled propagator in order to keep the temperature constant.

Nemesia *'Blue Gem'*

Nemesia *'Orange Prince'*

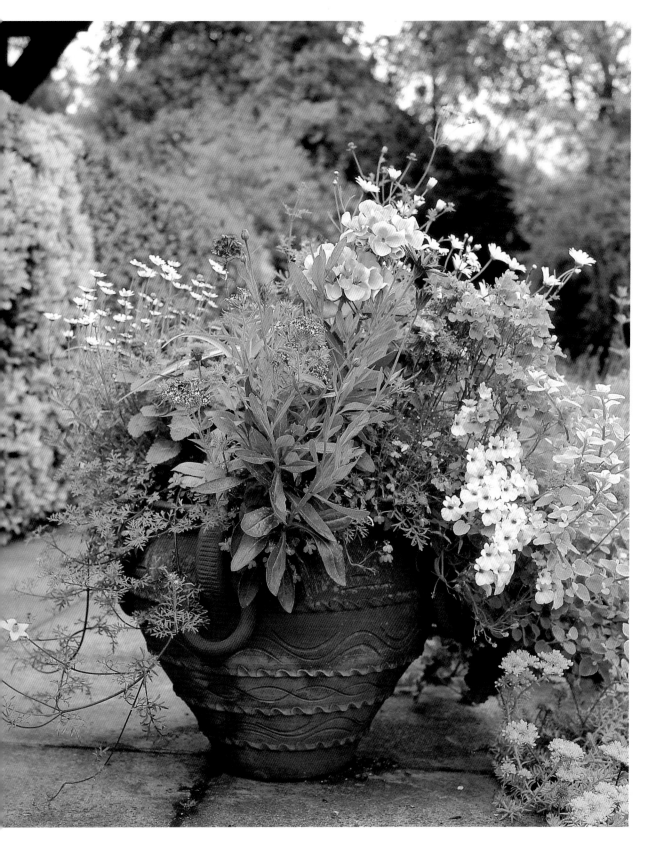

LEFT *At first sight this container looks as if colour planning has never even crossed the gardener's mind. Not so. Some of the plants in this container are there for the long haul, for the all-season display for which so many container plants are valued. Others, in particular the nemesias, are short-term expedients. The conscious thought has been both to create a connection with the colour of the yellow evergreen hedge behind and to maintain an inner harmony. The orange nemesia makes the hedge connection boldly from the day it's planted. In the longer term, the bidens will do the job. That orange is a little strident with the rose-pink geranium and phlox, but the white nemesia holds everything together, connecting with the white* Chrysanthemum paludosum *on the other side of the tub.*

# *Nicotiana* Ornamental Tobacco

Gardeners who grow tobacco plants fall into two groups. A sad few are determined to ruin their health with the least possible expense in taxation and for them the seed of smoking tobacco is still available. The rest of us, intent on enjoying our gardens into old age, grow only the ornamental nicotianas and these represent a rare example in which the plant breeder's enthusiasm for reducing the height of their new varieties has actually led to a more versatile plant.

For many years the tall and swaying 'Sensation' and 'Evening Fragrance' types were the standard nicotianas. Reaching 90cm/3ft or more in height, they tend to close their flowers by day, the petals relaxing to limpness, coming alive to release their exotic scent only in the evening. They can be spectacular: given space they develop an attractive rounded, rather airy habit, and their colours show a strange luminosity in evening light. Sadly, they're available only in the unpredictable mixtures rarely required in the borders of colour-conscious gardeners.

It is true that the blend of shades is less offensive in these types than in many mixtures – the soft reds and purples, the pinks, mauves and whites harmonize rather than clash in a mass planting. But for planned associations sow early and move the individual seedlings steadily on into 12cm/ 5in pots. Then, by planting time in late spring, the first flowers should be open and each plant can be given a place with the appropriate neighbours.

Nicotiana *'Sensation Mixed' (one colour)*

Nicotiana *'Domino Salmon Pink'*

Among the plants in these mixtures, look out in particular for the rather uncommon white-flowered type, where the backs of the petals are stained red. At the edges, where the petal tissue is at its least substantial, the red shows through to give a striking picotee effect.

Two valuable single colours, the pure white and the lime-green, have long had their fanciers. White comes in the form of *N. alata*, also known as *N. affinis,* an elegant plant with height, size of foliage and flowers, degree of branching and quantity of flowers open at any one time, all in scale. Although reaching 75–90cm/2½–3ft in height, it has foliage which is sufficiently discreet to allow it to be grown in large tubs. Its pure white flowers are bold enough to make a visual impact and it has a scent to add its own intoxication to a relaxing drink on a summer's evening. Placing a clump in the sunny angle of a hedge in a city garden ensures that the flowers are set off well and the scent held in the evening air.

Nicotianas have always been known for their unique green shade. This probably derives from decades of selection following a cross made between *N. alata* and the green-flowered *N. knightiana*, itself now available again. Here the modern $F_1$ hybrid types have let us down. 'Domino Lime' and 'Havana Lime' are a thin and watery shade, quite without passion. As they are the result of a further cross involving a white parent, the rich green is diluted. Most of the old open-pollinated types are stronger in

colour but even these vary, so search out, please, the shimmery, more truly lime green found in 'Lime Green' from Unwin's Seeds. Its depth of colour is outstanding.

The development of $F_1$ hybrid nicotianas has enabled their height to be reduced and the best (such as the 30–40cm/12–15in Domino Series) have sacrificed little of their natural elegance. But with low plants we tend to look on the flowers from above, rather than view them from the side. The breeders have dealt with this by creating individual flowers whose flat faces are angled upwards so that we see the most colour as we look down. Very neat. The flowers also stay open all day but the scent, sad to say, is much lessened.

In the Merlin, Havana and Starship series the height has been further reduced – and here the elegance is lost. The resulting plants are too squat for almost anything save display as individual plants in containers. There is, however, temptation in some of the colours: I especially like the warm pink 'Merlin Peach'.

There are three purple and white bicolours in the Domino Series: 'Domino Picotee' has the largest white centre; 'Domino Purple' has a small white centre; while 'Domino Purple Bicolour' falls in between. The flowers can provide a link to white plants, the stiff spikes of *Salvia farinacea* 'Cirrus' or the small silver foliage of *Helichrysum petiolare* 'Goring Silver', for example, and are useful where a change in scale is needed after the larger nicotiana foliage and flat-faced flowers. 'Havana Appleblossom', a

unique white with pink backs to the petals, also has a certain charm, despite being sadly dumpy with floppy, untidy flowers.

The soft yet vivid colouring of 'Domino Salmon Pink' looks charming among the small silver leaves of *Plecostachys serpyllifolia*. For a bolder look, it gleams in front of purple *Cotinus coggygria* 'Notcutt's Variety' or behind the new American dark-leaved heucheras such as 'Stormy Seas', yet is never garish.

But two unaltered wild species remain the most useful and effective of the whole group, especially in mixed borders. The dainty, waisted green bells of *N. langsdorffii* on their slender wiry stems are spectacular in a fluttery, airy mass. In milder areas this nicotiana often behaves as a good perennial and makes a dense stand of shoots in its second year. This too is wonderful in front of the sultry purple cotinus, although those with a more harmonious turn of mind might find a combination with the smoky pink flowers of *Cotinus coggygria* Purpureus Group more tasteful.

Altogether more majestic is *N. sylvestris*. This is occasionally diminished by a strangely appealing cultivar name, 'Only the

LEFT *Tall and swaying* Nicotiana sylvestris, *discreetly supported, shines out against the shrubby background in this mixed border. In the front, pink verbenas, 'Black Prince' antirrhinums,* Salvia verticillata *'Purple Rain' with its flowers resembling mauve millet and* Heuchera *'Palace Purple' pick up the colour of the purple-leaved cotinus in the background.*

RIGHT *White flowers set against fresh and healthy green foliage always make an impact, without the garishness of bolder contrasts. This planting is themed around the 'Iceberg' Floribunda rose, matching it with* Nicotiana alata, *which grows through, falling forward into the soft and spreading fragrant foliage of* Pelargonium *'Chocolate Peppermint'. In the following summer, an entirely different grouping in the same colours could complement the rose.*

Nicotiana langsdorffii

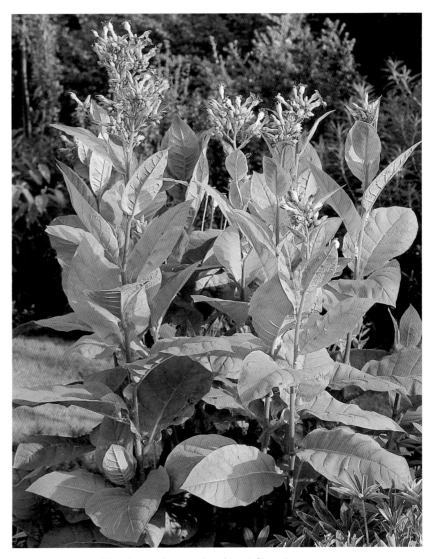

Nicotiana tabacum *(smoking tobacco)*

Lonely'. The soft, rather sticky, pale-green foliage is impressive from early on but its vital supporting midrib can be damaged in strong winds and then the leaf flops. Give it shelter. (Aphids also have a habit of nestling among the sticky glands, gaining a little protection from sprays. A systemic insecticide applied to the upper surface of the leaves will kill them.) Sown late, or kept pot-bound before planting, each plant will produce a single stem, topped by its compact head, with the exceptionally long-tubed flowers with wavy-edged white faces hanging down.

This is a handsome plant, again a perennial in mild areas, and a fine back-of-the-border spectacle best seen against a simple and unfussy background such as a hedge or a dark wall (which will also provide the necessary shelter), or soaring up into a clear blue sky. It's a splendid participant in a subtropical summer scheme; placed alongside a large purple ricinus, the white flowers mingle magnificently with the bold shiny foliage of the castor-oil plant. Show off the early leaves by planting late-comers in front: plants that will not interrupt the view of the leaves in early summer but will hide their imperfections later on in the season. Cannas, perhaps. And, although the leaves do not strike out away from the plant, allow sufficient space for them to develop without smothering their neighbours.

# Nigella *Love-in-a-mist*

The Mediterranean region has been the source of some of our most delightful, easy-to-grow and adaptable annuals – including the invaluable nigellas. That they originate in this area, and a knowledge of their adaptations to the climate, should enlighten us to ways of growing these plants which might not otherwise come to mind. We should also recognize that their companions in the wild, with which nigellas look so captivating, can also be their companions in the garden.

Sadly, when most gardeners plan a dry garden or a Mediterranean garden, annuals are forgotten. Shrubs and bulbs predominate and if annuals self-sow from other parts of the garden they may even be removed. But annuals are such a striking feature of many Mediterranean habitats that we should foster a role for them in gardens, where we should grow them in the same way they grow naturally.

In the wild, nigellas germinate in late summer and autumn, build up a strong root system in autumn and winter, and flower prolifically in spring. As summer draws near, their extensive root system is better able to sustain the plant in the increasingly high temperatures and reduced rainfall. In gardens, this approach will also encourage an extended flowering season in dry summers.

Most nigellas are no more or less fussy than other Mediterranean annuals, although some of the less familiar species come from the Aegean islands where the winters are especially mild. But sowing in the autumn and allowing a substantial and very attractive rosette to develop ensures that plants start flowering early, yet have the power to continue for as long as those sown in the spring and which begin flowering later.

Nigella *'Miss Jekyll'*

Nigellas have three features of interest. Their finely dissected foliage creates a pleasing contrast with broader-leaved or more substantial neighbours like euphorbias, acanthus or irises. The flowers are usually blue in the wild, and clear blue is always a valuable colour, although other colours such as white and mulberry have been developed in cultivation; then, when the flowers are over, the fat, inflated seed pods with their surrounding spidery bracts continue their appeal.

*Nigella damascena* is the species from which most cultivars are derived, with 'Miss Jekyll' by far the most popular. 'One of the annuals

LEFT *The low tumbling growth of the 'Raubritter' rose with its delightful rounded flowers falls into* Nigella hispanica, *creating an attractive contrast with both the finely cut foliage and the five-petalled flowers. Overwintered seedlings of the nigella become well established during autumn, winter and early spring when the rose is without its leaves, then flower in conjunction with the rose.*

that I think is entirely spoilt by dwarfing is Love-in-a-Mist,' wrote the good lady in 1899. A hundred years later she would be horrified by the 20cm/8in 'Dwarf Moody Blue' ('compact and miniature hedge-like' according to one catalogue) – as am I. She found her eponymous nigella in an old Kentish garden and picked it out especially for its 'double flower of just the right degree, and of an unusually fine colour'. She begged some seed and grew no other until a darker-blue type, known as 'Miss Jekyll, Dark Blue', appeared amongst the pale blues; this too is still found, along with the equally dark, but usefully taller, 'Oxford Blue', reaching 75cm/30in.

'Miss Jekyll Rose' and 'Miss Jekyll White' are still sometimes seen. Both are valuable. The rose is especially pretty amongst blue-leaved euphorbias such as *E. characias* 'Portuguese Velvet' and the white is lovely with pink cistus. The 'Persian Jewels' mixture is perhaps a little shorter at 38cm/15in and contains both dark and pastel shades. 'Mulberry Rose' has been picked out from the 'Persian Jewels' for listing separately and is disconcerting in opening almost white and steadily darkening to a warm and sumptuous shade.

In recent years, nigella seed heads have been increasingly prized for drying and *Nigella orientalis* has been introduced for its especially dark, fat seed pods, which follow its small yellow-green flowers; it often appears with the redundant cultivar name 'Transformer'. *Nigella hispanica* has also appeared and both of these are best allowed simply to self-sow in gravel amongst drought-loving shrubs and perennials. None are so overbearing that their neighbours will be smothered and their demure qualities ensure they fit in anywhere.

RIGHT *At Christopher Lloyd's garden at Great Dixter, Sussex, permanent and temporary plantings mingle together. The bold magenta spikes of* Gladiolus communis *subsp.* byzantinus, *taking over from the metallic footballs of* Allium cristophii, *are surrounded by* Nigella *'Oxford Blue' and the rich, dusty-purple foliage of the red orache,* Atriplex hortensis *'Red Plume'. The orache needs careful attention. It can self-sow too prolifically and smother smaller plants and as it does so its colour may vary; remove those plants which are badly placed or which show pale, watery-coloured foliage.*

# *Papaver* Poppy

The cornfield poppy has a strong pull on our emotions, connecting with romantic notions of an agrarian idyll. It's comforting to see the return of poppies to the landscape as fields are temporarily taken out of production or soil is disturbed by less sympathetic developments in the countryside. The ephemeral fragility of each poppy flower, petals falling as buds are opening, grips our attention and reminds us of our own transience. As emblems of those killed in the Great War, poppies are for remembrance each November, lest we should forget the battlefields bloodied by poppies soaking the landscape as trenches were dug and soil mounded. And wherever the British colonized, emigrants took poppies with them – as stowaways in their precious wheat – to become reminders of home.

Variants of the scarlet poppy, *Papaver rhoeas,* must have appeared regularly in the wild before the days of selective weed-killers; occasionally, they still do. But it was not until 1879, when the Reverend Wilks of Shirley in Surrey, noticed a wild form with a white flower edge, that the potential of these annual poppies as garden flowers was recognized.

From this one plant the vicar developed single- and double-flowered strains in softer colours, and twenty years later he had also eliminated the black blotch at the base of each petal. Then in the middle 1900s, the English painter Cedric Morris selected poppies, retaining those with misty and smoky tints, picoteed flowers and subtle whiskering; anything red was banished. These are variously known as 'Angel's Wings', 'Fairy Wings', 'Mother of Pearl' or 'Cedric Morris'.

More recently, 'Angel's Choir', the double-flowered form of 'Fairy Wings', has been developed; the fuller flowers lack the simplicity of their progenitors, but last a little longer.

The simplest way to raise these poppies is to scatter the seeds through mixed borders or along the edges of gravel drives; late summer is the best time. Plants then develop an extensive root system and a spreading rosette of foliage during the warm days of autumn and mild spells in winter. When the days begin to stretch in spring, at about the time for a spring sowing, the plants are already well established and ready to capitalize on longer days and increasing temperatures well ahead of spring-sown poppies. Much larger plants with far more flowers are the result, together with a noticeably longer flowering season. However, sowing in spring can also produce good results; prompt thinning and no check to growth enable plants to establish quickly and flower prolifically.

As plants develop from a spring or autumn scattering, you can easily remove those in unsuitable places. Any flowering in colours which are out of harmony with neighbouring plants can be pulled as their first flowers open. Unless dead-heading is faultless, you will have poppies for ever.

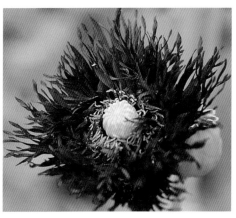
*Papaver somniferum* 'Peony Flowered Mixed'
(single colour)

*Papaver rhoeas* 'Shirley Single Mixed'
(single colour)

RIGHT *Just a few poppies can make a big difference. In one sense the annual chrysanthemums,* C. segetum, *dominate this natural blend of spring-sown, British native cornfield annuals. But the few fully open poppy flowers,* Papaver rhoeas, *and the spattering of soon-to-be open buds are enough to deflect our attention. Cornflowers,* Centaurea cyanus, *and corn chamomile,* Anthemis arvensis, *complete the picture.*

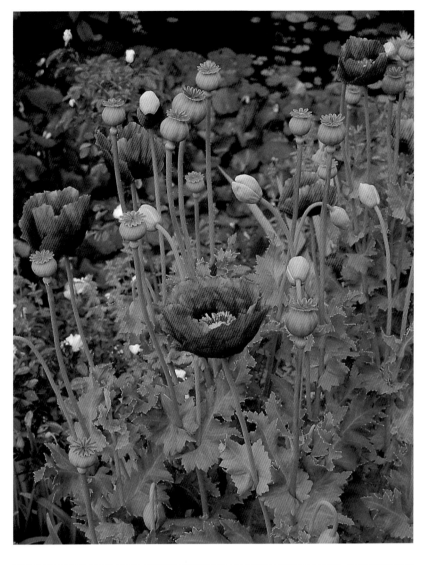

From Shakespeare to Keats and beyond, opium poppies have also gripped our emotions . . . one way or another. Some gardeners are wary of growing the opium poppy, *Papaver somniferum*, believing that the drug squad will drag them off to jail. Suffice it to say that growing them as ornamentals is not only legal but will add some valuable and fascinating flowers to your garden flora. Forms of this species have one special additional feature which other annual poppies lack: superb foliage. For this reason it's important to grow them well; in badly grown poppies the substance of the plant and the leaves suffer first.

In most areas, opium poppies are insufficiently hardy for an autumn sowing, but do develop strongly from a spring sowing. From an early stage their glaucous, blue-grey foliage is an attraction; set against the freshness of succulent delphinium shoots, it's a treat. Later it will also mask the cut-down delphinium spikes.

Garden varieties have diverged from the simple wild single mauve in both colour and flower form. There are some astonishing fluffy doubles, usually called peony-flowered, in mixtures, or better still, in single colours like 'Black Peony', a shimmering, rich maroon-purple. There are also frilly-feathered doubles, again in separate colours; the white, sometimes called 'Swansdown', is particularly gorgeous. Even more unexpected is a form with especially large seed pods, a form with especially *small* pods and even a hen-and-chickens form with tiny seed pods tightly clustered around a single larger pod.

Again, dead-heading is vital. Nip off the pods before they drop their seeds, or cut them on long stems to dry, and leave just a pod or two on plants whose flowers you especially like to shed their seed. If the colour is crucial, dead-head them all and resow bought seed the following spring.

ABOVE LEFT Papaver somniferum

LEFT *Poppies and climbing roses may seem an unlikely combination, but here, the simple but enticing flowers of a self-sown opium poppy are carried on tall-enough stems to reach in amongst the flowers of Rosa 'Compassion' as it scrambles around the window. A few snaking twirls of jasmine and clematis foliage feature in the background.*

# *Pelargonium* Geranium

You have to be so careful with geraniums. For the summer bedding outside Buckingham Palace they go to great lengths to match the colour of their geraniums with that of guardsmen's jackets. But those vast beds so full of geraniums and lined up in rows: no one else plants them like that any more. Fortunately, there are other ways.

I plant scarlet geraniums and so should you; the important question is: how? You may have a house in Tuscany where a straggly potful of red geraniums is just what you need to complete the rustic picture. But nowhere except outside Buck House should they be planted in such unrelenting red. And that old red-white-and-blue style, with the alyssum and the lobelia: that's out, be it salvias or geraniums which provide the scarlet.

Of course, there's nothing intrinsically wrong with red – far from it. And look at the wonderful range of seed-raised geraniums now available: you can have any shade of red you like; there are plenty, and any shade of pink too, and cerise and orange and purple and white with an increasing range of bicolours.

So within an admittedly limited spectrum there's a valuable range of shades from which to choose and also an increasing range of styles: the habit of growth and the type of flower head vary greatly. Some are close to traditional cuttings-raised geraniums with big, bold heads and this was the aim of plant breeders when

they developed 'Nittany Lion', the first F$_1$ hybrid geranium back in the 1960s. Some series incorporate genetic material from uncultivated wild species to create cultivars like those in the Sensation Series with more florets, but less crowded petals.

Frankly it's all too complicated to set out in detail without filling half the book. So let me summarize by use. For a traditional scarlet geranium to grow with 'Limelight' helichrysum, or with bronze beet and sparks of bidens, or with silver cinerarias, go for 'Horizon Deep Scarlet', with its impressive leaf zoning; 'Maverick Scarlet' is a chunkier alternative.

In a more informal arrangement, with daintier companions like the sinuous trails of *Plecostachys serpyllifolia* or that new favourite *Lobelia* 'Regatta Blue Splash', *Pelargonium* 'Sensation Scarlet' is superb. 'Sensation Picotee', in white with a red rim and red speckles, is the most gorgeous geranium yet created and would also fit. Even grown in a tub on its own 'Sensation Picotee' is simply captivating. The Sensations produce more flower heads than any other

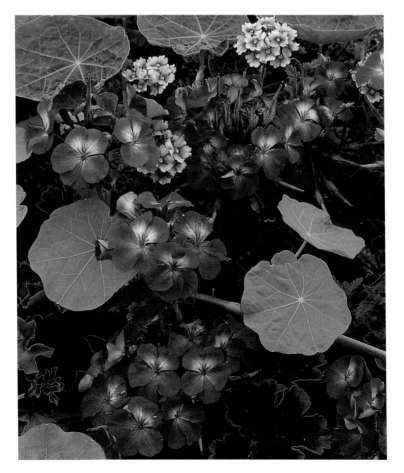

LEFT *Breeders have given up developing yellow- and pink-leaved geraniums; it's simply not possible genetically. Now they've adopted a different approach to foliage colour, and this soon-to-be-released cultivar boasts an unusually large dark zone on the leaf with a narrow green edging. Here, it grows with nasturtium foliage and the cuttings-raised* Verbena *'Pastel Pink'.*

variety available and they're almost never attacked by botrytis; the fading petals drop off rather than stay in place to rot.

For bedding in a traditional style, the Avanti and Multibloom series are best in a large expanse, where they'll get little special treatment. There are bold colours and more subtle and unusual shades in both series. 'Multibloom Lavender', for example, is a soft yet strong lavender-pink shade and perfect for the pastel combinations that we all still secretly love; try it with silver foliage, with the pink daisies of *Brachyscome* 'Strawberry Mousse', or with *Antirrhinum* 'Floral Showers Lavender'. 'Avanti Apricot Bicolour', also known as 'Rosy Sunset', is orange with a hint of pink and a white eye, and is stunning with purple perilla, with the picotee *Impatiens* 'Tempo Peach Frost' peeping out from underneath or with those bronze beetroot leaves about which I'm always enthusing. On a smaller scale, in good soil, the Sensations are impossible to beat.

Another for this multi-mixed intermingling style, and for ground cover, is the superb Tornado Series of ivy-leaved geraniums with their almost flat habit of growth and flower heads in carmine, lilac-pink or white, standing up from the foliage. 'Breakaway Scarlet', a denser ground cover geranium incorporating blood from wild species, is unjustly overlooked.

For containers, especially the jostling plantings which are so much more interesting than those in the old-fashioned blockier style, you'll find that in the moist, rich conditions which prevail when containers are well looked after, most geraniums develop a taller, slightly more open habit than they do in the open ground. The result is a plant which may spread out a little more, but which also smothers its neighbours less pugnaciously. So any plants like trailing lobelia, helichrysum, plecostachys, bushy convolvulus, bidens, petunias, and even violas and pansies – any with a

LEFT *Red geraniums can find a home anywhere, even at a garden like Hidcote Manor, Gloucestershire, but they need the right companions. Here, in a timber tub set against blue painted boarding, they're interplanted with Helichrysum petiolare 'Limelight', the long stiff stems emerging amongst the foliage and flowers of the geranium to create a bright but not uncomfortably flashy association.*

tendency to develop slender stems – will penetrate the geranium foliage and peep through to create interesting associations.

Before discussing how to raise them, perhaps it's worth selecting a few special cultivars from the many, many series available: 'Horizon Deep Scarlet' (deep red, well zoned); 'Multibloom White' (best all-round white); 'Raspberry Ripple' (red and white stripes); 'Sensation Picotee' (unique white with red edge and specks); 'Tango' (best orange); 'Tornado Felix' (white ivy-leaved for ground cover); 'Venus' (white with pink eye); and 'Vogue Appleblossom' (soft appleblossom pink).

Geraniums are not the easiest of plants to raise from seed, although modern seed technology has ensured that they're a great deal less difficult than they once were. The seed is expensive, so now that the seed is pre-prepared to make germination speedier and more even, it represents somewhat better value than in the past.

Space sow the seeds in late winter or early spring in a 7cm /3in pot of moist, peat-based compost, cover with their own depth of sifted compost, cover the pot with clingfilm and place in the dark at a temperature of 21°C/70°F. Move them into the light (but not the sun) as soon as they germinate, usually in about ten days. When they've developed their first true leaves, move the seedlings into individual 6cm/2.5in or 7cm/3in pots to grow on. There's no need to pinch them, but try to allow enough space on the greenhouse bench to encourage branching.

When planted out, geraniums in particular seem to benefit from watering in with a liquid feed, and I find it also pays to pick off any flowers and buds. Then they romp away.

RIGHT *This densely planted red bed contains no more than three plants of any one variety – and sometimes only a single plant.* Pelargonium *'Breakaway Red' is being invaded by 'Hermine Grashoff' nasturtiums which will need to be controlled.* Dahlia *'Scarlet Emperor' is just about to start to flower while to its right* Amaranthus *'Hopi Red Dye' is reaching its peak.* Salvia coccinea *'Lady in Red' peeps out all over the place and, in front of the wild white petunias, 'Rambo', the tallest and bushiest of all the* Salvia splendens *varieties, is filling out well.*

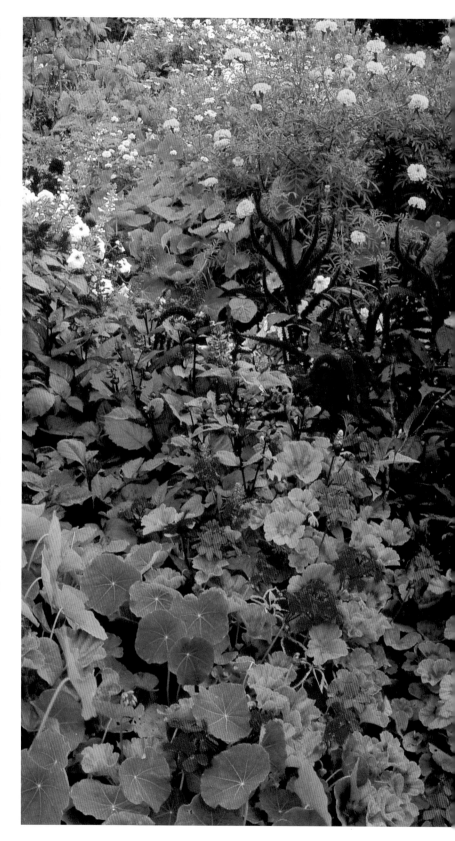

# *Petunia* **Petunia**

The petunia embraces every current trend in the development of annuals and bedding plants. While some annuals are popular for borders and some for containers, petunias are spectacular in both. Breeders are fixated upon producing ever more dwarf varieties of some annuals – and vigorous, trailing varieties of others; petunias are developing in both directions. Reviving old cultivars is popular in some annuals, new introductions fuel interest in others; in petunias it's both.

Gardeners and garden centres, seed companies and plant breeders are taking an interest in them all, using a wide yet still increasing range of varieties in both traditional and newly creative ways. So there's a great deal to say about them in a relatively small space.

Petunias are nothing if not colourful. And with breeders developing so many (one catalogue lists 162 different cultivars – not including mixtures; this parallels the asters of a century ago), the fine variations of colour and the huge range of colour combinations allow the most precise selection for carefully colour-themed plantings. Petunias sparkle; they're vibrant, quintessentially summersome, stunning in dry summers and more colourful than many annuals in dull ones; some are even scented.

The most recent trend looks to the past. Two wild species, both of them early participants in petunia devel-

Petunia *'Horizon Lavender Sunrise'*

Petunia *'Prism Sunshine'*

opment, have emerged from botanic gardens and into seed catalogues and garden centres. *Petunia axillaris*, its white flowers delicately patterned in speckled streaks the colour of Dijon mustard, has proved a vigorous and surprisingly weather-resistant plant. Its relaxed, open habit endears it to those of us frustrated at the impossibility of using the many more compact petunias in informal mixed border plantings.

And *P. integrifolia*, in bold magenta-purple, with its more spreading habit, has been used in the breeding of some of the cuttings-raised hanging-basket varieties like the Surfinias. This too is a good border petunia, without the intense branching and discordant density of colour which would disrupt plantings of perennials and old-fashioned annuals.

At the other extreme is the still-evolving Fantasy Series, sometimes known as the Junior Petunia. Small, flat or slightly rounded plants, their flowers are also unusually small, and the whole plant is rather stiff in its bearing. Although so weak as to be useless in beds and borders unless fed and watered almost daily, in containers, and especially when unfettered by competition, this can be a very pretty plant; a blend of harmonizing shades looks delightful in a terracotta strawberry pot.

By contrast, seed-raised trailing varieties to complement the cuttings-raised Surfinias are also benefiting

Petunia *'Fantasy Pink Morn'*

RIGHT *Unlikely companions: two matching colours from the Petunia 'Plum Pudding' mixture fill in cleverly around the bare leaf stems of Geranium palmatum, which can be wheeled under cover in late autumn for extra winter protection. The 'Florence White' cornflower is probably an unnecessary addition. Around the tub, the billowing green flowers of Alchemilla mollis make a soft frame. When they fade, and the astrantias in the background are cut down, the petunia will have developed sufficiently to capture the attention regardless of its surroundings. A stray yellow petunia from the mix has been set to the side to blend with the alchemilla.*

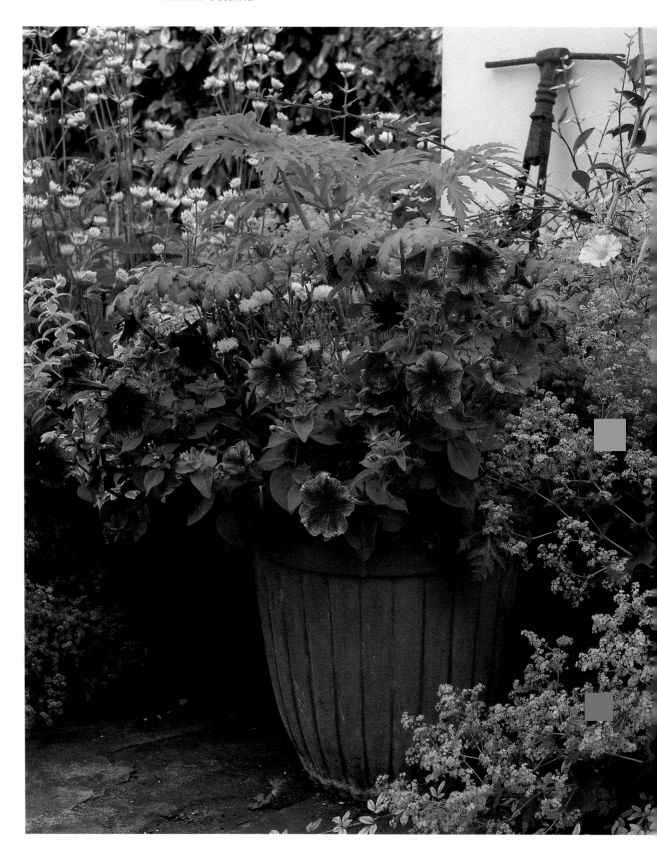

from determined attention and proving unexpectedly adaptable. Frankly, these petunias are less than elegant falling in curtains from baskets. They are, though, undeniably colourful, and grown on the flat as ground cover they can be both arresting and stylish; those in the Wave Series hold up their flowers more dependably than the cuttings-raised types. Even the almost-lurid 'Purple Wave' will make you gasp – with delight, as clumps of late-

summer colchicums surge through. 'Pearly Wave', in softest lilac-pink, is a cool background for white colchicums or can be planted through an enriching spring mulch to snake out from under and up into roses.

In cool damp summers the weather can ruin petunias; somewhere, during the journey from wild species to $F_1$ hybrid bedding plant, intolerance of bad weather was allowed to become almost endemic, especially in the larger-flowered Grandiflora types. (This may well have been because the breeders work almost entirely in areas with warm, sunny summer climates.) The smaller-flowered Multifloras have always shown more tolerance and better recovery, and in both groups the rich rose is the most weather-resistant colour, with dark red showing particular susceptibility. Now that weather resistance has become a priority, the Storm Series is one of the best for tolerating wet weather and recovering afterwards.

But it's colour that drives so much development, and new colours are now both tempting and bewildering gardeners. 'Prism Sunshine' marked a big step forward in yellow petunias, as much in seed quality as in colour, productivity and reliability. In the garden this is splendid grown with 'Curlina' parsley, curly kale 'Redbor' or pretty 'Seven Star Red' Afro-French marigolds.

'Horizòn Lavender Sunrise' is the most dramatic of the newer yellow-throated varieties, which are almost impossible to use in the garden – except on their own or, in the case of this petunia, with *Helichrysum petiolare* 'Limelight'; paler shades with paler throats are more accommodating to other nearby colours. Pale yellow- or cream-centred Morn types are a recent development; the cool and captivating 'Celebrity Chiffon Morn', so prolific as well as being almost ethereal in its colouring, combines

LEFT *The airy growth and wiry stems of* Gaura lindheimeri *look their best against a more rounded background, and the eye goes straight to them. When the occasional flower of* Petunia *'Pearl Rose & White' sparks through from behind, it adds a third dimension to an intimate planting. The small-flowered but prolific Pearl Series is again finding favour in reaction to the bigger, brighter and blowsier types.*

perfectly with the silver foliage of helichrysums or cineraria, with palest watered-blue petunias and with clean whites.

Veined types, such as the Plum Multifloras and Daddy Grandifloras, are good in small spaces where the two, usually harmonious, colours of background and veining bring adaptability. The startling red-on-blushed-white 'Strawberry Sundae' and the seven individual shades of the Mirage Reflections Series are the most choice, and provide the opportunity to co-ordinate neighbouring colours with either the background colour or the veins. Even a single plant from these series has character.

Doubles always create interest but are poor in wet summers. The Multiflora Duo Series of semi-doubles combines enough fullness of flower with the best weather resistance to create a viable series; 'Duo Silvery Shades', purple-veined pale lilac, is the pick in character, colour and performance. The Grandiflora Pirouettes are the Dolly Partons of the petunias: bigger, blowsier and altogether more fulsome. But a downpour ruins the colourful display with no compensating diversions. In porches and conservatories (where the Victorians always grew the doubles) and reliably sunny climates, they truly amaze.

There are so many series, some very similar, that it might be helpful to narrow down the range. This is my choice:

Grandiflora Double: Pirouette Series
Multiflora Double: Duo Series
Grandiflora Single: Storm Series or Daddy Series (veined);
Multiflora Single: Mirage Series or Celebrity Series
Trailing: Wave Series

RIGHT  *Two petunias, both in shades of rose-pink, show how carefully selected varieties from entirely different series can look good together. In the background is the taller 'Marshmallow', which fades as the flowers age, and in the foreground, the paler 'Celebrity Chiffon Morn'. In this planting, both provide the background against which to admire the unusual smoky pink of Cynoglossum 'Mystery Rose'. The blue is more common but this pink cynoglossum is altogether more subtle yet stands up well against the larger flowers of the petunias. It can be raised as a biennial, though it appreciates good winter drainage, but has here made a well-branched plant in rich soil from a spring sowing.*

But which varieties are scented? Most petunias have a little perfume but few modern cultivars are well scented. You'll have to go back to the old (and cheap) open-pollinated mixtures and also the $F_2$ mixtures, mostly in watered pinks and mauves; there you'll find scent. But not the flower power, the colours or the dependability of modern varieties; however, the breeders are working on it.

# *Phlox* **Phlox**

The popularity of the perennial border phlox has been constant for decades and the dependability of the alpine phlox may make them as popular amongst new gardeners than the border perennials. At the same time, interest in the smaller woodland phlox has broadened with a growing enthusiasm for shade gardening and the arrival of new introductions. But it's a little bewildering . . . Only quite recently, with the introduction of some superb new varieties, have annual phlox again found favour. For, as is the case with many annuals, phlox have known good times before the recent lean years. Let's look back . . .

In the late 1880s, Suttons Seeds listed 39 cultivars, including a double and a semi-double form, plus various mixtures; by the 1920s the total was still a very respectable 28. In the 1980s and early 1990s many catalogues were down to just three or four cultivars, and quality deteriorated (hence the red rogue amongst my 'Blue Beauty' in the picture on page 144). Then interest amongst breeders was revived: new pot plants were the first aim, followed by new doubles and semi-doubles, then taller mixtures then the reapperance of old cultivars such as 'Leopoldii'.

There are two features which make annual phlox so delightful. First, the colour range: the variety of colour combinations possible, and now becoming available, is the most diverse of all the annuals except perhaps pansies and violas. Second, the habit of the plants, except the very smallest, is naturally conducive to the style of intimate intermingling planting, which suits today's gardens. For the plants branch rather strongly, given space, yet the rigidity of the stems

and the occasional natural openings which develop allow other plants to intertwine without smothering the phlox.

The smallest varieties are the least suitable for the garden. 'Dolly Mixed' and the double-flowered 'Chanal' are good as autumn-sown pot plants for frost-free greenhouses, as they are less inclined to stretch; both are too dumpy in the garden. 'Palona' has a good range of colours and a slightly more relaxed habit, but the look is spoiled by the edges of the petals of some colours curling rather than lying flat.

If we move up in size, 'Cecily' has been revived as 'Cecily Old & New Shades', a lovely blend of colours with some unusual lavenders, pinks and creams. The expanding Buttons Series comes in bolder colours, is ideal in size and habit and its separate colours are increasingly easy to find, as is its formula mixture of separate colours, 'Buttons and Bows'. 'Buttons Blue Shades' is a rich but cool-harmonious blend of purplish blues with pale eyes and is lovely with *Salvia farinacea* 'Strata' and

LEFT *The vivid magenta-tinted red of this single colour from the 'Buttons and Bows' mixture of annual phlox mingles intimately with* Anagallis *'Skylover', whose slender, inquisitive stems insinuate themselves amongst the more rigid stems of the phlox to create a delightful picture.*

RIGHT *Although the dark red is a little tall and the scarlet a little bold, 'Fantasy Mixed' phlox shows an appealing harmony in colour tones and a reasonably even height across the colours. There are some especially delightful colours in the mix.*

silver foliage; 'Buttons Cherry White Eye' is bright, clean and looks good with dark-red geraniums and *Hibiscus acetosella*.

Stocks of the old favourite, the taller Beauty Series, are less true than they were and almost unavailable in separate colours, but the cream, when you can find it, is simply gorgeous. Then there are two particularly enticing taller mixtures, 'Coral Reef' and 'Tapestry', at about 35cm/14in. 'Coral Reef', also known as 'Phlox of Sheep' ('Dolly Mixed'? 'Phlox of Sheep'? Please, no more), comes in a blend of pinks, peach, apricot and coral shades, and yellows and creams. You can pick from its shades of languidly summery harmony to use individually. 'Tapestry' may be naturally less companionable as a blend but features rare colours and colour combinations; here too, you can pick out individuals to make themed groupings. One special feature of the mid-height 'Tapestry' and 'Cecily Old & New Shades'

mixtures is the presence of so many bicolours. This allows bi-coloured individuals to be used as transitional plants, linking with other plants in each of the two colours.

The tallest (at 45cm/18in) of those easily available, and a superb cut flower and mid-border variety is 'Leopoldii', introduced from Texas in 1835 yet still surviving. The rose-pink flowers have a white centre and a lovely scent, especially late in the day. We need more colours in this height.

Raising phlox is not difficult, although all varieties appreciate space to encourage branching and the smaller ones appreciate regular liquid feeding. Starting them in pots gives them the best chance to develop well. All benefit from careful dead-heading; this is fiddly, best done with the point of the kitchen scissors, but the improvement is dramatic – dead-headed plants flower for weeks or even months longer than those left untouched.

RIGHT *Evidence that when the best-laid plans go awry, the result may not necessarily be a disaster. Heliotropium 'Marine' dominates the foreground here, with the arching branches of the grey-leaved* Helichrysum petiolare *making an attractive contrast to the metallic flush in the heliotrope foliage. Phlox 'Blue Beauty' emerges behind with Salvia farinacea 'Victoria', but a single rogue red phlox, which came unexpectedly in the 'Blue Beauty', adds a fiery spark amongst the Anagallis 'Skylover'.*

# Primula *Polyanthus and Primrose*

Primrose, cowslip . . . don't those words just take you off into some dreamy rural idyll? Shakespeare, Thomas Hardy, Devon banks, unchilled bitter beer, lying on your back with grass stems framing your view of the sky, a few puffy white clouds in the clear blue. Polyanthus . . . sounds so vulgar, doesn't it? Brash seaside swimsuits, own-brand cola, sand in the sandwiches, Jeffrey Archer, parks bedding and diesel fumes in the coach home.

Oddly enough, those first two plants came together to make the third, for the polyanthus was developed from the hybrid between the primrose (*Primula vulgaris*) and the cowslip (*P. veris*). Most $F_1$ hybrid polyanthus now grown for bedding are vulgar, marred by overlarge flowers which weigh down the stems, especially after spring showers. So many are intentionally bred with garish yellow eyes to the flowers, the better to create a contrast with the basic colour, that they're impossible to use except in old-fashioned spangly mixtures or in last-resort combinations with yellow tulips.

The 'improved' primroses sold as pot plants also have their faults: they're weak, the flowers are gross and the colours are garish. Even the flowers of those in a true primrose colour are usually so disproportionately large as to have no place in the garden. But enough – let's turn to the real beauties amongst the polyanthus.

Fortunately, there was Florence Bellis of Gresham, Oregon, and Major Knocke of Cowichan Station, British Columbia, and to them we owe the fact that this chapter even appears in the book. For without these two, across the Atlantic from the plants' natural homes, there would be so few beautiful

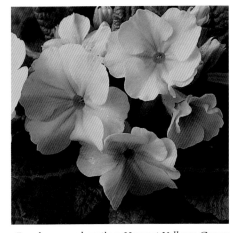

*Barnhaven polyanthus Harvest Yellows Group*

*Barnhaven polyanthus Cowichan Amethyst Group*

primroses and polyanthus to write about that I would be tempted to leave them out altogether.

In 1934 Florence Bellis spent $4.90 of her last $5 on some polyanthus seed from Suttons in England. Her good eye and her innocent enthusiasm led to the selection of her Silver Dollar strains (so-called from the size of the flowers) and the huge range of Barnhaven polyanthus and primroses that we have today.

Then in a Cowichan garden in the early 1930s, Major Knocke spotted a polyanthus which lacked the usual bright yellow eye. It seemed sterile, but the good major split it and passed it around, and ten years later Florence Bellis was able to find some pollen in its flowers. This was the beginning of what is now a five-colour series of lustrous polyanthus without garish contrasts.

The Cowichan Group polyanthus come in five groups of shades: Garnet, in garnet, blackish garnet and ruby shades; Amethyst, in violet and amethyst blue; Blue, in various rich blues, some with black eyes; Venetian, in strawberry and hot pink shades; and Yellow, with dark stems and bronzed foliage.

Sadly, the trials of these plants at the Royal Horticultural Society's garden at Wisley showed that we may have more florid catalogue prose than fine flowers, since all were too variable to be depended upon for carefully planned displays. But amongst them were a few plants of such poise and such elegant posture, such deep colour and such sumptuous richness, such lustre, such calm restraint, such prolific flowering and such harmonious association of flower colour, stem colour and leaf tone

– well, I've grown them for years, either from bought seed or my own, and they are gorgeous.

As an example, try yellow Cowichans with Bowles' golden grass (*Milium effusum* 'Aureum'), blue forget-me-nots such as 'Light Blue' with its pale flowers and tall open habit, or blue wood anemones. Plant them too amongst *Euphorbia donii*, whose red-tinted emerging stems pick up the colour in the Cowichans, or under *Daphne* x *houtteana*.

Florence Bellis's original Silver Dollar Series still comes in almost two dozen different colours or shades. Some are clean and pale, some rich and lustrous, some have dark stems and dark leaves, some a white or blue rim to the petals. Even some of those with a large yellow eye are pretty because the surrounding flower colour is so serene.

These and her other strains are all so superior in terms of colour that only uniformity recommends the $F_1$ hybrids; if you must, choose the Rainbow or Crescendo series.

Primroses have also developed enormously but they're rarely used in spring bedding. Almost all cultivars are bred as pot plants and are without the hardiness required to thrive after a wet winter in the open ground. The Barnhaven primroses are an exception, though they come in far fewer shades; many have the dark leaves and dark stems which set off the flowers so well. Most maintain the general habit of the wild primrose but are much more prolific; some of the colours, especially the apricot shades in Osiered Amber Group and the sultry reds of Tartan Red Group, are captivating.

Grow them with species crocus and other dwarf spring bulbs (even in a windowbox), with *Cyclamen coum*, with the fresh fronds of dwarf ferns like the beech fern, *Thelypteris phegopteris*, or with celandines and wood anemones. Wood anemones are increasingly available in the pinks and pale blues which associate well with these primroses, and *Anemone* x *lipsiensis*, the hybrid between *A. nemerosa* and *A. ranunculoides*, with its pale, yellow flowers and bronze-tinted foliage is an ideal companion.

At Barnhaven, they recommend this sowing procedure: sow the seed in February (March or April in especially cold areas) using seed trays and a peat-based compost; do not cover the

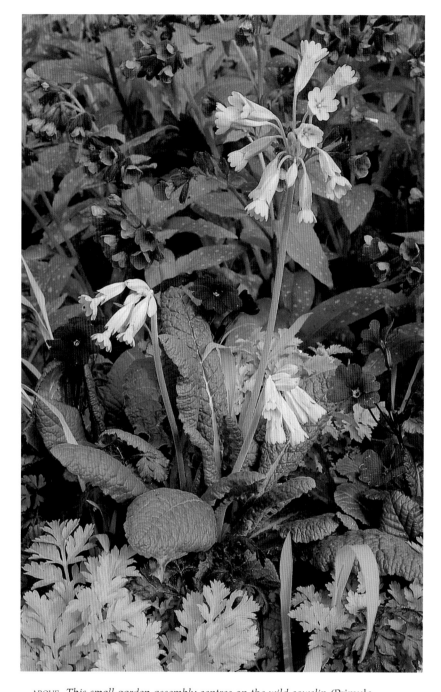

ABOVE *This small garden assembly centres on the wild cowslip (Primula veris) with blue Cowichan Group polyanthus on either side; they could be the start of some strange hybrids. The yellow-leaved feverfew seedlings will fill the space in summer, along with the foliage from the Pulmonaria saccharata in the background and the few slender yellow leaves of Bowles' golden grass (Milium effusum 'Aureum'), which will expand into bolder, but still delicate, clumps.*

seed. Water well, then cover the seed tray with another identical upturned tray and place in the shade. Germination should take place, they say, in two to three weeks; uncover them then, and prick out the seedlings when they have at least four true leaves.

Needless to say, I've adapted this system – partly so that half a dozen varieties can be sown in a smaller space than that occupied by six seed trays. Sowing in February is fine, especially as bought seed may not arrive until early autumn. The seed does not require frost to spark germination, so keep the seed in the fridge to prolong its viability before sowing in late winter. Home-saved seed is best sown as soon as possible after collection, in midsummer – as long as you can keep it cool.

I sow in 9cm/3½in pots of equal parts peat-based compost and soil-based compost. Then I firm the compost gently and top it with 6mm/¼in of sharp grit; I sow the seed on the grit and water it in carefully. Finally, I place the pots in a cold frame and cover it with something solid to keep out the light – I use an old wooden door. The trick is to keep them shaded and moist; the seeds must not dry out.

Modern $F_1$ hybrids are more vigorous and can be sown as late as June, but keeping the temperature below the 18°C/65°F at which germination is impeded can be very difficult in summer. After germination, I prick out into 7cm/3in pots, three seedlings in each, then split them and move them on into individual 9cm/3½in pots later.

Choosing the right time for planting out is not easy. Both primroses and polyanthus need time to establish themselves before the winter, but planting too early, or in excessively rich soil, can sometimes promote a mass of soft growth susceptible to disease.

The big pest problem with primroses and polyanthus is vine weevil. The adults nibble the edges of the leaves and their ginger-headed white larvae feed on the roots; primulas are their favourite food. Pesticides are ineffective but biological control in the form of parasitic nematodes, though expensive, often works well on young plants in pots – less so in garden soil.

One of the joys, and drawbacks, of Barnhaven polyanthus and primroses is that most are very variable. When the seedlings flower in their first spring there's an opportunity to select your favourites and retain them for future years, splitting them regularly after flowering. Collecting seed from them, however, will provide unpredictable results. The flowers of all primulas are constructed to prevent self-pollination and facilitate cross-pollination, so the seed from any one plant is unlikely to produce a batch of identical seedlings. Go back to new seed each year.

*Barnhaven primrose (single colour)*

*Barnhaven polyanthus Striped Victorian Group (single colour)*

# *Ricinus* *Castor oil plant*

Big, bold and beautiful effects are enjoying a come-back and with them the castor oil plant. If you have *Fatsia japonica* in the garden many visitors will quickly identify it as the castor oil plant – but they'd be wrong. *Ricinus communis*, with its poisonous but gloriously fat and speckled seeds (just opening the packet is a treat), is the true castor oil plant. Since the last century, it has been a vital constituent of the once-fashionable, now reviving, sub-tropical bedding schemes. Palms and bananas were wheeled out of greenhouses and bedded out for the summer; seed-raised castor oil plants fitted in perfectly.

For the largest and most dramatic castor oil plants – and that, after all, is the point – seeds should be sown early, a single seed in a 7cm/3in pot at 20°C/70°F. The seedlings should then be moved into increasingly large containers so that when they're planted out from 20cm/8in pots they hit the border running, so to speak, and romp away to produce plants with real impact. Of course, a long growing season implies a heated greenhouse early in the year when keeping temperatures high is at its most expensive, but there's no other way to provide that lushly tropical effect.

These large and luxuriant leaves do pose a problem – they're easily damaged in windy situations. So, use castor oil plants in sheltered places; once the vein along the centre of each leaf is broken, the leaf hangs limp. The leaves can also be disfigured simply by their rattling against each other.

A whole grove of castor oil plants in their various colour forms is an impressive sight. Unfortunately, a harmonious effect is less easy to achieve than it might appear, as catalogues can be unhelpful. What can you do when a cultivar is listed as 'Mixed', yet described as having leaves in 'bright green'? Don't buy it, of course. Fortunately, the colours are usually obvious by planting-out time, and individuals can be selected for their precise planting sites at this stage; fortunately again, the heights given in catalogues are usually a little more dependable – allowing for a little exaggeration in the dwarfness of the recently introduced smaller varieties.

The form usually listed as *Ricinus* var. *zanzibarensis* will reach 1.8m/6ft and often more in most suitable gardens without special treatment. It usually comes in a mix of dark green, various greens with a silvery grey sheen, and purplish or bronze shades. 'Gibsonii', a bronze selection, is equally tall.

'Impala', at 1.2–1.8m/4–6ft, in deep and shimmering bronze, has been one of the best of all for many years but is disappearing in favour of the similar but even shorter 'Carmencita', with red flowers, and 'Carmencita Pink', both of which at least have the benefit of flowering dependably.

As well as creating spectacular groves, castor oil plants can be used with other bold or exotic seed-raised plants such as *Nicotiana sylvestris*, cleomes, sunflowers, the tall forms of *Lupinus hartwegii* such as 'Sunrise' and 'Pink Javelin', *Convolvulus* 'Star of Yalta' and climbing nasturtiums. If they're available, add bananas, palms and other tender plants which can spend the summer in the garden and boast a similar boldness. Then staying at home in suburbia will feel like holidaying in the tropics.

Ricinus communis

LEFT *Single specimens of castor oil plant can add quite a punch to mixed borders. Here, a few plants of 'Carmencita' have been slipped in between Rosa 'Heritage', one of David Austin's English roses, and 'Sonata Mixed' cosmos and give the whole planting a quirky and strangely intriguing air.*

# *Rudbeckia* Coneflower

The independent, distinctive and sometimes contrary point of view is what saves society, and our gardens, from becoming banale. So consider the rudbeckias. These are amongst the most valuable of summer annuals, combining good colour, a long flowering period and robustness. But they remain on the fringes of fashion, spurned by those who consider superficially more refined flowers more tempting. Their quirky style, which takes them beyond the range of their relations, the French marigolds, and into a class where character has survived the plant breeders' inclination towards miniaturization, remains unappreciated. Even 'Toto', one of the smallest of them all at about 25cm/10in, with flowers in a flat plane at the top of the plant, has retained some individuality (although 'Becky', a mixture with larger flowers on shorter plants, has not).

But, at the same time, rudbeckias will never be as uniform as marigolds. So the consistently double flowers of 'Goldilocks' made it a well-deserved award winner in its time, but now you'll find plants with intensely double flowers mixed with those carrying far fewer petals. 'Kelvedon Glory', reintroduced as 'Sonora', should have single or slightly semi-double flowers with a mahogany blotch on each petal but some may be unblotched. 'Nutmeg' should be semi-double but only some of the flowers will have the dark blotch at the base.

All this is disconcerting only by contrast with rigid expectations. In my favourite mahogany and yellow plantings, the variation in doubling is irritating only if it reduces impact at a certain point in the border. There may be variation in colour too, but in

Rudbeckia *'Irish Eyes'*

Rudbeckia *'Rustic Dwarfs Mixed'*
*(single colour)*

the rough and tumble of such plantings this can even be an advantage – as long as you expect it. Plants of 'Rustic Dwarfs Mixed', for example, are all in the same gold/orange/mahogany /rusty-red colour range and so make a most harmonious grouping, introducing a little pace into a planting without upsetting the colour theme.

One of the most useful attributes of rudbeckias is that, apart from 'Toto' and the ignorable 'Becky', they have a highly companionable habit. The foliage is not so dense that neighbours are crowded out but, instead, allows them to sneak in amongst the rasping stems to provide an elegant background. The looser French marigolds, 'Coral Reef' phlox in beigey and creamy pink tones, or the old phlox 'Cream Beauty' make congenial partners. For something more startling, the dramatic flowering stems of *Verbena* 'Homestead Purple' will snake in between and then surge up to open in close and exciting companionship with the rudbeckias.

Raising rudbeckias from seed presents no special problems, although it's wise to move new plants into individual pots as soon as possible and give them plenty of root room to ensure that they develop productively.

However, unlike many summer annuals they will flower fairly well even if treated badly; their recovery from being starved and constricted in small pots is remarkable. This makes them ideal for gardeners wishing to raise their own half-hardy annuals from seed and create a brilliant show yet who tend to disappear for long weekends without watering first.

# *Salpiglossis* Salpiglossis

In the early 1980s I visited a British plant breeder's research station in cold, windy Norfolk. Out in the trials field was a large square plot of what looked like hundreds of dead twigs. These were the remnants of the salpiglossis trials, and a few of these sad remains had canes pushed in alongside them as markers.

The breeder's aim was to transform the salpiglossis from a greenhouse ornamental, or an outdoor plant for warm climates, to a summer bedding plant for cooler areas while ensuring that it could be raised in the same way as petunias. They were to be made shorter, so that strong winds actually left them standing up, and were selected for their ability to flower well in cool climates. The result of selecting these few specimens was, many years later, the Casino Series, followed more recently by the ten-colour Royale Series.

The Royales have brought the sumptuous and slightly exotic salpiglossis into cooler gardens for the first time. The addition of a completely new colour in the form of 'Royale Chocolate', often listed as 'Chocolate Pot', has brought new style to the dark, rich and sumptuous plantings which are now so popular.

So add 'Chocolate Pot' to dark-leaved *Hibiscus acetosella*, to rusty and deep crimson dahlias or to *Cosmos atrosanguineus*, and the result is truly impressive. The petals have a sheen to them which adds an unexpected touch of light to the planting. And the higher profile of salpiglossis has led to the reintroduction of the long-neglected, deep moody blue 'Kew Blue', which is splendid with *Salvia farinacea* 'Victoria' and 'Bobby Sox'

phlox. 'Yellow Chilli' is a sumptuous yet brilliant yellow from the Royale Series which has the flower power, along with the style, to be the perfect choice where a taller rich yellow is needed; other than rudbeckias there are few such options with a dependably long season. Try it with 'David Howard' dahlias, whose bronze foliage and fully double orange flowers need a little airiness and grace around them, or with the coppery foliage of *Haloragis* 'Melton Bronze' underneath.

'Royale Pale Blue Bicolour', with its pretty pattern of blue and white veining and its yellow throat, requires more carefully chosen neighbours. Consider picking up the dark, almost brown, throat colour with *Heuchera* 'Palace Purple' or, a little more of a gamble as it needs rich soil, the perennial *Rumex flexuosus* with its snaking brown shoots and slender brown foliage.

'Gloomy Rival' must have the strangest cultivar name in the history of plants. It's a strange colour too, a sort of grey with brown veins and brown throat. This is best as a modest clump near the path with purple-leaved shrubs in the background.

Start off salpiglossis in the same way as petunias until they're growing strongly. Then, because they make plants which grow larger more quickly, they're best moved into 12.5cm/5in pots where they're less likely to become pot bound.

Even the most modern varieties of salpiglossis tend to run up on a single stem without branching. Ensuring that the pots are well spaced as the plants develop encourages them to branch from low down, producing a superior plant.

Salpiglossis *'Royale Blue Bicolour'*

Salpiglossis *'Chocolate Pot'*

# _Salvia_ Salvia

Don't turn the page! You can relax. Would I advise filling your garden with salvias so savagely scarlet that you need to carry smelling salts every time you stepped outside? No, you're safe; I assure you.

That a relatively attractive Brazilian wild plant has been turned into a horticultural monstrosity, to be packed into the flower beds of public parks, surrounded by neatly alternating white alyssum and dark blue lobelia, is a discredit to a noble genus. And look in the catalogues: can you tell one from another? Grow them side by side in a trials field, as the big seed companies do, and it's still practically impossible.

Fortunately, in recent years dwarf bedding salvias have undergone something of a revolution. Firstly, new colours have appeared. First deep purple, crimson and creamy white, then various pinks and mauves have been introduced in a number of series. Subsequently we were hit with striped types, and more recently with varieties whose calyx is a different colour from the flower or in which the individual flowers are bicoloured. They are good, but all have the same fault: they're too squat. What we need are taller, bushy varieties reaching 38cm/15in, 45cm/18in or even 60cm/2ft, with a long succession of much smaller, more open spikes. We have 'Rambo' in this vein, but we need something similar in all these new colours; the breeders think I'm mad.

The Salsa and Sizzler series are the best. They're early flowering and have summer-long staying power in the open garden when cosseted; grown in tubs in which they're fed, watered and dead-headed regularly they last the season with a swagger and can be invaluable.

Salvia _'Rambo'_

They also have a slightly angular habit, with the flower spikes striking off at a slant rather than being determinedly upright, and this allows other plants to sneak in between the spikes to make interesting associations. For example, the dainty zinnia relative _Sanvitalia procumbens_, with its small, dark-centred lemon flowers is a real sparkler peeping out amongst the flowers of 'Sizzler Purple' then streaming over the sides of a container.

But there are at least four other salvia species, less Lilliputian in their habit, which fit sympathetically into informal annual plantings and into mixed borders. And these are now finding their way into catalogues.

The Texan _Salvia farinacea_, with its slender tuberous roots, may come in a very restricted colour range – basically it's blue or it's white – but is nevertheless an important species. The foliage is narrow, dark and glossy; its flowering stems stand strikingly vertical and each is lined with small flowers which have the unusual habit of opening at the same time at different points along the stem. The stem itself is slightly downy, in dark blue or white.

Varieties range in height from about 38cm/15in to over 60cm/2ft. 'Rhea' and the slightly taller 'Victoria' and the taller still 'Blue Victory' have dark blue flowers on dark blue stems; 'Cirrus' and the taller 'Victoria Silver' and then 'White Victory' have white flowers on silver stems; the neat and sparky 'Strata' and the slightly taller 'Reference' have blue and white bicoloured flowers on silver stems. Mingle them, allow them to surge through the blue and white _Browallia_ 'Sapphire' in a container or border, or set 'Victoria Silver' to make a bold

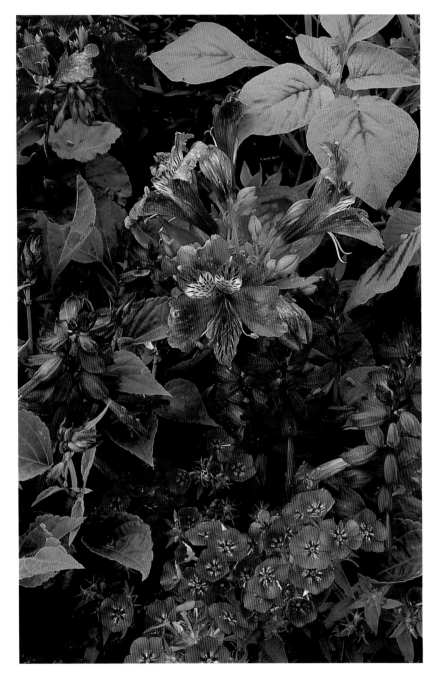

ABOVE *'Sizzler Lavender' is one of the newer salvia colours with the flower power of the reds. Here, it fronts the neat growing* Alstroemeria *'Deep Rose', the first F₁ hybrid type, and a single colour from* Phlox *'Cecily Old and New Shades' in a mauve grouping with white highlights from the alstroemeria and phlox.*

yet sympathetic contrast in front of a dark-leaved dahlia such as 'Tally Ho'.

*Salvia coccinea* is a scarlet salvia, but in a more comely style than most red bedding salvias, which have the bloated arrogance of an undersized bouncer outside a seedy basement club. In contrast, 'Lady in Red', the pink and white 'Coral Nymph' and 'Snow Nymph' have the assured elegance of the dancers we're queuing to see.

These three all reach about 60cm/2ft and, although they start to flower a little later in the summer than other salvias, they fit so well into borders with perennials and taller, naturalistic annuals that we can forgive their late appearance.

Create a rosy harmony with 'Coral Nymph' and the tall pink and white annual phlox, 'Leopoldii'; 'Snow Nymph' may be a fraction less prolific but playing cool with pale lemon *Chrysanthemum* 'Primrose Gem' it's the only tall and elegant white form. And with 'Lady in Red' it's possible to create a more satisfying version of the tired old red, white and blue bedding that this book is aiming to banish for good. So combine it with the sultry *Salpiglossis* 'Kew Blue' and *Cosmos* 'Sonata White'; or front it first with *Salvia farinacea* 'Blue Victory', then clouds of the trailing *Lobelia* 'Regatta Blue Splash' planted on the flat with that most captivating of all bedding geraniums, the eagerly awaited 'Sensation Picotee'.

In a quite different style, and colour range, is *Salvia patens*. This is a plant with modest impact but real class – the absolute antithesis of dwarf-bedding shockers such as 'Blaze of Fire'. It could hardly be said to produce a forest of growth and for much of the time each 60–90cm/2–3ft stem may carry only two or three open flowers – but it's easily the largest of any salvias which could conceivably be used for bedding and it has an intriguing parrot-beak shape. Most forms of this slightly tuberous species are best used in containers, where their flowers can be appreciated more closely.

Seed production in *Salvia patens* is an unpredictable business, especially on a commercial scale; perhaps we lack the wild pollinators found in their natural South American habitat. The result is that forms of this plant rarely appear in seed catalogues, although what little seed is produced is usually true to type.

The natural species is a bright royal blue; 'Oxford Blue' and 'Royal Blue' seem little different; 'Cambridge Blue' is a lovely clear sky shade; 'Chilcombe', named for the Dorset garden of the painter John Hubbard where it originated, is an unusual misty mauve; and 'White Trophy' is . . . of course, white, though with a faint blue smudge at the base. The only variety best grown in borders is the astonishing 'Guanajuato', a wild-collected form growing to twice the normal height and with flowers almost twice the normal size.

The last of this important genus (which also contains several other useful species) are a true annual and three true biennials – all the rest are perennials in their natural habitat.

In *Salvia horminum* (now properly called *S. viridis* and best known, but not quite correctly, as clary) the colour comes from the bracts. For drying or as an all-summer annual, sow outside; for more carefully planned intimate plantings, sow relatively late and bring on in pots.

The profoundly silvered rosettes of the biennials *Salvia argentea* and the more cut-leaved *S. aethiopis* are irresistible at the front of well-drained sunny borders – they just demand to be touched. But they can be difficult to accommodate there since their flower stems stretch up to 60cm/2ft in the late spring and summer, and their flowers are rather open in form and not quite dense enough to be overwhelming or impressive; they sometimes seem uncomfortable in such a position. Then they die and leave an ugly gap – eventually filled with their own seedlings.

Better suited to the back of the border is the true clary, *S. sclarea*. This is a chunkier plant with much larger rosettes in dark green and with a noticeable network of veining. It enjoys the same sunny site and well-drained soil but produces surging stems with, again, relatively insignificant flowers with bold bracts attached. These bracts hang down beneath the flower and can be purple or, more striking in var. *turkestanica*, white with purple tints.

You may be sceptical about my enthusiasm for some salvias, but this is one which even the most unreconstructed banisher of bedding can enjoy.

Salvia farinacea *'Blue Victory'* and *'White Victory'*

Salvia patens *'Cambridge Blue'*

Salvia argentea

RIGHT *The long-lasting colour in this purplish-blue form of* Salvia viridis *is provided by bracts, which provide colour in cream with green veins, blue or pink; the tiny two-lipped flowers are relatively insignificant. With the unruly and ever-changing double Shirley poppies around them, the upright stems bring an air of calm in spite of their bold colouring.*

# Tagetes *African and French marigold*

I hate marigolds. Well, says he quickly, I don't hate them all, for such sweeping scorn would make this chapter singularly unhelpful. Just bear with me while I say my piece before I come to some of the most valuable and stylish of all garden annuals. But really, why grow African marigolds? If a lorry backed up to your gate and tipped out a huge load of those yellow playballs you see at nursery schools, would you set about arranging them in your borders? If a salesman called at your door and offered you plastic oranges on sticks, would you plant them in your tubs?

You get my point. African marigolds may be colourful but so is paint. And the heads of the Discovery (discover how horrid they are), Sumo (as bloated as you'd expect) and Perfection (perfectly ghastly) Series marigolds are jammed together so tightly that you might as well have bought them by the yard from the DIY centre and rolled them out like carpet. This is the only time when you could possibly be grateful for botrytis.

So, having written off one of the four main groups of marigolds, can I recommend any of their more desirable relations? Of course. There are French marigolds, there are the Afro-French hybrids and there are 'tagetes'.

In French marigolds, eschew all the unnaturally tiny varieties like 'Boy O'Boy'

Tagetes *'Seven Star Red'*

Tagetes *'Mischief Mahogany'*

(how could you do otherwise?), and concentrate on two particular groups of varieties: the rusty doubles and the taller singles.

The rusty and mahogany doubles, often insulted with the appellation 'red', can be gorgeous; 'Scarlet Sophie' is the best (but by no means scarlet). Brighter shades with the vibrancy of 'Safari Tangerine' are difficult to place – though pink verbena is a possible companion . . . !

The taller single French marigolds are both more elegant and more adaptable and, in private gardens, where plants are carefully tended, you can often add 25% to the heights given in catalogues. Two series stand out, Favourite and Mischief. The former is easier to find but I like the (British-bred) latter.

The Favourites come in five colours, Mischief in six, of which the mahogany with its finest of yellow wiring round the petals is the pick. Peeping through the lemon-lime leaves of *Helichrysum petiolare* 'Limelight', it's unexpectedly stunning; with the unusual bronze of *Haloragis erecta* 'Wellington Bronze' and the fleeting little yellow stars of *Bulbine annua* on their juicy green stems it's surprisingly refined. Unfortunately, these are rarely available in separate colours, so grow them to first flower and then make a selection for planting.

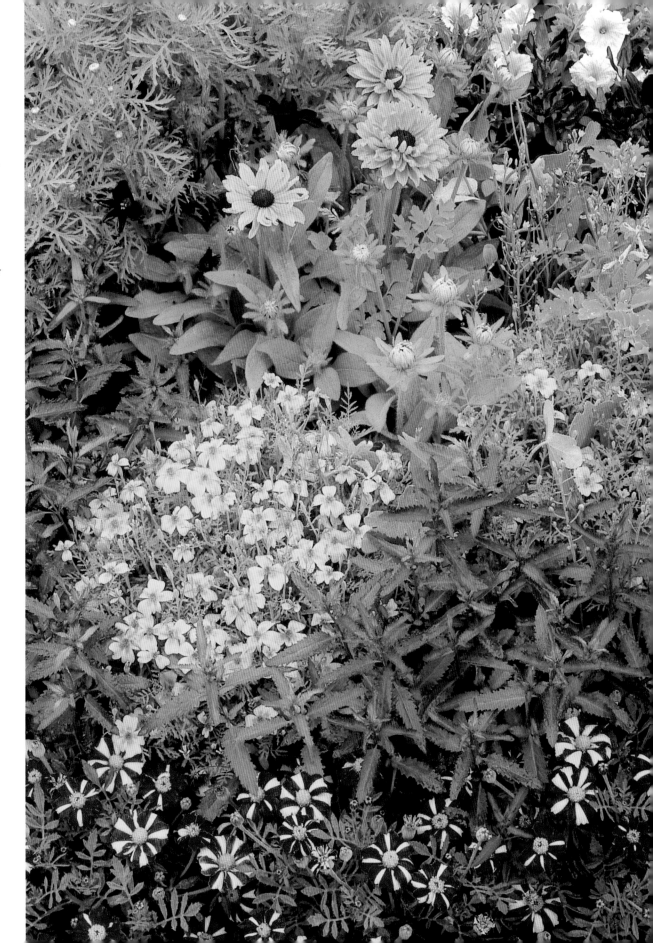

RIGHT *The essence of good bedding. Thoughtfully grouped plants in ones, twos and threes mingle together as the season progresses. The supposedly double-flowered* Rudbeckia *'Goldilocks' has many buds still to open and 'Golden Gem' tagetes, darker than 'Primrose Gem', melds in well colour-wise. In front, the mahogany in the stripes of 'Dwarf Harlequin' marigolds, much like 'Legion of Honour' from the nineteenth century, picks up the dark eyes of the rudbeckias and the rarely seen foliage of* Haloragis erecta *'Wellington Bronze', a real find, holds it all together. Great!*

Of all the French marigolds, the recently revived Victorian striped forms are the most choice; modern names like 'Jolly Jester' have replaced originals like 'Old Scotch Prize'. The Victorians grew singles and doubles, tall and short, some with a single mahogany stripe through each petal, some striped at the edges. They were rarely illustrated in old catalogues and the simple description 'beautifully striped' failed to distinguish them.

The taller forms are the best. Reaching 60–90cm/2–3ft and excellent for cutting, they carry their flowers on long stems with an unexpected airiness. They mingle contentedly in mixed borders with yellow grasses or sedges like *Carex stricta* 'Aurea'; they fit into temporary summer plantings in front of dark-leaved dahlias; and they colour match *Calendula* 'Indian Prince' in strictly annual plantings. The one problem is that flowers which develop under stress may temporarily lose their stripes.

For simple flowering power the hybrids between the African and the French marigolds cannot be beat; they might also give you a headache, some are so unnervingly bright, but they are prolific. Known as Afro-French, Super French or triploid marigolds, they seldom produce seed and so flower prolifically without dead-heading.

'Seven Star Red' is gorgeous – indeed it's one of the most valuable of all marigolds. Its deep mahogany flowers slowly become rustier, then more orange, but it's a harmonious fading. Try it with tightly curled 'Curlina' parsley, with one of the new, neatly trailing bidens like 'Goldie' snuggling through it, with

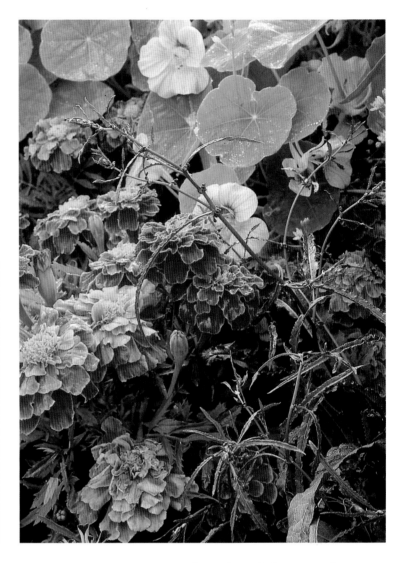

*Coprosma* 'County Park Purple' or with *Rudbeckia* 'Goldilocks'.

The so-called 'tagetes' can be difficult to use in the garden. Occasionally, they're seen in a dwarf hedge lining a path to a cottage door but they are so dominant that plants behind are visually overwhelmed. One answer is to use them with close neighbours like salpiglossis which will disrupt their form by surging through them, or with rudbeckias, which are sufficiently robust to break up their slightly suffocating growth.

The pure colours, like the helpfully descriptive 'Primrose Gem', 'Paprika' and 'Golden Gem' are the most effective. All have that sharp, fresh scent to the foliage which makes weeding amongst them a pleasure – although their dense growth usually smothers weeds before they become established.

ABOVE LEFT *Fragrances come together in this end-of-season combination. The marigold is an unusual one: 'Tessy' is a hybrid between what is usually referred to as a 'tagetes' (Tagetes tenuifolia) and a French marigold, and retains some of the scent of the former in its foliage. Surging though are the waiting-to-shed seed heads of Anethum graveolens.*

ABOVE *Even the russet tones of 'Scarlet Sophie' marigolds could be a little too truculent in some plantings, especially as they become more orange as they fade. Here, softened by the coolness of both foliage and flower of 'Tip Top Apricot' nasturtiums and the wavy wands of the bronze-leaved Rumex flexuosus, they look just great. The rumex is a perennial whose slender shoots sneak through neighbouring annuals, creating interesting associations. Planted with them in late spring, it is a substantial plant, but never overwhelming.*

# *Tanacetum* *Feverfew*

Feverfew has two valuable features: foliage and flowers. The yellow-leaved feverfew, *Tanacetum parthenium* 'Aureum', is one of those much-appreciated plants which turns up unannounced in most well-cultivated gardens. It may come as a seedling in a pot from a nursery or may intentionally be bought in the form 'Gold Ball', which makes neat little yellow domes but which, in succeeding self-sown generations, stretches and matures into an altogether more elegant plant. But once arrived it's always enjoyed. The yellow leaves (not 'gold', please) are invaluable and its white daisies too; the leaves are fragrant, the stems good for cutting and it deserves to be treated with more respect than simply allowed to self-sow.

But there are more feverfews, plenty more. The Dutch have raised a succession of forms intended as cut flowers; some, like 'Virgo', have clean, cream-eyed white buttons, while 'Santana' is more intentionally yellow. Reaching 60–90cm/2–3ft, 'Virgo' makes a fine border plant with the dusky red spikes of *Veronica spicata* 'Rotfuchs', and in well-drained soil all these forms will behave as short-lived perennials.

There are few good seed-raised, silver-leaved annuals but *Tanacetum ptarmiciflorum*,

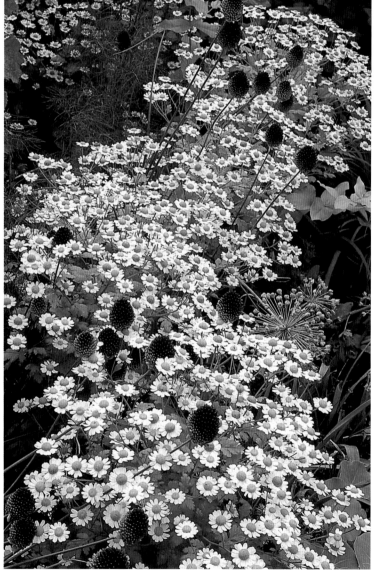

sometimes unnecessarily overdignified with the cultivar name 'Silver Feather', is one with a great character. It never flowers the first summer but its flat, pewter-grey foliage, finely and prettily dissected, is a fine companion in containers with diascias, twiggy nemesias and other not-too-pugnacious plants. However, unless started inconveniently early, it rarely makes a good-sized plant in the less pampered conditions of the bed or border.

Feverfew, I should say, is so-called from its traditional use as a medication against fever and colds. Botanically, the yellow-leaved and cut-flower types have in the past been assigned to both *Matricaria* and *Chrysanthemum*. while the silver-leaved type has usually been billeted in *Pyrethrum*; now, all are classified as *Tanacetum*.

LEFT *Yellow-leaved feverfew,* Tanacetum parthenium *'Aureum', is an invaluable plant. Its fresh foliage creates a bright speck of sunlight all winter, then stretches before revealing its white daisies. Planted, as here, with the deep purple heads of* Allium sphaerocephalon *falling through it, or self-sown in happy, and sometimes less than happy, combinations, the sharp fragrance of its leaves is released as you remove unwanted seedlings or simply brush against it.*

# *Tithonia* **Tithonia**

Strong and vigorous annuals which create a real presence in a border are becoming increasingly uncommon as plant breeders strive to reduce everything to the size of a French marigold. There are signs that the magnificent *Tithonia rotundifolia*, which I've grown to 1.8m/6ft, may be destined for this treatment. But why turn a uniquely bold and expressive plant into an approximation of a commonplace and characterless one?

Tithonia is a boisterous, rough-and-ready plant with flowers rather like those of a single dahlia, orange-red in colour with a yellow eye; it's an ideal component of hotter autumn borders. 'Torch' is a little shorter and bushier, while 'Goldfinger', at 90cm/3ft, is even shorter yet still an effective plant. The orange-tinted 'Yellow Torch' seems to have disappeared but may well be the same as 'Sunset' and 'Aztec Gold'.

I was dreading the development of even shorter varieties and now, with the arrival of 'Fiesta del Sol', that most feared prophecy has come to pass. This 30cm/12in tithonia has all the floral elegance of an orange brick – so throw it through the seed company's window. If you need a dwarf cultivar in orange or yellow, please choose a rudbeckia or a marigold.

With so few really substantial seed-raised plants available 'Goldfinger' and 'Torch' are invaluable components of larger annual plantings. Dark-leaved dahlias or amaranthus could go alongside, taller rudbeckias could go in front and canary creeper (*Tropaeolum peregrinum*) could sprawl through. 'Goldfinger' would look very fine with *Mina lobata*, but, as it is not sufficiently robust to take the mina's weight, the climber would have to be planted on a fence behind and trail forward into the tithonia.

Such is the vigour of tithonias that they're best sown in early spring, pricked out into 7cm/3in pots, then moved into 12.5cm/5in pots so that the roots never become too restricted; they will branch if not crowded in their early stages. In exposed sites, stake the main stem, as the broad leaves catch the wind effectively.

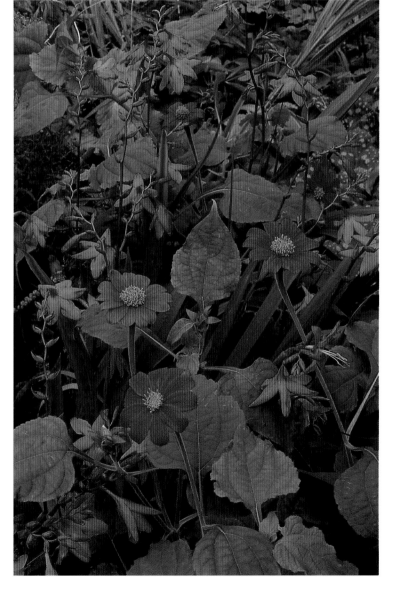

LEFT *'Goldfinger', one of the shorter tithonias, is planted here around an established clump of the large-flowered* Crocosmia *'Star of the East' and creates an unexpected harmony of flower colours, together with an intriguing contrast in foliage. The tithonia will continue to flower well into the autumn and also become increasingly bushy, so hiding the ragged end-of-season leaves of the crocosmia after its flowers are over.*

# *Tropaeolum* Nasturtium and Canary Creeper

Nasturtium . . . many people feel this is a word which sounds a little suspect. Like Battenburg cake, council house and antimacassar there was a time in Britain not so long ago when the more snobbish amongst us looked down on all these – and sneered. Some still do. Across the Atlantic, of course, things are different. There's a more egalitarian, less class-ridden attitude to cake, housing, furnishing and plants, and nasturtiums are accepted for what they are – valuable, if unexpectedly fussy plants.

The climbing sorts seem least particular; these are the most closely related to their South American ancestors and they certainly can grow. In recent years we've been limited to those with such dispiriting names as 'Climbing Mixed', but a few remain from their Victorian heyday, including the pale lemon 'Moonlight' and 'Jewel of Africa' with its marbled leaves.

If you start them off in 7cm/3in pots and plant under evergreen hedges, the seedlings remain sufficiently starved to give a good account of themselves. Starving is crucial: feed them and water them as you do your family when they come for Christmas and they'll react in the same way; they'll expand heartily, then begin to look rather green . . . and their less appealing characteristics will emerge.

It's always said that, given conditions which are too rich, nasturtiums produce leaves at the expense of flowers. What actually happens is that the petioles, the leaf stems, grow longer than they do in

Tropaeolum *'Whirlybird Scarlet'*

more Spartan conditions so the sandwich-sized leaves simply hide the flowers. At the base of an established hedge or shrub, which will suck up most of the water and nutrients, the balance is often better and the show a fine one. Plant them under a wigwam of canes in a richly manured flower bed and they will romp to the top, a juicy, leafy spire – then a gale will blow them all over.

Bushy nasturtiums are similar: rich fare produces luxuriant leaves. Fortunately their leaves are amongst the most striking of all annuals but the flowers will still be hidden if the soil is too rich. If you add humus to the soil in your flower bed, leave some soil unimproved; if you spread fertilizer, leave an area untreated. Then make a sign: here be nasturtiums.

Breeders have been aiming for bushy varieties which hold their flowers above their leaves, even in rich conditions. The Whirlybird Series is the best so far, the flowers spurless and held up to face the viewer. 'Alaska Mixed' is second class in this respect – but its speckled foliage is superb; 'Tutti Frutti' has a better blend of

ABOVE LEFT *In spite of the mass of fluted yellow provided by the 'Primrose Jewel' nasturtiums, doesn't this simple combination have a quiet coolness about it? The flowers of* Nemesia *'Bluebird', brightly contrasting in colour yet content to be overwhelmed in scale, mingle with the nasturtium in a quietly confident way, so different from the brashness of much annual planting.*

flower colours. The old dark-leaved varieties also score more on foliage than habit; the wonderful 'Empress of India' is the only variety which is far more dependably bushy.

All this talk of strong and luxuriant growth might lead you to believe that nasturtiums are easy to grow; but no, they're martyrs to pests. Black aphids, leaf miners, flea beetle plus pea and bean weevil can all be devastating – and nasturtiums are also unexpectedly sensitive to many insecticides. I now use a systemic insecticide every week – but at half strength to prevent the leaves being damaged. It works.

ABOVE LEFT *Perhaps the best hosts for annual climbers are other climbers. Here,* Clematis × jouiniana, *with its dark foliage and blue-tinted white flowers, supports the long trails of canary creeper,* Tropaeolum peregrinum. *The spikes of red buds and creamy flowers of* Mina lobata *are perhaps more striking.* Mina *may need heat to start it off but it's worth the effort.*

ABOVE *With the red blotch, the old-style 'Peach Melba' and the pure-yellow of 'Primrose Jewel' sprawl through the delicate grey* Senecio viravira. *The clean lines of the neatly dissected senecio foliage are set against the rounded nasturtiums and the speckled leaves of* Tolmiea menziesii *'Taff's Gold'.*

# Verbena *Verbena*

Verbenas are a surprisingly mixed bunch. Most are neat and perhaps even a little blocky in habit, although few are so tight and rigid as to exclude their inquisitive neighbours from intermingling to create happy associations. The one unexpectedly tall and wirily slender species is also a blender by nature. And verbenas boast both rich velvet shades and cool pastels.

The Sandy, Novalis and Romance Series, forms of *Verbena* x *hybrida*, all are compact and rather upright, 25–30cm/10–12in high, with flowers gathered in a horizontal plane at the top of the plant; all are susceptible to mildew (though spraying usually works) and they germinate poorly. However, the colour range is superb, especially in the Romance Series, and the colours so cool or intoxicating that they beg indulgence.

The palest lavender pink of 'Romance Lavender' is delightful with the sympathetic silvery trails of *Plecostachys serpyllifolia*. The Quartz Series boasts the best germination; 'Quartz Burgundy' is a distinctive deep shade, great with the yellow-veined leaves of *Pelargonium* 'Crocodile' or the deep purple-leaved shiso, *Perilla frutescens* 'Atropurpurea'; *Verbena* 'Blue Lagoon', by far the best blue, also appreciates this sultry purple-leaved neighbour. 'Peaches and Cream' has a unique colouring and is lovely with *Phlox* 'Cream Beauty'; interplanted with the dainty *Platystemon californicus*, which peeps out amongst the flower heads, it's a treat. But its germination is especially poor.

*Verbena* 'Imagination', derived from *Verbena tenuisecta*, is an award-winning plant with an arching, spreading habit, finely dissected foliage, clouds of smaller, deep purple flowers and less mildew. It's stunning with the dainty yellow buttons of *Sanvitalia procumbens* running through it.

'Polaris', a form of *V. rigida*, is probably the prettiest colour of all verbenas – a warmly icy, soft lilac-blue – but is difficult to find in catalogues. Although reaching 30–35cm/ 12–14in, 'Polaris' is less congested than the more widespread bedding types and makes a cool combination with small blue hostas like 'Hadspen Heron'. Its progenitor, *V. rigida* (often listed as *V. venosa*), may be familiar from municipal displays; interplanted with red geraniums it creates a shimmering purple haze above the bright scarlet flowers. This works even better on a more intimate scale.

The cooler counterpart of those colours is 'Polaris' in concert with 'Vogue Appleblossom' geraniums.

The most fashionable verbena amongst plantsmen is *V. bonariensis*. Stiff and absolutely vertical, it makes 1.2–1.5m/4–5ft with its purple flowers gathered at the top. This is a good perennial in many areas but flowers well in its first year from seed. It's superb set at the very front of a border where you look through it like a sparse curtain to the plantings behind, or at the back interplanted with tall and fiery red-hot pokers, *Kniphofia* 'Prince Igor'. Sow the dainty yellow *Tropaeolum peregrinum* to clamber through them all. Once you have it you always will, for *V. bonariensis* self-sows freely. In addition, this is the one verbena which germinates easily.

Verbena *'Peaches and Cream'*

Germination is a problem with most verbenas owing to the almost impermeable waxy layer immediately under the seed coat. But to try and compensate by keeping the seed moist is a mistake, as verbena seed germinates poorly in damp compost. Instead, prepare the seed pots and water the compost the day before sowing. Then sow the seed and cover either with vermiculite or dry seed compost and keep it in the dark at 18–21°C/65–70°F until germination; higher temperatures can also be inhibiting. Keep relatively dry until the seedlings are growing well.

BELOW *Intermingling plants works as well with tall, substantial varieties as it does with more compact types, provided enough space is available. Here,* Nicotiana sylvestris *has been interplanted with* Verbena bonariensis, *the wiry stems of the verbena standing out against the nicotiana's broad foliage, and the haze of purple enlivened by the glints of the white flowers of the tobacco plant. 'Purity' or 'Pied Piper Red' cosmos also make good companions.*

# *Viola* **Pansy and Violet**

We all have an urge to deal with large quantities of information by organizing and classifying it. We group together material which has clearly distinguishable common features and separate it from other groups with different factors in common. If only it were that simple with pansies and violas.

Of course, they all have the same distinctive flower structure. Unfortunately, they vary so much in their other features, and have so many intermediates, that classifying them is almost impossible. True, it is possible to correlate four main features: flower size, leaf size, degree of branching and rate of flower production. As a rule, large flowers go with large leaves, sparse branching and a modest rate of flower production; small flowers go with small leaves, repeated branching and prolific flowering.

But it's the vast range of in-betweens which muddle the issue between the larger pansies and the smaller violas. With terms like Mini-pansy, Miniola, Large-flowered Viola and Small-flowered Pansy blurring the edges between what were once clearly distinct groups, it's best to invoke some personal criteria, the better to reduce the range to manageable proportions.

First, I must exclude most of those primarily intended for summer flowering. We have enough flowers for summer and too few for spring, so

Viola *'Padparadja' with* Tulipa *'Giuseppe Verdi'*

Viola *'Jackanapes'*

transforming pansies from their natural spring-flowering period into summer flowers is to be discouraged. The Imperial and Banner series are therefore excluded, in spite of the subtle and startling colour combinations in the former. Let's also exclude those boasting flowers larger than those of the familiar Universal Plus and Ultima series (about 5cm/2in). Large flowers are a disadvantage in pansies: they're disproportionate to the size of the plant on which they're carried and the tissue of the petals is often insufficiently robust to support their weight; the edges collapse, giving the flowers a ragged look. So the Super Majestic Colossal Giants (I kid you not), Crown, Royal, Happy Face, Majestic, Mammoth Giants and Atlas series are all excluded. I feel better already.

Most pansies and violas are produced in series, some of which, like the Ultima Series, can run to almost thirty colours. Catalogues tend to offer either mixtures of all the colours in the series, or colour-themed mixtures selected from the series, such as the pastel 'Ultima Silhouette', plus a few exceptional separate colours. I would always urge that you choose separates so that you can plan colour associations more carefully. Pansies and violas often feature faces, blotches, eyes or whiskers in contrasting colours, enabling fluid and inclusive plant

Viola *'Bowles' Black'*

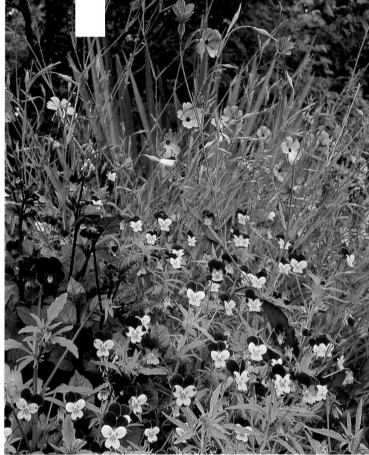

groupings to be created. This ability to create links with other plants in two colour ranges is invaluable.

Catalogues list individual colours from larger series as well as one-offs. 'Springtime Lemon Splash', in pale lemon with a blotch in deep blackcurrant-purple, is unique in its colouring; slipped amongst a permanent planting of larger daffodils like 'King Midas' and dark-leaved *Heuchera* 'Stormy Seas', it creates an invaluable cohesion.

Older one-offs like the bicoloured yellow and purple 'Jacka-napes', named after Gertrude Jekyll's pet monkey, tend to be much looser, even sprawling in habit. 'Jackanapes' will scramble up into a purple cut-leaved maple or over and around the emerging shoots of *Cryptotaenia japonica* f. *atropurpurea* to make delightful combin-ations. The almost black 'Midnight Runner', an improved version of the old 'Bowles' Black', is pretty set amongst the bright yellow leaves of *Lysimachia nummularia* 'Aurea' or white grape hyacinths.

ABOVE LEFT *Early in the summer season, this 'Fanfare White Blotch' pansy is little more than a tufty little plant amongst the overwintered heliotrope and the steadily increasing 'The Crocodile' ivy-leaved geranium. But as the season advances, the pansy will fill out just as the bare stems of the geranium and heliotrope would otherwise become obtrusive, and that bare middle ground will be filled with sympathetic colour, the delicate purple face of the pansy picking up the colour in the flower of the heliotrope.*

ABOVE *This swarm of the slightly variable* Viola tricolor *'Johnny Jump Up' is close to the wild species whose blood is in all these pansies and violas. Its consistent purple element connects it with similar shades in the dark-leaved dahlia and, in a paler range, Silene 'Rose Angel'. Sometimes listed under* Viscaria, *these latter are easy and underrated annuals for direct sowing whose colours have been improved in recent years. Silene 'Cherry Blossom', in white-eyed rose-pink, is especially pretty.*

LEFT *Self-sown viola seedlings can be invaluable. If you don't mind their unpredictability you can let them loose amongst the stems of* Allium cristophii *and with the almost imperceptible clouds of* Agrostis nebulosa, *the more solid yet decidedly lacy* Artemisia alba *'Canescens' dispatching its steadily running roots amongst the whole planting until the allium is set against silver and the violas mingle in front. With careful thinning of the flower colours, year by year you can manipulate the shades of the violas.*

ABOVE *Looking in close often gives you an entirely new view. The dark stems and foliage of* Anthriscus sylvestris *'Ravenswing' stretch to 90cm–1.2m/3–4ft in height but, down at the base, the 'Ultima Pink Shades' pansy is just the right colour to create a little gleam amongst those dark stems and leaves, without a stark contrast.*

Most violas will trail if given the opportunity; truly trailing types are the next development. The tiny yellow 'Sunbeam' is delightful in a basket, though hardly flamboyant, and also makes a very pretty ground cover with the tiniest of purple crocus, *C. sieberi* 'Violet Queen' perhaps, peeping through. Look for its larger-flowered successors like 'Purple Rain'.

The Ultima, Universal Plus, Springtime and Challenge series flower in the autumn and mild spells in winter, and are at their peak in spring; the mixtures are far easier to find than separates. Simply filling a windowbox or trough with a sparkling mixture can be very cheerful but since plants will often be carrying their first flowers at planting time you can select by colour for more thoughtful planting. For example, pick out the blue and white bicoloured 'Ultima Marina' or 'Universal Plus Marina' to go with a blend of blue and white *Muscari azureum*.

But the smaller the flowers, the better I like them, and the easier they are to accommodate with dwarf bulbs and spring perennials. While 'Fanfare', described as a Large-flowered Viola or a Floribunda Pansy, and 'Velour', described as a Mini-pansy, may have some superb individual colours, neither has as wide a range as the smaller-flowered Sorbet Series of violas, whose twelve colours, many in delightful combinations, are perfect with dwarf bulbs. This series is a triumph. 'Sorbet Blueberry Cream', with its continuous succession of neat flowers in pale lavender blue with gold on the lower lip and short dark whiskers, could be set amongst *Crocus tommasinianus*; 'Sorbet Blackberry Cream' has purple edges to a white flower and a neat yellow eye which makes *Narcissus* 'Hawera' an ideal companion.

There is, though, one difficulty in growing pansies and violas for autumn and spring: seed must be sown in early summer. This may seem very convenient as space will be available after all the summer flowers are planted. But pansies germinate poorly in high temperatures and keeping them cool is difficult. A temperature of 15–18°C/60–65°F is ideal; germination drops off above 18°C/65°F, so choose a cool shady place outside for the seed pots. Rich compost can also cause problems, so use a specific seed compost, rather than a multipurpose type which contains more nutrients, and soak it well with fungicide the day before sowing as a protection against damping off.

Move the seed pots into good light as soon as the seeds germinate, as they can stretch quickly, and prick out into trays or 6cm/2½in pots to grow on. Overwatering leads to a loose and flabby plant, so be cautious, and keep the plants cool – they can be stood outside once established in their pots. An occasional low-nitrogen liquid feed is useful.

RIGHT *Nestling at the front of this spring border, at the base of a taller planting of perennials,* Viola *'Baby Lucia', one of the first of the modern seed-raised violas, is set around the emerging shoots of the perennial* Lobelia *'Queen Victoria'. Alongside, recently planted and just taking hold, is purple-leaved basil. This harmony of colouring, created from a disparate group of plants and set against a green background, is typical of imaginative small garden planting.*

171

# *Zinnia* **Zinnia**

It may be tempting to skip this entry, for the reputation of the zinnia as a difficult and unpredictable plant is a familiar horticultural hand-me-down, but don't be misled. The truth is that this reputation was, once, partly justified; but no more.

The flamboyant larger-flowered cultivars were regularly defeated by wet summers; in the warmer summers of the turn of the twentieth century they've become more successful. Of these larger types, the Dasher and Oklahoma series are undeniably spectacular, the purity of their colours unrivalled. The striped 'Candy Cane' and 'Scabious Flowered Mixed' are less impressive.

Smaller-flowered zinnias, more closely related to the wild species, such as the daintier *Zinnia peruviana*, and looking far more relaxed than the familiar, stiff and starchy large-flowered types, have always been easier to grow. Sadly, when these more delicate cultivars are seen in gardens, the news that they're zinnias is often enough to deter prospective growers.

But no one could despise the petite 23cm/9in Star Series. In orange, yellow, white and the 'Starbright' mixture they're easy to grow, tolerate drought, flower for months and they have an unusually open habit, so make companionable neighbours with camissonias and small linarias such as 'Gemstones'.

'Persian Carpet' sits between the small-flowered *Zinnia peruviana* and the Star Series in plant and flower size; its neat double flowers come in warm, exotic yellows, golds, orange and rust shades with some maroon, plum, white and rose in a huge range of colour combinations. It thrives on sowing direct in a sunny place, and for dry banks is supreme.

As the supposed problems of raising zinnias still deter many gardeners from growing them, the technique deserves discussion. In general, sowing seed where the

plants are to flower is usually more successful than sowing in pots and pricking out; the lack of disturbance seems to ensure better establishment. Delay sowing until about a week or two before the last frost date in your area. Sow in damp drills (see page 177), placing the conveniently large seeds 5–7.5cm/2–3in apart, then thinning them out as advised on the seed packet. All groups respond well to this simple approach.

You will need to sow indoors, where the rate of growth during the summer months may not allow a sufficiently long period of flowering, or outdoors, where you need to place them precisely in the border amongst established plants. This requires care. Zinnia seedlings, especially those of the larger-flowered, more flamboyant kinds, are notorious – show them a mere molecule of damping-off disease and they keel over like the bridegroom on his stag night. Do not use 100% peat composts, improve the drainage by adding up to 50% perlite and restore the nutrient balance by mixing in granules of all-season container feed.

It's important to keep the plants growing strongly; avoiding root disturbance is crucial. Sow the seeds singly in individual cells of compost and germinate at 21°C/70°F. Watering from below is best and keep the seedlings well ventilated. As soon as the compost in the cells is sufficiently full of roots to hold together, move the plugs on into 9cm/3½in pots, setting the surface of the cell a little above the compost in the pot. This ensures that the base of the seedling does not

Zinnia peruviana

RIGHT *The smaller-flowered zinnias like this 'Persian Carpet' are amongst the most adaptable, partly because they're variable but within a clearly confined colour range. Here, with* Tagetes signata *'Lulu' and the neat poms of* Lonas annua *at front and back, they add depth to a basically yellow planting.*

become too wet and so is less likely to rot. Water from below again, so that the surface of the compost remains the driest.

Before the pot fills with roots, either move the plants on into 12.5cm/5in pots for later planting or plant out. After planting out, soak them thoroughly then leave them unwatered. The natural vigour of the plants should then ensure that the roots establish well.

Problems could still arise at a later stage, especially in cool, damp summers and when growth is slow. Rainwater collects amongst the petals of the larger, fully double flowers and the result is botrytis infection; this also attacks the neck immediately behind the flower, causing the stem to fold and the flower to flop. In long damp spells botrytis may also attack at the points on the stems where they branch, sometimes leading to a greater part of the plant collapsing.

All these symptoms are at their most prevalent in the large-flowered, fully double types, and spraying with an appropriate

ABOVE LEFT *A new take on formal bedding . . . Pelargonium 'Multibloom Salmon' is grown by the thousand all over the world, but only at Landesgartenschau at Böblingen in Germany would they think to combine it with Zinnia 'Dreamland Coral' – and not just combine it, but interplant it. The zinnias must be well grown; if too many fail (as they so often do) the display is ruined, but here it captures the eye and inspires admiration.*

ABOVE *Backing these Persian Carpet zinnias with plants from the bigger and brighter Oklahoma Series makes a sparkling but not overwhelming combination. In front are the yellow buttons of Lonas annua with occasional clumps of the rich, egg-yolk yellow of Coreopsis 'Early Sunrise' erupting on their vertical stems.*

fungicide certainly helps. But the smaller-flowered forms are inherently less troublesome. They also have a more natural look, and forthcoming developments will widen the range and make them even more desirable. Start with them.

# *Practicalities*

Whether an annual is hardy or half-hardy depends on whether it can be sown directly outside or must be started indoors first. The range of temperatures at which a plant will germinate well and produce the highest proportion of good seedlings varies from plant to plant. In any given area some annuals must be raised in the warmth of protected conditions whereas some will germinate well when sown outside. While this distinction gives us the two familiar groups – hardy annuals and half-hardy annuals – the boundary between these two groups of plants varies according to where they are grown.

In cooler areas many plants such as nicotianas and zinnias must be treated as half-hardy and sown in cosy conditions in a greenhouse or propagator, while in warmer regions they can be sown directly outside. A few plants, like cosmos which are normally treated as half-hardy annuals, are sufficiently vigorous to be sown outside later in the spring when soil temperatures have increased.

You can also raise many annuals which are tough enough to be grown outside in the same way as half-hardy annuals to make them available in pots for careful planting in containers or when small numbers are required for intimate plantings with other varieties. A few perfectly tough plants are raised as half-hardy annuals because their seeds are expensive and the packet contains relatively few; the percentage of losses is always higher from seeds sown in the open ground.

## Seed sowing inside

You don't need to have a greenhouse to raise half-hardy annuals: many a successful garden has been planted with annuals raised on a shelf in the kitchen or on the conservatory windowsill. Nevertheless, a greenhouse is still the best environment.

### The greenhouse

Any glass or polythene greenhouse is suitable, with certain provisos: it must have good ventilation and some form of heating, the glass or polythene must be clean, and it should be situated to benefit from the best of the early season light.

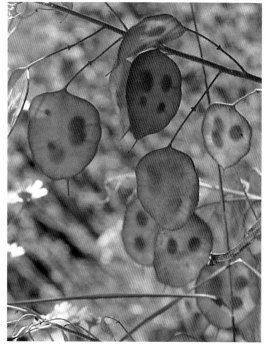

Lunaria annua *seedpods*

For raising more than just a very few plants, the most practical arrangement is to divide the greenhouse into a larger area, which is left unheated or given little more than frost protection, and a smaller area, which is kept warmer. The warm area can house an electric, thermostatically controlled propagator in which to germinate seeds and a second propagator in which to wean the newly germinated seed pots at a slightly lower temperature. From there they can go on to the open greenhouse bench. When raising large numbers of annuals, electric heating mats are invaluable. Always have your electricity supply fitted using waterproof sockets by a qualified electrician. Greenhouses without an electricity supply can be heated by paraffin or bottled gas but take care with your fuels. Bottled gas heaters can be fitted without professional help but be sure to follow the instructions from the manufacturers and bottled gas suppliers. Never let paraffin heaters run low as they may fill the greenhouse with smoke.

Good shading and ventilation are vital for those spring and early summer days when the sun is strong, and you need a supply of clean mains water, not a rainwater butt, for watering. Ideally, you should fit benches with a capillary watering system to ensure that pots and trays stay constantly moist and can conveniently be left without attention.

### In the house

Most annuals can adapt to less than perfect conditions indoors but it helps if the temperature is constant and the light is good. Most plants don't need light in the first week or two before the seedlings emerge. Some gardeners use an airing cupboard to provide warmth, but temperatures here can be damagingly high and seedlings must be checked frequently and removed the moment they peep through. A propagator in a warm place is the most practical idea.

In the house or conservatory, where light may be highly directional, turn the propagator with its seedlings, or the young plants, frequently, so that all receive equal amounts of light from each side; uneven light encourages lank and unbalanced growth.

The most difficult problems arise from dealing with inadequate and strongly directional light, and from trying to fit pots and trays on to shelves and windowsills and other makeshift spaces.

### Timing – summer annuals

The timing of seed sowing is a tricky subject. When a delay of three weeks in sowing can make the difference between a variety flowering well and hardly flowering at all, the differences in climate between Cornwall and the Scottish Highlands and the variation in conditions from one year to another make it impossible to give specific advice on the best time to sow a particular variety. Most half-hardy annuals are sown in March or April, although begonias and geraniums benefit from an earlier sowing. Start by following advice on the seed packet, perhaps making adjustments according to your local practice, then adapt in the light of experience and of extremes in seasonal conditions.

Each plant, sometimes even each variety of a plant, will flower or reach a particular size in a certain length of time from sowing under particular conditions. So, tuberous begonias, for example, should be amongst the first of your seeds to be sown in late winter or early spring; marigolds grow faster so can be sown later.

The size of the plant you need can also influence sowing time. For large tubs in prominent positions, where an instant effect is a great advantage, substantial plants in flower at planting time are preferable to younger, smaller plants still waiting to flower.

There's another way of looking at it: early sowing demands extra heat to ensure that the best use is made of the additional time. This extra heat, in the coldest season, is expensive. Planning a careful succession of varieties can minimize this expense. Unfortunately, early sowings are also the most difficult – light levels are low, days are short and cosy growing space may be limited; so careful daily attention is required to ensure that they thrive. Keep in mind also that if seeds are sown too early, plants will be ready to plant out before conditions in the garden allow it, so they must either be potted on, occupying additional valuable space, or they will become increasingly pot bound and so need more frequent watering and additional feeding. This will mean they have problems establishing when they finally go outside.

If you sow seeds too late, the plants may still be small at planting time; not having grown sufficiently to thrive outdoors, they will flower late and perhaps be unable to hold their own against more established plants in the rough and tumble of the border.

### Pots and trays

Forget about seed trays. Long gone, except in the largest of gardens, are the days when seeds were sown in seed trays. What is the point of filling a whole seed tray with seeds that you don't really need, or spacing out the few you *do* need to fill an unnecessarily large area? It's simply a waste of space.

If you use 7cm/3in square plastic pots instead, you'll fit fifteen pots in the space occupied by a standard seed tray – and even sixteen large dahlia seeds will fit comfortably into a single pot, so you'll usually only need the one pot for each variety.

### Compost

Never sow seeds in pots of garden soil. In the unnatural habitat of a pot in a propagator, the micro- (and not so micro-) organisms in soil multiply quickly and many of them will attack seeds and seedlings. Garden soil also drains poorly in containers and this exacerbates disease problems.

Of course, there's always the occasional gardener who raises a superb batch of fibrous-rooted begonias in solid clay left over from excavating the foundations for the new garage – but opening the oven door is not an essential element of baking technique simply because the sponge didn't sink the first time you took a look. Use fresh compost from the garden centre.

Garden centre seed and multipurpose composts are very variable. Coir-based composts in particular vary dramatically from one brand to another, and there hasn't been enough research yet into how best to formulate and use them. Soil-based composts should not be used for most annuals. So, although environmental concerns prompt us to keep searching for substitutes, peat-based composts are still the most dependable.

It's often tempting to add extra drainage material to all-peat composts; I've done it myself: adding 25% perlite was my normal practice. But by adding drainage material, the feed incorporated in the compost is distributed more thinly through a greater volume, and I came to the conclusion that this disadvantage was not outweighed by any extra leeway in watering.

It is, however, crucial to leave the peat-based compost almost entirely unfirmed – over-firming can close the natural water drainage channels in the compost so it quickly becomes waterlogged. The dreaded damping-off disease is then more likely to attack; firmed compost is also more difficult to rewet once it has dried out. So if you're a determined firmer and cannot change the habits of a lifetime, by all means add 25% perlite or grit – but be sure you liquid feed your young seedlings from when they first appear.

### Sowing seed in pots

Make sure the compost is moist, then fill your seed pot loosely, tap it smartly a few times on a hard surface to settle it and wipe off any compost standing above the rim of the pot using a plant label, or something similar. Then use the bottom of another pot, or a purpose-made presser, to firm and level the compost very gently.

Cut the top off the seed packet with a pair of scissors. You'll often find a smaller packet or foil sachet inside: snip the top off this too. Don't sow all the seeds in the packet simply because they're there; consider how many plants you need.

Keep in mind too that seeds are much less likely to rot if given space to develop from the start, so sow thinly. It's impossible to be precise about this as seeds vary so much in their size and rate of development; usually the packet will give guidance. But err on the side of wide spacing and use two or even three separate pots if you need a large quantity of one variety, rather than try to cram them all into one pot.

The 'tap from the packet' method is my preferred seed-sowing technique as it combines precision and control. First, make a crease halfway along one cut edge of the seed packet. Next, hold the edges of the packet between the thumb and second finger, tilt the packet slightly, and tap the edge of the packet gently with the index finger. You can then watch the seed drop off the cut edge on to the compost and adjust the rate of tapping and the movement of the packet to give an even spread. Large seeds like marigolds and zinnias can be sown individually by hand.

After sowing, cover all but the finest seed with seed compost. Shake the compost through a coarse sieve made from a piece of fine mesh plastic netting tacked to a simple wooden frame; the mesh of a wire kitchen sieve is too fine. Cover the seeds with their own depth of compost; the finest seeds like begonias and lobelia are better left uncovered until germination begins and then given a light dusting of compost. Finally, label the pot with the name of the plant and the date plus, if you like, the name of the seed company.

It's often suggested that, after sowing, pots be stood in a tray of water to allow them to soak up moisture from below without disturbing the seeds on the surface. I find that as the surplus water drains away, the compost shrinks from the sides of the pot so that later, when you water from above, both water and seed wash down the gap at the side. A small watering can, fitted with a fine rose and used carefully, is best.

### Germination

Place the pots in the propagator and cover with newspaper, brown paper or a couple of sheets of greenhouse shade netting. Check every day for germination: marigolds take only a few days, lobelia takes much longer. As soon as the first tiny shoots are evident, uncover the pot to give the seedlings maximum light. It pays to cover the pots individually so that each can be uncovered as its seed germinates, leaving the rest covered. Better still, move the pots of germinating seeds into a second propagator and put more pots of freshly sown seed in the first.

After germination, the temperature can be reduced slightly. The next stage is pricking out – moving the developing seedlings to give them more space to grow naturally without competition from their neighbours.

### Pricking out

The correct stage for pricking out is usually said to be when the seedlings are large enough to handle. This is a good general guide, although it's fair to say that plants with tiny seedlings, like begonias and lobelia, will always be more difficult to handle than the larger seedlings of cosmos and calendula. Again, pots are better than seed trays for pricking out. I transfer individual seedlings into 6cm/2½ square pots, 7cm/3in pots for more vigorous varieties. Individual pots give the seedlings more compost into which to grow without competition and they can be removed for planting without root disturbance. It's also easier to fit small individual pots into a confined space.

Fill the pots in the same way as for seed sowing (see above). Prepare all the pots for each variety at the same time, but do not firm at all. Then carefully remove the compost and seedlings from the seed pot by sliding it out on to a hard surface and break up the compost with your fingers to loosen the seedlings.

Using a dibber or an old pencil, make a deep hole in the centre of the first pricking-out pot. Lift a good strong seedling from its compost, holding it gently by its leaves and never by its stem, then slide it into the hole so that its lowest pair of seed leaves rests on the compost. Tap the pot sharply on a hard surface to allow the compost to settle.

When you've planted each batch of seedlings, water in well with a liquid feed in the water; this will complete the settling of the compost around the seedling. Do not firm the compost, as this damages fragile roots and leads to poor drainage and damping-off disease.

An increasing number of annuals are now bought as seedlings or plugs. This eliminates the tricky germination phase and allows inexperienced growers, or those with no special facilities, to raise annuals. Seedlings dispatched by post are often of better quality than those bought from garden centres and usually come with excellent instructions.

**Growing on**

Once settled, the seedlings can be grown in cooler conditions; this not only saves on the cost of heating but encourages root development rather than leafy legginess. After about six weeks, when the plant food content of most composts has been exhausted, regular liquid feeding will be necessary; a tomato fertilizer is ideal. Avoid high-nitrogen feeds which cause lank growth.

Try to keep the plants uniformly moist. If you're concerned that they might become too spindly or too large, keep them slightly dry, but without letting them actually dry out, as this has been shown to reduce growth and increase bushiness; however, this is a technique which calls for delicate balancing.

Vigorous plants, like the taller nicotianas, asters and zinnias as well as cosmos, chrysanthemums and other naturally strong-growing plants, including climbers, may need potting on as they develop to ensure that they have sufficient room. Move them into 10cm/4in or 12.5cm/5in pots as necessary. There is often a temptation to pinch out the tips of seedlings to encourage bushiness but, while this can be helpful with less highly developed species, modern $F_1$ hybrids are bred to branch and require no pinching. Best of all, if facilities are available, simply space the plants more widely on the bench or windowsill as this in itself will encourage branching.

Some plants may need support. Tall nicotianas, cosmos and chrysanthemums need a single split cane with a couple of ties. Climbers like ipomoeas and eccremocarpus are more difficult, as they can quickly become unwieldy with wands waving all over the place, and a single cane is often insufficient. A cane in each corner of a 12.5cm/5in square pot allows the stems to be wound round and tied in; any that become uncontrollable can simply be shortened.

**Hardening off**

One of the most critical stages in raising half-hardy annuals is the transition from a protected environment to planting outside. The process, known as hardening off, involves acclimatizing the plants to increasingly cool temperatures so that they eventually cope with life in the outside world. This transition is most difficult to manage when plants are raised in the house without special facilities. A divided greenhouse (see page 175) is the most practical environment. The cooler growing area can be ventilated increasingly freely from three to four weeks before planting out, then the plants can be moved outside from a constantly fully ventilated greenhouse area.

In the house, plants can be moved from the windowsill in a warm room to a cooler one; they can then be moved to a cool sun room or a porch – but taking the plants straight from warm, cosy conditions and planting them outside can be fatal.

A cold frame was once an invaluable help in the hardening-off process but, as gardeners have realized that a basic greenhouse can often be bought for the price of a cold frame which covers a smaller area, they've become less popular. However, in gardens where there's no space for a greenhouse, or where one would be aesthetically unsatisfactory, a timber-sided, glass-topped frame is very useful – and can be used for growing melons once the annuals are planted!

## *Seed sowing outside*

The plants most frequently sown outside are hardy annuals, those which can germinate and grow in cool conditions, like alyssum and nigella. You can sow plants which are less cold-tolerant such as cosmos outside, but you will need to sow them later in the spring than hardy annuals. Both these groups are almost invariably sown where they are to flower. Biennials like wallflowers and sweet William are also sown outside, but in summer, and are usually moved to their flowering positions in autumn.

**Conditions**

Most hardy and half-hardy annuals should be sown in an open sunny place where they will flower best. They grow well in any soil which is not too heavy and waterlogged; their seedlings especially dislike wet soil. In wet conditions, create a friable soil structure and firm cautiously.

Biennials, which will be moved on to their final flowering place, need a fertile soil which holds together well – the fact that the vegetable garden is so often suggested as a good location for them indicates the right kind of soil.

**Timing – hardy and half-hardy annuals**

Being specific about when to sow is difficult, as this varies enormously from region to region according to the climate. Observing when self-sown seedlings germinate in your own garden can provide a good practical guide, as can the seed packets from your favourite seed company.

Seed packets often give a range of sowing times, e.g. March to May or September to November, and this helps in two ways. It indicates that in relatively mild areas the plants will develop well from an early sowing, while in colder areas it's wise to wait; but it also shows that a late sowing will still have time to develop and flower before the season ends.

### Timing – biennials

Biennials are usually sown in early summer: wallflowers, daisies and sweet William in the open ground; pansies, violas, primroses and polyanthus in pots. My experience, especially in smaller gardens, is that all biennials are best started in pots.

In areas where plants set out in autumn may be damaged by severe winter weather (cold or wet), spring planting can be more successful. In this case, I recommend delaying sowing by another month (or more).

### Preparing the soil

Soil for sowing should be fertile, though not rich; never add compost or manure immediately before sowing or in the previous autumn, unless the soil is in especially poor heart. Many annuals grow naturally in relatively impoverished conditions and, while richer fare will certainly produce more prolific and long-lasting flowers, there is a danger of promoting growth which is *too* lush with relatively sparse flower production. Use a balanced general fertilizer cautiously before sowing, never a high-nitrogen feed.

### Sowing in position

Ensure that the area where the seeds are to be sown is both weed-free and open in texture by forking the soil over to the depth of a border fork (sometimes called a lady's fork!) and removing any weed roots. If you need to improve the soil, fork in organic mater at this stage – old potting compost or any fine-grade, bagged soil improver is best as the nutrient levels will not be too high and the fine texture will mix easily with the soil. Firm the area well to eliminate any air pockets then rake level, removing stones, sticks and other debris.

It's always best to sow seeds in rows. You can then cover them with soil from between the rows without disturbing other seeds and they will germinate in distinct lines – anything not in a row is therefore clearly a weed. As the plants develop, the lines will disappear.

Check the seed packet or catalogue for instructions as to spacing and depth of sowing.

Use the tip of a cane, the corner of a rake or a dibber to make small furrows (drills) in the soil as wide apart and as deep as recommended for the particular variety; if in doubt, give more space rather than less, and less depth rather than more. If the soil is dry, carefully water along the drill with the spout of a watering can, using your thumb over the spout to control the water flow. This will provide a reservoir of moisture for the young seedlings.

Open the packet as described above (page 177) and use the same technique to sow the seeds; move the packet along the drill watching the seeds drop into the soil and ensuring that spacing is even. You can sow large seeds like zinnias or sweet peas individually to ensure the necessary spacing. Use the back of the rake to draw soil over the seeds from the side of the drills, then use the flat of the rake to gently firm the soil on top.

You can sow sunflowers and other tall annuals in clusters of three rather than in rows; after germination retain only the most vigorous seedling. Since biennials will eventually be transplanted into their flowering positions elsewhere, you can simply sow them in straight rows in the vegetable garden or any bright corner.

Immediately after germination, remove weeds from between the rows – by hoeing if the rows are sufficiently widely spaced, otherwise by hand. You must also remove weeds from within the rows, by hand, and you can remove (thin) crowded seedlings at the same time. Check the seed packet or catalogue for advice on the final spacing. Thin first to one quarter of the eventual spacing; then, a few weeks later, reduce the number of seedlings to half those eventually required; then the last thinning can be to the final spacing.

## *Planting out*

Most plants raised as half-hardy annuals should be planted out as soon as possible after your last frosts. In some ways, of course, this is a preposterous recommendation: how can you possibly know which frost is the last? Your experience, and that of your neighbours, will guide you but it's worth remembering that the lie of the land and the configuration of the garden can make a significant impact on where the last light frosts actually bite. In general, the last week of May is safe in most areas, although in colder parts of the country and cold gardens, allowing an extra week or two is advisable. In some warm gardens, plants can go out in early May. It's also worth remembering that some plants are more frost resistant than others: antirhinnums, for example, are tougher than begonias.

Biennials are usually put out in late September or early October. The problem at this end of the season is that summer flowers may still be looking good, but biennials must be allowed time to establish before winter; sometimes you may have to be ruthless to make room for them.

### Preparation

In general, half-hardy annuals can take richer conditions than hardy annuals but the soil preparation can be the same as for sowing hardy annuals (see page 179). In some cases, you may want to plant your pot-raised half-hardys singly or in small groups amongst other plants so you should prepare individual planting places.

To prepare the plants, gather them together after hardening off and give them a generous liquid feed to help them develop new root growth promptly.

### Planting

Whether you're planting a few single plants, or a whole display devoted entirely to annuals, set out all the plants in position in their pots before planting any of them. Then take a step back, and consider whether they really are in their best positions. Once you have settled on where, exactly, they are to go, small plants can be planted with a trowel, while you may find it easier to plant those in larger pots with a spade. After planting, water each plant with more liquid feed – much of which will soak into the soil beneath the plant ready for when its roots start to stretch.

Plant pot-raised biennials as above. Those raised in the open should be lifted carefully with as much soil as possible on their roots and moved quickly to their flowering positions. In spring schemes, always plant the biennials first and bulbs afterwards – so that you avoid spearing the bulbs with the trowel as you plant the biennials.

## *Aftercare*

Planting annuals in the garden is only the beginning. In an unpredictable climate, their aftercare must be tailored to the season and to the individual requirements of each cultivar as it thrives or languishes. No two seasons are ever quite the same.

### Watering and feeding

Overhead watering can be as brutal as a thunderstorm; using a seephose (soakhose) eliminates this problem and is also far more water-efficient. Put it in place immediately after planting; use it infrequently but leave it on long enough to provide a thorough

soaking. Apart from this, no other feeding or watering should be required during the whole season – unless individual plants are used as gap fillers later in the season, when a thorough drench, or perhaps two, with liquid feed is all that is necessary.

### Support

Climbing annuals obviously require support from trellis, netting, a wigwam of canes or some more elaborate timber or steel support, or they may utilize other plants. It's important that the supports are in place before planting; setting them in afterwards may damage roots. Some other annuals may also require support. The taller nicotianas, cosmos, antirrhinums and annual chrysanthemums, together with cleomes, amaranthus, asters, hollyhocks and sunflowers, may all benefit from support; usually a single cane with two or three ties is sufficient.

In windy or wet areas where shorter plants are subject to damage, plastic pea-and-bean netting spread horizontally and kept taught between canes or stakes is highly effective.

### Dead-heading

Regular and thorough dead-heading makes more impact on a display of annuals than anything else except water. However, some annuals are easier to deal with than others. The flowers of bedding lobelia are almost impossible to dead-head individually; a thorough drench to encourage regrowth followed by a quick snip with the shears is about all that's possible. Plants with larger flowers, like asters, are much simpler and flower-cutting scissors, which grip the stem after cutting, are often easier to use than secateurs.

It's worth taking the trouble to dead-head some seemingly tricky plants thoroughly. Annual phlox, nemesias and linarias all benefit enormously from a little careful attention from the kitchen scissors.

### Pests and diseases

In general, annuals are relatively free of pests and diseases but damping off and aphids are especially troublesome and others may also be damaging.

**Aphids** Aphids, in various shades, are universal. If present in the greenhouse on mature plants these insects will quickly move to the smallest of seedlings; they will also colonize a wide variety of annuals in the garden.

Keeping more mature plants pest-free over the winter is a good first step, as is lining the ventilators with fine mesh to keep insects out. In the garden, useful preventatives include growing plants like buckwheat, *Limnanthes douglasii* and bushy annual convolvulus which all attract hoverflies, the aphid's most voracious predator.

For a spray, I prefer to use one based on pyrimor which kills only aphids and leaves their predators and other insects unharmed.

**Botrytis** This is usually a problem only in wet seasons on double flowers like zinnias, African marigolds and dahlias. A fluffy grey mould grows on the soggy flowers; picking off the damaged flowers promptly is the best cure.

**Capsids** The first signs of infestation are slightly ragged holes in the young leaves at the tips of shoots. As the leaves grow the holes expand with them, creating an increasingly tattered appearance. A systemic insecticide deals with the problem.

**Caterpillars** Many different caterpillars attack many different plants. Columbines and geraniums are often the most severely affected, but the culprit, the victim and the severity vary from garden to garden, region to region. Simply picking caterpillars off can often be treatment enough; otherwise I find *Bacillus thuringiensis* biological control is usually effective.

**Damping off** The main symptom of this destructive disease is the collapse of seedlings at the surface of the compost; the disease usually starts in one area then spreads to the rest of the seedlings. Germinating seeds can also be damaged; they start to germinate, then cease to grow – then rot. There are two main factors which promote infection: poor hygiene and waterlogging.

Always use clean equipment, fresh compost and clean tap water to avoid introducing infection, and avoid overfirming and overwatering. Wash out the watering can regularly with a fungicide known to kill these organisms; not all do – liquid copper is the usual stand-by. This can be watered on to the compost after sowing, during germination and after pricking out.

**Earwigs** Chewed petals on double dahlias and zinnias are often signs of earwig damage. Earwigs hide in dark places during the day so can easily be trapped in rolls of corrugated paper. You can also spray the flowers with insecticide at dusk.

**Leaf miner** Columbines and chrysanthemums are the main victims of these tiny grubs which tunnel under the surface of leaves. You can pick off the unsightly leaves, squash the grubs between thumb and finger, or use a systemic insecticide to deal with them.

**Powdery mildew** A fungus, most common in hot, dry conditions; a white powdery coating appears on the leaves, which turn dry and crisp and then die. Affected plants mainly include zinnias, verbena, alyssum and calendula. Choose resistant varieties when these are available; spray with an appropriate fungicide.

**Red spider mite** A pest of dry climates and dry seasons; pale mottling of the leaves is followed by fine webbing around the plants. In the greenhouse these mites can spread from mature plants to seedlings, and they also occur outside in warmer regions and warmer seasons. Keep the greenhouse atmosphere moist as temperatures rise and use *Phytoseiulus persimilis* biological control.

**Rust** This disease affects only antirrhinums, geraniums and hollyhocks; deep brown or rusty red spots appear on the underside of the foliage, which is soon killed. Rust can wipe out antirrhinums in a couple of weeks; there are no rust-resistant varieties. Always use a preventative fungicide which kills rusts (not all do) on these plants.

**Slugs and snails** These are beasts. In the greenhouse they sneak out in the dead of night and munch through your seedlings, leaving little but flimsy stumps behind. In the garden they will start at one end of a row of seedlings and chomp through to the other – then find the end of the next row and start back the other way. Biological control is partially effective, but expensive; use pellets, but sparingly – a pellet every 10–12.5cm/4–6in is enough.

### Replacements and additions

It's inevitable that there will be casualties after planting. Occasionally a plant may just fade away instead of taking root; slugs and cats can cause losses. Some annuals, like nemesias, are naturally relatively short-lived. In many cases, neighbouring plants will quickly move in and dominate the vacant spaces, though a little encouragement may sometimes be helpful. But it can also be useful to have a few plants in reserve for emergency gap filling.

Any spares left after planting can be moved on into larger pots and kept in a sheltered place outside, and it's also worth making later sowings of particularly quick-growing plants like nemesias, mimulus and linarias – some varieties of the last two will flower in as little as six weeks from sowing and so can be very useful.

### Managing growth

The intimate, intermingling planting schemes featured in this book sometimes require intervention to keep plants from overwhelming each other or to keep their growth in proportion. Snipping off shoots which are upsetting the harmony of the planting rarely leaves an ugly space for long and often the removal of a relatively substantial branch is unnoticed the next day. But it's important to look out for this over-vigorous growth. Nasturtiums, with their dense foliage, cabbages and kales can be smothersome. The removal of a single leaf is often sufficient to give neighbouring plants the light they need.

# Glossary

**Annual** A plant which completes its entire life cycle in one season; e.g. alyssum. Also, a seed-raised, naturally perennial plant whose useful life cycle extends only to one season; e.g. petunia. See also: ephemeral, winter annual.

**Bedding plant** Any plant set out specifically for a spring or summer display then removed; e.g. bellis, geranium.

**Bicolour(ed)** Used to describe a flower in which two colours appear.

**Biennial** A plant which completes its entire life cycle over two seasons; e.g. *Eryngium giganteum*. Seed germinates and the plant establishes during the summer and autumn of its first season, then flowers, sets seed and dies in its second season. Also, naturally perennial plants treated in this way: e.g. wallflower.

**Calyx** The group of small, leaf-like structures enclosing and protecting a flower bud; each segment is known as a sepal.

**Coir** Fibrous material derived from the outer husk of the coconut; used as an environmentally friendly replacement for peat in potting composts but usually less easy to manage. Sometimes known as coconut fibre.

**Cold frame** A low structure usually with solid sides in timber, brick, concrete, steel, aluminium or sometimes plastic with a removable clear top (known as the 'light') in glass or transparent plastic. Provides protection from the most severe weather and used especially for hardening off (see below).

**Cultivar** A distinct special form of a plant which has been selected in cultivation; sometimes confused with 'variety', which is a distinct special form of a plant which is found growing in the wild.

**Damping off** A fungus disease which attacks young seedlings, causing them to collapse and die suddenly (see also page 176).

**Dibber** A slender device for making a planting hole in potting compost or garden soil for large seeds or for seedlings. Usually wood or plastic.

**Drill** A shallow furrow in garden soil made with a cane or the corner of the rake and along which seeds are sown.

**Ephemeral** An annual plant with a very short life cycle, often weeks. Usually a weed.

**Eye** The centre of a flower, in colour often contrasting with the rest of the flower.

**$F_1$ hybrid** (In this context) the result of crossing, often by hand, two specially selected and highly bred parents. The resultant plants are uniform, often very prolific. Most familiar bedding plants such as petunias and geraniums are $F_1$ hybrids. Seed taken from $F_1$ hybrids usually produces plants unlike both the $F_1$ hybrid and its parents.

**$F_2$ hybrid** (In this context) the result of allowing $F_1$ hybrids to pollinate themselves and each other, often indiscriminately. The result is usually variable, but predictable within broad limits. The resultant plants usually retain some, but not all, of the qualities of their $F_1$ hybrid parents but are less expensive. The relatively few bedding plants that are produced in this way include geraniums and pansies. Plants grown from seed saved from $F_2$ hybrids can be variable and unpredictable.

**Field-grown mixture** Seed collected from plants in mixed colours growing together. The resultant balance of colours is usually slightly variable and unpredictable.

**Formula mixture** Seed collected by the seed producer from plants grown separately in individual colours and blended later in a pre-determined proportion. The resultant balance of colours is constant and predictable.

**Fully double** A flower in which the number of petals is dramatically increased so that it appears to consist entirely of petals.

**Germination** The development of a seed from an apparently inert object to a young plant (seedling).

**Half-hardy** Used to describe annual or perennial plants which thrive out of doors in summer but whose natural life cycle is cut short by the first autumn frosts or by low winter temperatures.

**Harden off** To acclimatize plants raised in a greenhouse or other protected environment to cooler conditions outside by steadily exposing them to less protection.

**Hardy** Used to describe plants not normally killed by frosts.

**Leggy** Used to describe plants, especially seedlings, which have become unnaturally thin and stretched owing to their being grown in low light conditions.

**Open-pollinated** Used to describe cultivars derived from allowing a stand of plants to be pollinated by bees or other relatively uncontrolled means. The resulting plants vary in their uniformity according to the care with which rogues (see below) are removed.

**Pelleted seed** Individual seeds enclosed in a clay pellet which breaks down on contact with water. Allows very small seed to be handled and sown more easily.

**Perlite** White, lightweight, inert material derived from volcanic rock and used to improve drainage in potting composts.

**Picotee** Used to describe flowers or petals with a pale background colour and a dark band of the same or a different colour around the edge, or a dark ground with a pale band around the edge.

**Pinching out** The removal of a shoot tip, usually from a young plant, to encourage the development of side shoots.

**Plug plants** Young plants, usually seedlings, grown in individual cells of compost enabling them to be pricked out or transplanted without disturbing the roots.

**Pricking out** Transferring seedlings to individual pots, or giving them more space in a seed tray, to allow uncrowded development.

**Ray floret** The colourful petals of plants in the daisy family; the central eye of daisy flowers is made up of disk florets.

**Rogue** An off-type, of any sort, in a stand of plants grown by a seed producer for their seed; e.g. a blue-flowered individual in a stand of plants of a white-flowered cultivar. If the rogue is not removed (rogued) the resulting seed will usually produce a few off-types amongst those which are correct when grown in the garden; e.g. blue-flowered plants amongst the white.

**Seed crop** A stand of plants grown by a seed producer specifically to provide seed.

**Seed stock** The batch of seed of a particular cultivar from a given supplier. Seed stocks from different suppliers may vary according to

the attention given to roguing (see above).

**Self-colour** Describes a flower in which the colour is even and uniform.

**Self-sow (v)** Used when a plant in the garden sheds its own seed which then germinates near by.

**Self-fertile** Used of a species or cultivar which will set seed when pollinated with its own pollen.

**Self-sterile** Used of a species or cultivar which will not set seed when pollinated with its own pollen.

**Sepal** Segment of the leaf-like structure enclosing a flower bud, collectively called the calyx.

**Series** A range of cultivars, usually of a popular bedding plant, which are similar in all respects except the colour of their flowers.

**Set seed** To produce viable seed following pollination.

**Space sow** To place (usually large) seeds individually in the soil at consistent spacing.

**Spur** The slender tube at the back of some flowers, e.g. aquilegia, usually producing nectar.

**Sterile** Used of a cultivar or an individual plant which is incapable of producing seed. Sometimes refined as follows: male sterile, producing no viable pollen but capable of producing seed; female sterile, incapable of producing seed but producing fertile pollen.

**Stopping** Removal of the shoot tip, usually from a young plant, to encourage branching.

**Tender** Highly susceptible to frost damage.

**Thin/thin out** To remove some seedlings from a row in order to allow those remaining enough space to develop without crowding.

**True/true to type** Used to describe a plant which matches the accepted description of the cultivar to which it is assumed to belong.

**Winter annual** An annual which germinates late in the season and flowers early the following season; it will also develop normally from a spring sowing.

# The Problem of Names

In recent years changes have taken place in the botanical names of some annuals, as has been the case with other groups of plants. Gardeners are often irritated or confused by botanists changing plant names, however good the reason, and the situation with annuals is confused by the fact that the seed trade is even more reluctant to take up new names than other branches of the horticultural industry. The result is that new names become widely accepted in botanical literature and serious garden writing but the catalogues and seed packets stick to the old names. What's more, in different countries, different conventions are followed.

The names used in this book are not, always, absolutely botanically correct. As you will see from some of the examples on the following list, if they had been used they would have been more confusing than helpful. But it's right to give these names here so that as they become more accepted over the years gardeners will be better able to understand to which plants they refer.

So this list covers both names which are now becoming accepted and also recent changes which may take some time to become familiar. It covers both plants in this book and other annuals you may find listed in seed catalogues.

| Incorrect old name | Correct new name |
| --- | --- |
| Althaea rosea | Alcea rosea |
| Alyssum maritimum | Lobularia maritima |
| Aster chinensis | Callistephus chinensis |
| Brachycome | Brachyscome |
| Calliopsis bicolor | Coreopsis tinctoria |
| Centaurea moschata | Amberboa moschata |
| Cheiranthus cheiri | Erysimum cheiri |
| Chrysanthemum carinatum | Ismelia carinata |
| Chrysanthemum coronarium | Xanthophthalmum coronarium |
| Chrysanthemum multicaule | Coleostephus myconis |
| Chrysanthemum nivellei | Nivellea nivellei |
| Chrysanthemum paludosum | Mauranthemum paludosum |
| Chrysanthemum segetum | Xanthophthalmum segetum |
| Cineraria maritima | Senecio cineraria |
| Clarkia elegans | Clarkia unguiculata |
| Consolida ajacis | Consolida ambigua |
| Convolvulus major | Ipomoea purpurea |
| Convolvulus minor | Convolvulus tricolor |
| Cosmidium | Thelesperma |
| Delphinium zalil | Delphinium semibarbatum |
| Geranium peltatum | Pelargonium peltatum |
| Geranium x hortorum | Pelargonium x hortorum |
| Godetia amoena | Clarkia amoena |
| Godetia bottae | Clarkia bottae |
| Godetia grandiflora | Clarkia rubicunda |
| Godetia rubicunda | Clarkia rubicunda |
| Helichrysum bracteatum | Bracteantha bracteata |
| Matricaria capensis | Tanacetum parthenium |
| Pyrethrum ptarmiciflorum | Tanacetum prtarmiciflorum |
| Quamoclit coccinea | Ipomoea coccinea |
| Tropaeolum canariense | Tropaeolum peregrinum |

| Correct new name | Incorrect old name |
| --- | --- |
| Alcea rosea | Althaea rosea |
| Amberboa moschata | Centaurea moschata |
| Brachyscome | Brachycome |
| Bracteantha bracteata | Helichrysum bracteantum |
| Callistephus chinensis | Aster chinensis |
| Clarkia amoena | Godetia amoena |
| Clarkia bottae | Godetia bottae |
| Clarkia rubicunda | Godetia grandiflora, G. rubicunda |
| Clarkia unguiculata | Clarkia elegans |
| Coleostephus myconis | Chrysanthemum multicaule |
| Consolida ambigua | Consolida ajacis |
| Convolvulus tricolor | Convolvulus minor |
| Coreopsis tinctoria | Calliopsis bicolor |
| Delphinium semibarbatum | Delphinium zalil |
| Erysimum cheiri | Cheiranthus cheiri |
| Ipomoea coccinea | Quamoclit coccinea |
| Ipomoea purpurea | Convolvulus major |
| Ismelia carinata | Chrysanthemum carinatum |
| Lobularia maritima | Alyssum maritimum |
| Mauranthemum paludosum | Chrysanthemum paludosum |
| Nivellea nivellei | Chrysanthemum nivellei |
| Pelargonium peltatum | Geranium peltatum |
| Pelargonium x hortorum | Geranium x hortorum |
| Senecio cineraria | Cineraria maritima |
| Tanacetum parthenium | Matricaria capensis |
| Tanacetum prtarmiciflorum | Pyrethrum ptarmiciflorum |
| Thelesperma | Cosmidium |
| Tropaeolum peregrinum | Tropaeolum canariense |
| Xanthophthalmum coronarium | Chrysanthemum coronarium |
| Xanthophthalmum segetum | Chrysanthemum segetum |

# Seed Suppliers

Almost all of these seed companies supply seed by mail order, you'll also find some seeds on sale in garden centres. All list a good range of cultivars (except where mentioned). Changes of address, together with details of any export arrangement, will be found at the *Discovering Annuals* website (see page 186).

**Barnhaven Primroses**
Langerhouad 2240
Plouzelambre
France.
Primroses and polyanthus only.

**Basically Seeds**
Risby Business Park
Newmarket Road
Risby
Bury St Edmunds IP11 8AS

**D.T. Brown**
Station Road
Poulton-le-Fylde FY6 7HX
http://www.users.globalnet.co.uk/~dtbrown

**J.W. Boyce**
Bush Pasture Lower Carter Street
Fordham
Ely CB7 5JU

**B&T World Seeds**
Paguignan
34210 Olonzac
France
http://www.b-and-t.world.seeds.com

**Robert Bolton & Son**
Birdbrook
Halstead
Essex CO9 4BQ
Sweet peas only

**S&N Brackley**
117 Winslow Road
Wingrave
Aylesbury
Buckinghamshire HP22 4QB
Sweet peas only

**Carters Seeds**
Hele Road
Torquay, TQ2 7QJ
(no mail order)

**Chiltern Seeds**
Bortree Stile
Ulverston
Cumbria LA12 7PB

**Dobies Seeds**
Long Road
Paignton
Devon TQ4 7SX

**Mr Fothergill's Seeds**
Kentford
Newmarket
Suffolk CB8 7QB

**Peter Grayson**
34 Glenthorne Close Brampton
Chesterfield
Derbyshire S40 3AR
Sweet peas only

**Johnsons Seeds**
Gazeley Road
Kentford
Newmarket
CB8 7QB
(No mail order)

**E.W. King & Co. Ltd**
Monks Farm
Coggeshall Road
Kelvedon
Essex CO5 9PG

**S.E. Marshall & Co. Ltd**
Wisbech
Peterborough PE13 2RF

**Mathewman's Sweet Peas**
14 Chariot Way
Thorpe Audlin
Pontefract
West Yorkshire WF8 3ERZ
Sweet peas only

**Milton's Seeds**
3 Milton Avenue
Blackpool
Lancashire FY3 8LY

**Moles Seeds**
Turkey Cock Lane
Stanway
Colchester
Essex CO3 5PB
(Large orders only)

**The Organic Gardening Catalogue**
Coombelands House
Addlestone
Surrey KT15 1HY

**Plants of Distinction**
Abacus House
Station Yard
Needham Market
Suffolk IP6 8AS

**Seeds-by-Size**
45 Crouchfield
Boxmoor
Hemel Hempstead
Hertfordshire HP1 1PA
http://www.seeds-by-size.co.uk

**Diane Sewell**
Overdene
81 Willingham Road
Over
Cambridge CB4 5PF
Sweet peas only

**Seymour's Selected Seeds**
Farm Lane
Spalding
Lincolnshire PE11 1TD

**Suttons Seeds**
Woodview Road
Paignton
Devon TQ4 7NG

**Suffolk Herbs**
Monks Ram
Coggeshall Road
Kelvedon, Essex CO5 9PG

**Thompson & Morgan Seeds**
Poplar Lane
Ipswich IP8 3BU

**Unwins Seeds**
Histon
Cambridge CB4 4ZZ

**F.A. Woodcock**
Lawn Road Nurseries
Lawn Road
Walmer
Deal
Kent CT14 7ND
Sweet peas only

# Finding out more . . .

## Further Reading

Books on annuals and bedding plants are relatively few and far between and it's interesting to note that the last burst of publishing on this subject, similar to that seen in the late 1990s, was in the mid 1950s.

**In print at the time of writing**

Clark, Ethne *Three Seasons of Summer* (David & Charles, 1998)

Lane, Clive *Cottage Garden Annuals* (David & Charles, 1997)

Lloyd, Christopher and Rice, Graham *Garden Flowers from Seed* (Penguin, 1997)

Platt, Karen, ed. *The Seed Search* (Karen Platt, 1998 and annually)

**Out of print at the time of writing**

Barber, Angus *Annual Flowers* (Faber and Faber, 1954)

Booth, Charles O. *An Encyclopaedia of Annual and Biennial Garden Plants* Faber and Faber, 1957)

Evison, J. R. B. *Gardening for Display* (Collingridge, 1958)

Jekyll, Gertrude *Annuals and Biennials* (Country Life, 1916)

Rice, Graham *A Handbook of Annual and Bedding Plants* (Croom Helm, 1986)

Rice, Graham *Bedding Plants* (Cassell/RHS,1993)

All these books, together with other relevant titles published after this book went to print, are reviewed or discussed on the *Discovering Annuals* website.

## The Discovering Annuals *website*

In a unique relationship between print publishing and the World Wide Web, this book is partnered by its own dedicated website.

The *Discovering Annuals* website can be found at:

http://discoveringannuals.com

It features additional information on the plants mentioned and described in this book ,together with background information for which there was unfortunately insufficient space in the book itself.

In addition to selected illustrated extracts from this book, the *Discovering Annuals* website also features:

- Photographs of additional plant associations
- Additional pictures of cultivars not illustrated in this book or newly introduced
- Reviews of each year's seed catalogues
- Background information on how new annuals are developed
- Reports of any new pests or diseases affecting annuals or developments in their control
- Advice on ordering seeds from American seed companies

The website also allows me to update information which appears in this book such as:

- Changes to seed company addresses
- Reviews of new books on annuals
- Opening times and visitor information for recommended gardens and trial grounds
- Changes to generic and cultivar names
- Changes in the availability of cultivars

This is the first gardening book to be linked to a website in this way. I hope you find it useful. Please e-mail me from the site if there are any features you would especially like to see added.

## Where to see annuals

Listing gardens in which to see annuals can be a hazardous business. An arboretum can be recommended with certainty as a place to see trees but, as annuals are short-term plants by their very nature, a garden which grows a good range of annuals one year may hardly grow them at all the next. However I have confidence that these will remain worth visiting.

Crathes Castle, Banchory, Aberdeenshire

Great Dixter, Northiam, East Sussex

Hadspen House, Castle Cary, Somerset

Harlow Carr Botanical Gardens, Harrogate, North Yorkshire

Hidcote Manor, Hidcote Bartrim, Gloucestershire

Nymans, Handcross, West Sussex

Old Vicarage, East Ruston, Norfolk

The Priory, Kemerton, Worcestershire

Royal Botanic Gardens, Kew, Surrey

Royal Botanic Gardens, Edinburgh

Sissinghurst Castle, Cranbrook, Kent

Wisley Gardens, Wisley, Surrey

At various times many of the seed companies (see page 185) have opened their trial grounds to visitors. Not only are they spectacularly colourful but these comparative trials provide a unique opportunity to assess similar cultivars side by side. At the time of writing, the following seed companies open their trials for a few days each summer: Thompson & Morgan Seeds, Ipswich, Suffolk; Suttons Seeds, Torquay, Devon.

Precise details will be posted on the *Discovering Annuals* website every year.

## Award-winning annuals

Every year new varieties of annuals are released by plant breeders all over the world and introduced by the familiar seed companies. Often, there is little information about these varieties available, other than the hyperbolic text in the seed catalogue, therefore, many gardeners appreciate guidance as to which of these many new varieties really are worth growing.

Both in Europe and the United States there are award schemes which recognize the finest new introductions. In Europe, Fleuroselect awards Gold Medals to the very best newcomers while other excellent cultivars are awarded a Quality Mark. These awards are given after each year's entrants to the scheme are voted upon in blind trials at sites all over Europe. In the United States, All-America Selections run a similar scheme.

Many fine plants have received awards under these two well-established schemes. There's a full list on the *Discovering Annuals* website together with a list of display gardens where award winners can be seen.

# Index of plant names

# Acknowledgments

It's customary for the author to begin this entry with the words 'This book would not have been possible without' and then list all his family, friends and relations down to the new puppy. So let's be realistic: a very different book would have been possible without anyone's help. *This* book would not have been possible without my picking the brains of all my friends in the seed trade (they're all listed on the *Discovering Annuals* website). It's not just that they've responded to my questions with as much, and occasionally more, information than commercial competitive concerns allowed. But their enjoyable enthusiasm has continually sparked mine.

I'd also like to thank photographer John Fielding, who almost every week in the summer of 1997 set his alarm clock at an utterly unreasonable hour in order to be out in my garden in the best possible light to photograph so many of the annuals for this book. John, your pictures are wonderful; thank you.

At the publishers, Frances Lincoln, I'd like to thank Erica Hunningher for her belief that the time had come for this book, Louise Kirby for her elegant design and thoughtful choice of pictures, and especially Kirsty Brackenridge for pulling it all together with such good humour and against odds which would, and indeed sometimes have, defeated lesser editors.

Finally, I want to thank jude for her constructive comments on my text, which has improved noticeably as a result, and for transforming the British edition into the American one so thoughtfully. And I'd also like to thank her for attending the 1997 Chelsea Flower Show.

## Photographic Credits

(A=above, B=below, L=left, R=right)

A-Z Botanical Collection © Moira C. Smith 114
**Nicola Brown** 34A (Sandra and Nori Pope, Hadspen Garden)
**David Cavagnaro** 21, 102B
**Bruce Coleman Limited/Liz Eddison** 101
**Eric Crichton Photos** 49A, 63B, 92A, 102A, 104L, 166
**John Fielding** 5, 6 (Graham Rice), 7 (Graham Rice),10 (Graham Rice), 12 (Graham Rice), 18, 20 (RHS Wisley), 22-23 (N & S Pope, Hadspen Garden), 24B (Graham Rice), 25 (Graham Rice), 28-29 (Graham Rice), 30 (Graham Rice), 38A, 41 (RHS Wisley), 43 (Graham Rice), 44AR, 45, 48 (Graham Rice), 51 (Graham Rice), 52-53 (RHS Wisley), 56 (Graham Rice), 58 (RHS Wisley), 67 (Graham Rice), 71 (Graham Rice), 73B (Graham Rice), 77 (Graham Rice), 82, 89A (Graham Rice), 90 (Graham Rice), 94A, 98 (Graham Rice), 103 (Graham Rice), 107 (Graham Rice), 109 (Graham Rice), 110 (N & S Pope, Hadspen Garden), 113, 127, 135 (Graham Rice), 137 (Graham Rice), 140 (Graham Rice), 141 (Graham Rice), 142 (Graham Rice), 144-145 (Graham Rice), 151A (N & S Pope, Hadspen Garden), 153 (Graham Rice), 154 (Graham Rice), 155A (Graham Rice), 158A (Graham Rice), 159 (Graham Rice), 161 (Graham Rice), 175 Photographer/Designer John Fielding 2, 9, 13, 15, 26, 34, 37, 39, 40, 42, 50, 59, 74L, 74-75, 81, 83,85, 86, 89B, 95, 97, 111, 116, 121, 122, 123L, 147, 150, 152L, 160, 162, 163, 164A, 165, 170R, 171
John Glover 44AL, 44B, 47, 62, 64, 129A, 130-131, 132B, 133, 143, 146B, 170L
**Sunniva Harte** 146A, 148
**Anne Hyde** 124, 139
**Andrew Lawson** 24A, 61, 65, 66, 72, 73A, 76L, 91 (Christopher Lloyd, Great Dixter), 106R, 120B, 125A, 128, 129B, 155BL, 155BR, 156-157, 168AR, 168B, 169R
**Rob Leopold** 49B
**Tony Lord** 16-17, 19, 68-69, 173, 174
**David McDonald** 115
**S & O Mathews** 105, 167
**Clive Nichols Garden Pictures** 8, 63A, 84, 106L, 108B, 126, 151B
Oxford Scientific Films © Deni Bown 117, © Bob Gibbons 136
Photos Horticultural 123R
**Peter Ray** 32, 60
**Graham Rice** 1, 27, 33AL, 33B, 38B, 76R, 79, 80, 87, 92B, 93, 94B, 100, 108A, 120AL, 120AR, 125B, 132A, 138AL, 138, 152R, 158B, 164B, 168AL
**Howard Rice** 36, 38B, 57, 99
**Derek St Romaine** 31, 35, 54, 78, 88, 96, 112, 134B
**Erica R. Shank** 33AR, 149
**Jörgen Schwartzkopf** 55
**Harry Smith Collection** 104R
**©judywhite/New Leaf Images** 46, 70, 169L, 172

The publishers would like to thank the following for their help in producing this book: Anne Askwith, Jo Grey, Sarah Mitchell, Sara Robin and Ann Barratt for the index.

Editor: Kirsty Brackenridge
Art Editor: Louise Kirby
Picture Research: Sue Gladstone
Picture Editor: Anne Fraser
Editorial Director: Erica Hunningher
Art Director: Caroline Hillier